great cookies

Also by Carole Walter

Great Cakes

Great Pies & Tarts

great cookies
SECRETS TO SENSATIONAL SWEETS

Carole Walter

PHOTOGRAPHS BY DUANE WINFIELD

Clarkson Potter/Publishers

NEW YORK

Published by Clarkson Potter/Publishers, New York, New York
Member of the Crown Publishing Group, a division of Random
House, Inc.
www.randomhouse.com

CLARKSON N. POTTER is a trademark and POTTER
and colophon are registered trademarks of Random House, Inc.

Printed in China

Design by Marysarah Quinn

Library of Congress Cataloging-in-Publication Data
Walter, Carole.
    Great cookies : secrets to sensational sweets /
Carole Walter.—1st ed.
        p.   cm.
1. Cookies.   I. Title.
    TX772.W355   2003
    641.8'654—dc21   2003007633

ISBN 0-609-60969-6

10 9 8 7 6 5 4 3 2

With love, from . . .
    The one who fills the cookie jar with sweets,
To . . .
    My "sweets" who make the cookies disappear.

My children,
Frank and Marla
Pam and Andy,
and
grandchildren,
Zach and Samantha
Jeffrey and Neil

contents

I The Cookies

1 Drop Cookies

oatmeal raisin cookies

MAKES ABOUT 4 DOZEN 3-INCH COOKIES

Savor the flavors of this favorite comfort cookie made with old-fashioned oatmeal, brown sugar, molasses, cinnamon, raisins, and lots of toasted pecans. The orange zest really complements these ingredients.

PAN: Cookie sheets

PAN PREP: Moderately buttered

OVEN TEMP: 350°

BAKING TIME: 15–17 minutes

DIFFICULTY: ✪

2 cups all-purpose flour, spooned in and leveled

1½ teaspoons ground cinnamon

1 teaspoon baking soda

1 teaspoon salt

1 cup (2 sticks) unsalted butter, slightly firm

1 teaspoon grated navel orange zest

⅔ cup lightly packed dark brown sugar

½ cup granulated sugar

¼ cup dark unsulfured molasses

2 large eggs

2 teaspoons pure vanilla extract

2 cups old-fashioned oatmeal

1 cup broken, toasted pecans or walnuts

1 cup dark raisins, plumped (see page 391), drained, and patted dry on paper towels

Cookie Characteristics

Homestyle

Moderate shelf life

Travel well

1. Position the shelves in the upper and lower thirds of the oven. Heat the oven to 350°. Moderately butter the cookie sheets.

2. Strain together the flour, cinnamon, baking soda, and salt. Set aside.

3. In the large bowl of an electric mixer, using the paddle attachment, soften the butter with the orange zest on medium speed until smooth and creamy, about 1 minute; add the brown sugar, then the granulated sugar and mix until light in color, 2 to 3 minutes. Blend in the molasses and mix to combine. Add the eggs one at a time, then the vanilla and mix for 1 minute longer.

4. Reduce the mixer speed to low and pour in the dry ingredients, half at a time, mixing only to incorporate the flour, then blend in the oatmeal. Using a large rubber spatula, fold in the pecans and raisins.

5. Drop by rounded tablespoons 3 inches apart onto the cookie sheets. Bake for 15 to 17 minutes, or until the bottoms of the cookies are golden brown, rotating the pans top to bottom and front to back toward the end of baking time. Do not overbake or the cookies will be too crisp and difficult to remove from the pan. Let cookies stand for 2 minutes, then loosen with a thin metal spatula. Cool on wire racks.

STORAGE: Store in an airtight container, layered between strips of wax paper, for up to 1 week. These cookies may be frozen.

spiked apple cookies

MAKES ABOUT 4 DOZEN 2¼-INCH COOKIES

Here is a recipe that was inspired by hermits, the classic New England cookie. Flavored with cinnamon and nutmeg, the dough is flecked with bits of dried apples that have been macerated in apple liqueur. Try these along with a mug of hot mulled apple cider. What could be better to warm the tummy when there is a chill in the air?

AT A GLANCE

PAN: Cookie sheets

PAN PREP: Moderately buttered

OVEN TEMP: 350°

BAKING TIME: 12–14 minutes

DIFFICULTY: ✪

½ cup firmly packed dried apple slices

3 tablespoons Calvados or applejack liqueur

1½ cups all-purpose flour, spooned in and leveled

1 teaspoon ground cinnamon

½ teaspoon baking soda

¼ teaspoon salt

¼ teaspoon ground nutmeg

⅔ cup (1⅓ sticks) unsalted butter, slightly firm

½ cup lightly packed light brown sugar

½ cup granulated sugar

1 large egg

¼ cup sour cream

1 teaspoon pure vanilla extract

1 cup broken walnuts

1 recipe Vanilla Glaze (page 358)

1. Place the apple slices in a small bowl and cover with boiling water. Let stand for 2 to 3 minutes to soften. Drain well and cut into ¼-inch dice. Toss the apples with the Calvados in a small, deep bowl and let macerate while preparing the cookie dough.

2. Position the shelves in the upper and lower thirds of the oven. Heat the oven to 350°. Moderately butter the cookie sheets.

3. Strain together the flour, cinnamon, baking soda, salt, and nutmeg. Set aside.

4. In the large bowl of an electric mixer, on medium-low speed, using paddle attachment, mix the butter until creamy and lightened in color. Add the brown sugar, then the granulated sugar, and mix for 1 to 2 minutes. Blend in the egg, then the sour cream and vanilla.

5. Reduce the mixer speed to low and add the dry ingredients in three additions, mixing *just* until well combined. Using a large rubber spatula, fold in the apples and walnuts.

6. Drop from the tip of a teaspoon, making walnut-size mounds of dough (about 1¼ inches), onto the cookie sheets, spacing them about 2 inches apart. Bake for 12 to 14 minutes, until lightly browned. Toward the end of baking time, rotate the pans from top to bottom and front to back. Remove from oven and let stand for 2 to 3 minutes. Loosen with a thin metal spatula and place on wire racks set over wax paper.

7. Using the back of the spoon, apply ½ teaspoon of Vanilla Glaze to each warm cookie.

STORAGE: Store in an airtight container, layered between strips of wax paper, for up to 3 weeks. These cookies may be frozen before glazing.

Cookie Characteristics

Homestyle

Long shelf life

Travel well

Clockwise from top: Hermits (page 18), Peanut Jumbles (page 20), and Spiked Apple Cookies.

hermits

Hermit cookies are indigenous to New England and were a favorite among sailors working long voyages on ships. As with many baked goods popular during the colonial era, these sweets were made with dried fruits and nuts that were steeped in liqueur and flavored with molasses and spices. Because these ingredients improve with age, the name "Hermit" reflects their long keeping properties. But please don't wait to take to the waters before trying these. They are a real treat on land as well.

AT A GLANCE

PAN: Jelly roll pans

PAN PREP: Baking parchment

OVEN TEMP: 375°

CHILLING TIME: 1 hour

BAKING TIME: 11–13 minutes

DIFFICULTY: ○

2 cups diced mixed dried fruit, such as apricots, raisins, and figs, plumped (see page 391)

1 cup coarsely broken walnuts

½ cup Grand Marnier (or other orange liqueur)

2½ cups all-purpose flour, spooned in and leveled

1½ teaspoons ground cinnamon

1 teaspoon baking powder

¾ teaspoon salt

¾ teaspoon ground nutmeg

½ teaspoon ground allspice

¼ teaspoon baking soda

¾ cup (1½ sticks) unsalted butter, slightly firm

2 teaspoons grated navel orange zest

1 cup lightly packed light brown sugar

½ cup granulated sugar

2 large eggs

⅓ cup light unsulfured molasses

1 teaspoon pure vanilla extract

¼ cup sour cream

1. Combine the plumped dried fruits and walnuts in a medium bowl. Pour in the Grand Marnier and stir to coat the fruit and nuts. Set aside to macerate (see page 391) for at least 30 minutes.

MAKE THE DOUGH

2. Strain together the flour, cinnamon, baking powder, salt, nutmeg, allspice, and baking soda. Set aside.

3. In the large bowl of an electric mixer fitted with the paddle attachment, mix the butter and orange zest on medium-low speed until creamy and lightened in color, about 2 minutes. Add the brown sugar, ½ cup at a time, then the granulated sugar and beat for 2 to 3 minutes. Blend in the eggs, 1 at a time, mixing to combine. Scrape down the side of the bowl as needed. Add the molasses and the vanilla extract and mix for 1 minute longer.

4. Reduce the mixer speed to low, then add the dry ingredients alternately with the sour cream, three parts flour to two

rustic maple pecan date cookies

Reduce chopped pecans in the Master Recipe to ¾ cup. Measure 1 cup loosely packed dates cut into ¼-inch dice and toss them into 1 teaspoon of flour to prevent them from sticking together. Mix the dates with the pecans and proceed with step 5 in the Master Recipe.

Cookie Characteristics

Homestyle

Long shelf life

Travel well

crystallized ginger and macadamia wafers

MAKES ABOUT 4 DOZEN 3-INCH COOKIES

These thin wafers are speckled with bits of crystallized ginger and chunks of macadamia nuts. The buttery nuts and the refreshing bite of candied ginger make a tantalizing combination.

AT A GLANCE

PAN: Cookie sheets

PAN PREP: Moderately buttered

OVEN TEMP: 375°

BAKING TIME: 11–12 minutes

DIFFICULTY: ◯

1½ cups all-purpose flour, spooned in and leveled

1½ teaspoons ground ginger

¼ teaspoon salt

¾ cup (1½ sticks) unsalted butter, slightly firm

½ cup lightly packed light brown sugar

6 tablespoons granulated sugar

3 egg whites, at room temperature

1½ teaspoons pure vanilla extract

1 scant cup macadamia nuts, cut into quarters with a paring knife

1 (2.5-ounce) jar Australian crystallized ginger bits or ½ cup crystallized ginger chips

Cookie Characteristics

Versatile

Long shelf life

Fragile

1. Position the shelves in the upper and lower thirds of the oven. Heat the oven to 375°. Moderately butter the cookie sheets.

2. Strain together the flour, ground ginger, and salt. Set aside.

3. In the large bowl of an electric mixer fitted with the paddle attachment, mix the butter on medium-low speed until lightened in color, about 1 minute. Add the light brown sugar and then the granulated sugar, scraping down the side of the bowl as needed. Blend in the egg whites one at a time, then add the vanilla. (It is okay if the mixture appears to separate.)

4. Reduce the mixer speed to low and add the dry ingredients in three additions, mixing *just* until blended after each addition. Using a large rubber spatula, fold in the macadamia nuts and ginger bits. *Do not overmix.*

5. Drop 1¼-inch mounds from the tip of a teaspoon onto the prepared cookie sheets, placing them about 3 inches apart (these cookies will spread). Dip your fingertips in ice water and gently flatten the mound.

6. Bake for 11 to 12 minutes, or until the edges are golden brown, rotating the pans top to bottom and front to back toward the end of the baking time. Remove from oven and let stand for 2 or 3 minutes or *just* until set. Using a thin metal spatula, carefully loosen and transfer to cooling racks. If the cookies stick, return the pan to the oven and heat briefly.

STORAGE: Store in an airtight container, layered between strips of wax paper, for up to 3 weeks. Handle carefully; the cookies are fragile. These cookies may be frozen.

fudgy nutwiches with caramel mascarpone cream

MAKES ABOUT 3 DOZEN 1¾-INCH SANDWICHES

Imagine a rich chocolate cookie flavored with toasted pecans and a hint of honey, sandwiched with a filling of creamy mascarpone flavored with melted caramel candy. As the cookies mature, they develop an appealing chewy texture from the moistness of the filling that makes them absolutely addictive. While the sandwiched cookies will keep in the refrigerator for up to five days, the cookies may be frozen and then filled when you are ready to serve them. If you wish to omit the filling, you may do so. These tasty chocolate disks are delicious on their own!

AT A GLANCE

PAN: Cookie sheets

PAN PREP: Heavy-duty aluminum foil

OVEN TEMP: 350°

BAKING TIME: 8–9 minutes

DIFFICULTY: ○○

½ cup all-purpose flour, spooned in and leveled

2 tablespoons strained Dutch-processed cocoa powder

¼ teaspoon baking powder

⅛ teaspoon salt

8 ounces fine-quality bittersweet chocolate, such as Lindt Bittersweet, cut into small pieces

¼ cup (½ stick) unsalted butter, slightly firm

1 tablespoon honey

½ cup superfine sugar

2 large eggs, lightly beaten

2 teaspoons pure vanilla extract

⅔ cup toasted pecans, finely chopped with 1 tablespoon granulated sugar

1 recipe Caramel Mascarpone Cream (page 356)

1. Position the shelves in the upper and lower thirds of the oven. Heat the oven to 350°. Line the cookie sheets with heavy-duty aluminum foil.

2. Strain together three times the flour, cocoa, baking powder, and salt. Set aside.

3. In a 3-quart bowl set over a pot of simmering water, melt the chocolate. Remove from the heat and blend in the butter, then the honey. Using a wooden spoon, add the superfine sugar, eggs, and vanilla and beat 100 strokes to thoroughly combine. Stir in the nuts.

4. Strain the dry ingredients into the batter in four additions, folding in with a large rubber spatula. Do not overmix.

5. Drop ½ teaspoon of batter from the tip of a spoon, 2 inches apart, onto the cookie sheets, forming 1-inch mounds. Be sure that the mounds are uniform in size. Allow the dough to stand 5 to 10 minutes or until firm enough to roll into balls. Then shape each mound into a ball and bake.

6. Bake for 8 to 9 minutes. *Do not over-bake.* The cookies will feel slightly soft on top. Remove from oven and let stand for 2 or 3 minutes before loosening with a thin metal spatula. Transfer to cooling racks. When cookies are cool, sandwich each pair with about 2 teaspoons Caramel Mascarpone Cream. Refrigerate until firm.

STORAGE: Store in an airtight container, layered between strips of wax paper, for up to 5 days. These cookies may be frozen.

fudgy nutwiches with chocolate ganache

Substitute ¾ cup of thickened Ganache Glaze (page 360) for the Caramel Mascarpone Cream. Use about 1 teaspoon to sandwich each cookie pair.

Cookie Characteristics

Versatile

Moderate shelf life

Temperature sensitive

carole's really great chocolate chip cookies

MAKES ABOUT 40 2³/₄-INCH COOKIES

I really love this recipe for chocolate chip cookies. It was truly a challenge to create one that was different because so many exist.

What I tried to zero in on was the most common complaint that bakers have about their cookies: the spreading of the cookie dough during baking. As a rule, cookies spread because of too much moisture in the dough. To overcome this problem, I created a recipe using very finely ground oatmeal to bind the dough and prevent it from spreading. The presence of the oatmeal is not detectable and the end result is delectable.

snickerdoodles

One morning, my plumber, Bruce Robertshaw, walked in briskly to make a repair. Bruce, a no-nonsense man, said, "Hmmm . . . and what are we making today?" I recited my menu of cookies, one of which happened to be snickerdoodles. "Snickerdoodles," he said, "my wife makes the best! It was my grandmother's recipe and has been in my family for years." Needless to say, my curiosity was aroused and I had to try out the recipe for this book.

As Bruce left, he said with a gleam in his eye, "You know I timed this all wrong! I usually come at the end of the day so I can go home with a plateful of cookies!" For me, the timing was perfect. I put aside my own snickerdoodle recipe in anticipation of Grandma Robertshaw's. Grandma's snickerdoodles more than lived up to their reputation. Here is the Robertshaw family recipe. See if you don't agree!

AT A GLANCE

PAN: Cookie sheets

PAN PREP: Lightly buttered

OVEN TEMP: 350°

CHILLING TIME: 6–8 hours

BAKING TIME: 10–12 minutes

DIFFICULTY: ◯

2½ cups all-purpose flour, spooned in and leveled

2 teaspoons cream of tartar

1 teaspoon baking soda

½ teaspoon salt

½ cup (1 stick) unsalted butter, at room temperature

½ cup vegetable shortening

1¾ cups sugar, divided

2 large eggs

1 teaspoon pure vanilla extract

1–1½ teaspoons ground cinnamon

MAKE THE DOUGH

1. Strain together the flour, cream of tartar, baking soda, and salt. Set aside.

2. In the large bowl of an electric mixer fitted with the paddle attachment, mix the butter and vegetable shortening on medium speed until lightened in color, about 2 minutes. Add 1½ cups of the sugar in a steady stream and mix for another 2 minutes. Reduce the mixer speed to low and add the eggs one at a time, mixing well after each addition and scraping down the side of the bowl as needed. Stir in the vanilla.

3. Add the dry ingredients in two additions, mixing *just* until blended after each addition. Scrape the dough into a clean bowl, cover with plastic wrap, and chill for 6 to 8 hours, or overnight.

4. Position the shelves in the upper and lower thirds of the oven. Heat the oven to 350°. Lightly butter the cookie sheets.

5. Divide the dough into quarters. With lightly floured hands, shape each quarter into a log. Slice each log into 12 equal pieces and roll into small walnut-size balls.

6. Combine the remaining ¼ cup sugar with the cinnamon in a small mixing bowl. Working one piece at a time, place each ball in the mixture and briskly rotate the bowl in a circular motion to coat the dough evenly with the mixture.

7. Place 3 inches apart on the cookie sheets. Bake for 10 to 12 minutes, or until lightly browned. Toward the end of baking time, rotate the pans from top to bottom and front to back. (A shorter baking time will make these cookies chewier, while longer baking results in crispiness.) Remove the cookies from the oven and let rest for 5 minutes. Transfer with a thin metal spatula to wire racks to cool.

STORAGE: Store in an airtight container, layered between strips of wax paper, for up to 3 weeks. These cookies may be frozen.

Cookie Characteristics

Homestyle

Long shelf life

Travel well

crispy gingersnaps

MAKES ABOUT 40 2½-INCH COOKIES

What would a cookie book be without a recipe for gingersnaps? Here we have a cookie that is power-packed with ginger flavor. I have added a contemporary touch with the addition of chopped crystallized ginger. And unlike most gingersnaps, these are made without molasses, making them especially crispy. On a wintry day, with a hot cup of tea, this cookie really hits the spot.

AT A GLANCE

PAN: Cookie sheets
PAN PREP: Baking parchment
OVEN TEMP: 375°
BAKING TIME: 9–10 minutes
DIFFICULTY: ○

2 cups all-purpose flour, spooned in and leveled
1 tablespoon ground ginger
1 teaspoon baking soda
1 teaspoon ground cinnamon
¼ teaspoon ground cloves
¼ teaspoon salt
⅔ cup (1⅓ sticks) unsalted butter, slightly firm
¾ cup granulated sugar
½ cup lightly packed dark brown sugar
1 large egg
1 teaspoon pure vanilla extract
1 teaspoon cider vinegar
3 tablespoons finely chopped crystallized ginger

Cookie Characteristics

Homestyle

Long shelf life

Travel well

1. Position the shelves in the upper and lower thirds of the oven. Heat the oven to 375°. Line the cookie sheets with baking parchment.

2. Strain together the flour, ginger, baking soda, cinnamon, cloves, and salt. Set aside.

3. In the bowl of an electric mixer fitted with the paddle attachment, mix the butter with the sugars on medium-low speed until creamy and lightened in color, 2 to 3 minutes.

4. Add the egg and mix until well combined, about 1 minute. Scrape down the side of the bowl. Add the vanilla and the cider vinegar and mix for 1 minute longer. Reduce the mixer speed to low and add the dry ingredients in three additions, mixing *just* until combined. Using a large rubber spatula, blend in the crystallized ginger.

5. Break off walnut-size pieces of dough and roll into 1¼-inch balls. Place 2 inches apart on the cookie sheets. Bake for 9 to 11 minutes, or until golden brown. Toward the end of baking time, rotate the pans from top to bottom and front to back. Let rest on the cookie sheets for 2 minutes, then loosen with a thin metal spatula and transfer to cooling racks.

STORAGE: Store in an airtight container, layered between strips of wax paper, for up to 3 weeks. These cookies may be frozen.

BAKE THE COOKIES

4. Position the shelves in the upper and lower thirds of the oven. Heat the oven to 375°. Moderately butter the cookie sheets.

5. Roll the dough in the palms of your hands to form 1-inch balls and place on the cookie sheets, about 2 inches apart. Gently press a whole almond into the center of each cookie. Using the heel of your hand, flatten the cookie into a 1½-inch disk. Bake for 10 to 12 minutes or until the edges are golden brown. Toward the end of baking time rotate the pans from top to bottom and front to back. Let stand for 2 or 3 minutes before loosening with a thin metal spatula. Transfer to cooling racks.

STORAGE: Store in an airtight container, layered between strips of wax paper, for up to 3 weeks. These cookies may be frozen.

Cookie
Characteristics

Versatile

Long shelf life

Travel well

oatmeal almond jammies

MAKES ABOUT 5 DOZEN 2-INCH COOKIES

Oatmeal, almond paste, toasted almonds, and a touch of cinnamon make an exciting kaleidoscope of flavors for Oatmeal Almond Jammies. The center of this thumbprint-style cookie is chewy with almond paste, while the crust is crunchy with toasted almonds. While some recipes for thumbprint cookies have their cavities filled before baking, I think you achieve a prettier end result if the depression is made twice: once before the cookies are baked and again midway through baking. Although I love these cookies filled with blackberry preserves, you may use any flavor of preserves you wish.

AT A GLANCE

PAN: Jelly roll pans

PAN PREP: Baking parchment

OVEN TEMP: 350°

CHILLING TIME: 30–45 minutes

BAKING TIME: 20–24 minutes

DIFFICULTY: ○○

1½ cups all-purpose flour, spooned in and leveled

¾ cup old-fashioned oatmeal

1½ teaspoons baking powder

¾ teaspoon ground cinnamon

½ teaspoon salt

¾ cup (1½ sticks) unsalted butter, at room temperature

3 ounces almond paste, shredded (see page 390)

1¼ cups sugar

1 large egg

2 large egg yolks

1½ teaspoons pure vanilla extract

½ teaspoon pure almond extract

1½ cups sliced unblanched almonds, toasted

2 large egg whites, lightly beaten with 2 teaspoons water

½ cup blackberry preserves

MAKE THE DOUGH

1. Place the flour, oatmeal, baking powder, cinnamon, and salt in the bowl of a food processor fitted with a steel blade and process for 15 seconds. Pulse four times, then process for another 25 seconds. The mixture will be cakey in texture.

2. In the large bowl of an electric mixer fitted with the paddle attachment, mix the butter on medium-low speed until smooth and lightened in color. Add the almond paste and mix until completely smooth, 3 to 4 minutes. Add the sugar in three additions, scraping the bowl after the final addition. Add the egg, egg yolks, and extracts and mix until well blended, scraping the side of the bowl as needed.

3. Reduce the mixer speed to low and add the dry ingredients in two additions, mixing *just* until blended after each addition. Cover the bowl with plastic wrap and chill for 30 to 45 minutes, until firm enough to handle.

BAKE THE COOKIES

4. Position the shelves in the upper and lower thirds of the oven. Heat oven to 350°. Line the pans with baking parchment.

5. Place the almonds in a large, shallow dish, such as a pie plate, then break them up coarsely with your fingers.

6. Roll the dough into 1-inch balls. Roll each ball in the egg whites, then roll in the crumbled nuts to coat. Place 2 inches apart on the cookie sheets. Using the handle of a wooden spoon, poke an indentation in the center of each. (If dough sticks, dip the end of the spoon in flour.)

7. Bake for 12 to 14 minutes, remove from the oven, and re-press each indentation. Fill each with a scant ½ teaspoon jam and return to oven. (Do *not* overfill.)

Bake for an additional 8 to 10 minutes, until the edges are golden brown. Toward the end of baking time rotate the pans from top to bottom and front to back. Remove from the oven and let stand for 2 or 3 minutes before loosening with a thin metal spatula. Cool on a wire rack.

STORAGE: Store in an airtight container, layered between strips of wax paper, for up to 2 weeks. These cookies may be frozen.

Cookie Characteristics

Versatile

Long shelf life

Travel well

"On days when warmth is the most important need of the human heart, the kitchen is the place you can find it." —E. B. WHITE

oatmeal walnut crispies

MAKES ABOUT 5 DOZEN 2½-INCH COOKIES

These wonderfully crunchy cookies receive their texture from flakes of oatmeal, chopped walnuts, and egg whites. The buttery batter is heightened with a hint of cinnamon, creating one heck of a delicious cookie.

AT A GLANCE

PAN: Cookie sheets
PAN PREP: Moderately buttered
OVEN TEMP: 375°
BAKING TIME: 13–15 minutes
DIFFICULTY: ○

1¾ cups all-purpose flour, spooned in and leveled
1 teaspoon baking soda
½ teaspoon salt
½ teaspoon ground cinnamon
1 cup (2 sticks) unsalted butter, at room temperature
1⅓ cups sugar
2 large egg whites
2 teaspoons pure vanilla extract
2 cups quick (1-minute) oatmeal
1¼ cups medium-chopped walnuts

Cookie Characteristics

Versatile

Long shelf life

Travel well

1. Position the shelves in the upper and lower thirds of the oven. Heat the oven to 375°. Moderately butter the cookie sheets.

2. Strain together the flour, baking soda, salt, and cinnamon. Set aside.

3. In the large bowl of an electric mixer fitted with the paddle attachment, mix the butter on medium-low speed until smooth and lightened in color. Increase the speed to medium and gradually add the sugar over 2 to 3 minutes. Add the egg whites one at a time, beating well after each addition and scraping down the side of the bowl as needed. Blend in the vanilla.

4. Reduce the mixer speed to low. Add the dry ingredients in three additions, then blend in the oatmeal. Mix on low speed *just* until the ingredients are blended together. Using a large rubber spatula, fold in the nuts.

5. Using a teaspoon to portion the dough, make 1¼-inch walnut-size balls and place them 2 inches apart on the cookie sheets. Bake for 13 to 15 minutes, or until golden brown. Toward the end of baking time rotate the pans from top to bottom and front to back. Let stand for 2 or 3 minutes before loosening with a thin metal spatula. Cool on wire racks.

STORAGE: Store in an airtight container, layered between strips of wax paper, for up to 2 weeks. These cookies may be frozen.

Chocolate Chip Oatmeal Crispies

Reduce walnuts to ½ cup. Blend in ¾ cup mini semisweet chocolate morsels when you add the nuts. Proceed as directed in the Master Recipe.

Secrets for Making Hand-Formed Cookies

- Letting dough rest for a few minutes before shaping will reduce its stickiness.

- Scooping the dough out with a spoon before hand-shaping helps to ensure even-sized cookies.

- To divide cookie dough evenly, form into a square before chilling. When the dough is firm enough to handle, divide the square into cubes using a dough scraper. The size of the square is determined by the yield of the recipe. After the squares are cut, roll each into a ball.

- If cookie dough is too soft, chill it for approximately 30 minutes or until it is firm enough to handle. Always scrape down the side of the bowl before chilling the dough.

- Do not allow cookie dough to become too cold or it will crumble and be difficult to shape. Allow it to stand at room temperature until it is malleable.

- If the dough sticks to your hands, coat your hands with flour or sugar. Alternatively, if you have warm hands, periodically rinse them in very cold water, or put ice cubes in a metal bowl and hold the bowl to cool your hands. Washing your hands periodically will prevent the dough from sticking.

- When forming the dough into balls, the thickness of the finished cookies will be more even if the balls are first flattened. You can use the heel of your hand or your fingertips, but be sure to avoid your palm because it is the warmest part of your hand. Good results are also achieved by using a flat-bottomed glass or a bâtarde. If the cookie dough sticks, cover the glass or bâtarde with a piece of plastic wrap, dampened paper toweling, or a smooth dish towel. The glass or bâtarde may also be dipped in flour or sugar to prevent sticking.

- When rolling dough into balls, only roll the ball three or four times between the palms of your hands. If the dough is overworked, it will become too soft. This will cause the dough to lose its shape during baking and will toughen the texture of the cookie.

- Hand-formed cookies lend themselves to coatings like sugar, finely chopped nuts, cocoa powder, decorative sugars, jimmies, nonpareils, and spice-flavored sugars. To make the coating adhere, the balls of dough are sometimes dipped in lightly beaten egg white.

- If the balls of dough are to be coated, let them air-dry a few minutes before trimming. They will be easier to handle.

- To apply the coatings neatly and evenly, place the coatings in a shallow pan or pie plate. Instead of using your hands to coat the dough, shimmy the pan back and forth, working with only a few balls at a time.

- Use only a portion of the coating at a time to guarantee a fresh appearance for the finished cookie.

poppy seed thumbprints

MAKES ABOUT 40 1¾-INCH COOKIES

Here is an easy cookie that will add pizzazz to any platter of sweets. The centers of the cookies are usually filled with colorful preserves, but sometimes I vary this selection with a bull's-eye of thickened Ganache Glaze (page 360). While I love the crunch that poppy seeds add, they can be omitted if you wish.

AT A GLANCE

PAN: Cookie sheets

PAN PREP: Ungreased

OVEN TEMP: 350°

BAKING TIME: 14–15 minutes

DIFFICULTY: ◐◐

2 cups all-purpose flour, spooned in and leveled

¼ teaspoon salt

¼ cup poppy seeds

1 cup (2 sticks) unsalted butter, slightly firm

½ cup sugar

2 large egg yolks

1 teaspoon pure vanilla extract

Raspberry preserves

Apricot preserves

1. Position the shelves in the upper and lower thirds of the oven. Heat the oven to 350°.

2. Strain together the flour and salt in a large bowl. Whisk in the poppy seeds and set aside.

3. In the large bowl of an electric mixer fitted with the paddle attachment, mix the butter on medium-low speed until smooth. Pour in the sugar and mix *just* until incorporated. Add the egg yolks and vanilla, mixing only until blended. Using a wooden spoon, stir in the dry ingredients in two additions, mixing *just* to combine after each addition. *Note:* Do not overmix this dough or it will become oily.

4. Roll the dough into balls about the size of a large walnut and place 2 inches apart on the cookie sheets. Using a wooden spoon with a rounded handle no wider than ½ inch, make a deep indentation with the tip of the handle in the center of each cookie. If the dough sticks, dip the tip in flour before pressing.

5. Place the cookies in the oven. After 10 minutes, remove the cookies from the oven and re-press each indentation. Then fill the centers with preserves. To do this neatly, point the tip of the spoon down into the indentation and slide the preserves off with your fingertip. Do not overfill these or the preserves will run over.

6. Return cookies to the oven, rotating the pans top to bottom and front to back. Bake for 4 to 5 minutes longer, or until the cookies are golden brown around the edges. Using a thin metal spatula, loosen the cookies from the pans as soon as they are cool enough to handle. Cool on wire racks.

STORAGE: Store in an airtight container, layered between strips of wax paper, for up to 2 weeks. These cookies may be frozen.

almond thumbprints

Substitute ¼ cup very finely chopped toasted unskinned sliced almonds for the poppy seeds, then proceed with the Master Recipe.

Cookie Characteristics

Versatile

Travel well

Long shelf life

honey-roasted peanut butter cookies

MAKES ABOUT 40 2½-INCH COOKIES

Peanut butter cookies, an all-American favorite, are also a favorite of mine. Since honey and peanut butter are a tasty flavor combination, I add honey-roasted peanuts to my cookie dough along with a touch of honey. The honey adds moistness to the cookie and contributes a lovely but subtle flavor. If your family is not into nuts the way I am, it's okay to omit the peanuts and use smooth peanut butter instead of crunchy.

AT A GLANCE

PAN: Cookie sheets
PAN PREP: Ungreased
OVEN TEMP: 350°
CHILLING TIME: 1 hour
BAKING TIME: 11–13 minutes
DIFFICULTY: ✪

1¼ cups all-purpose flour, spooned in and leveled
1 tablespoon wheat germ (optional)
½ teaspoon baking soda
½ teaspoon baking powder
½ teaspoon salt
1 cup crunchy peanut butter
¼ cup (½ stick) unsalted butter, softened
¼ cup vegetable shortening
2 tablespoons honey
½ cup granulated sugar
⅓ cup lightly packed light brown sugar
1 large egg
1 teaspoon pure vanilla extract
½ cup coarsely chopped honey-roasted peanuts

MAKE THE DOUGH

1. In a large bowl whisk together the flour, wheat germ, baking soda, baking powder, and salt. Set aside.
2. Using an electric mixer fitted with the paddle attachment, mix the peanut butter, butter, vegetable shortening, and honey until well blended. On medium speed, add the granulated sugar and then the brown sugar and mix for 1 minute, until combined. Add the egg and vanilla and mix for 1 to 2 minutes, or until the batter lightens in color.
3. Reduce the mixer speed to low and add the dry ingredients, mixing *just* until blended. Fold in the chopped peanuts and chill for 1 hour or until firm enough to handle.

BAKE THE COOKIES

4. Position the shelves in the upper and lower thirds of the oven. Heat the oven to 350°.
5. Roll the dough into 1¼-inch balls, about the size of large walnuts, and place about 2 inches apart on the cookie sheets. Using a table fork that has been

dipped in flour, slightly flatten the cookies while making a crosshatch design across the tops. Bake for 11 to 13 minutes or until lightly golden. Toward the end of the baking time rotate the pans from top to bottom and front to back. Let cookies stand for 1 minute before removing with a thin metal spatula. Transfer to cooling racks.

STORAGE: Store in an airtight container, layered between strips of wax paper, for up to 2 weeks. These cookies may be frozen.

Cookie Characteristics

Homestyle

Long shelf life

Travel well

"What is sweeter than honey?" —JUDGES 14:18

peanut butter balls

MAKES 5 DOZEN 1½-INCH COOKIES

One day, my assistant, Kathie, and I were comparing our grandmothers' recipe boxes (they happened to be identical!). Kathie's, like mine, was filled with hand-written recipes. They were gathered over the years by her mother, an avid baker. One of the recipes that caught my eye was from the kitchen of Noel Rozint, a dear friend of Kathie's mom.

It was a simple "no-bake" cookie made with the irresistible combination of peanut butter and chocolate. So, I decided to try it. I loved the results! If you have youngsters who enjoy "hands-on" baking, by all means, ask for their assistance when making these cookies. And don't forget to taste, I mean *test*, for quality while making them!

AT A GLANCE   PAN: Jelly roll pans
PAN PREP: Baking parchment
DIFFICULTY: ◑

2⅓ cups strained confectioners' sugar, spooned in and leveled
1 cup graham cracker crumbs
½ cup (1 stick) unsalted butter, softened
¾ cup chunky peanut butter
10 ounces semisweet chocolate, coarsely chopped
2 teaspoons vegetable oil
2 cups salted peanuts, finely chopped

1. In a large bowl, stir together the confectioners' sugar and graham cracker crumbs. Add the butter and peanut butter and work with a wooden spoon or with your hands until thoroughly combined. Portion the dough into 60 1-inch balls and place them on parchment-lined jelly roll pans.

2. Combine the chocolate and vegetable oil in a medium heat-proof bowl. Place the bowl over a medium saucepan filled with simmering water and slowly melt the chocolate, stirring occasionally. When the chocolate is melted, remove it from the heat, but keep the bowl over the pot of water. Place about ½ cup of the chopped peanuts in a low flat dish, such as a pie plate.

3. Using a chocolate dipping fork (see page 383), or a 2-prong fork, dip one ball at a time in the melted chocolate. Tap the fork gently on the side of the bowl to help drain the chocolate from the cookie. The coating should be thin. Roll the dipped cookie in the chopped peanuts, and coat it evenly. Remove the cookie with a 2-prong fork and place it back on the jelly roll pan to set. Repeat with the remaining cookies, adding peanuts as needed. (It is easier to roll the cookies in a small amount of peanuts.) If the chocolate begins to

crackly cinnamon wafers

MAKES ABOUT 7 DOZEN 2¾–INCH COOKIES

Here we have thin butter cookies with a heady cinnamon flavor that are delicate and oh, so scrumptious! A light brushing of egg wash forms a whisper of a crust that twinkles with a sprinkling of coarse sugar. If these larger granules are difficult to obtain, granulated sugar may be substituted. The sparkly cookies are perfect to serve at teatime or on your best holiday table.

AT A GLANCE

PAN: Cookie sheets

PAN PREP: Moderately buttered

OVEN TEMP: 350°

CHILLING TIME: 1 hour

BAKING TIME: 10–11 minutes

DIFFICULTY: ✪

1¾ cups all-purpose flour, spooned in and leveled

1 tablespoon ground cinnamon

1 cup (2 sticks) unsalted butter, slightly firm

1 cup granulated sugar

1 large egg, separated

3 to 4 tablespoons sparkling white sugar (available from The Baker's Catalogue; page 403), for garnish

Cookie Characteristics

Versatile

Long shelf life

Fragile

MAKE THE DOUGH

1. Strain together the flour and cinnamon. Set aside.

2. Using an electric mixer fitted with the paddle attachment on medium-low speed, mix the butter until smooth. Add the granulated sugar in a steady stream and beat until combined. Add the egg yolk and mix for 1 minute longer, scraping down the side of the bowl as needed. Reduce the mixer speed to low, then add the dry ingredients in three additions, mixing *just* until blended after each addition. Cover with plastic wrap and refrigerate for 1 hour.

BAKE THE COOKIES

3. Position the shelves in the upper and lower thirds of the oven. Heat oven to 350°. Moderately butter the cookie sheets.

4. Roll dough into ¾-inch balls and place on the prepared cookie sheets, about 2½ inches apart. Using the bottom of a flat-bottomed glass that has been covered with plastic wrap and dipped in flour, flatten the dough balls into 2½-inch disks.

5. In a shallow dish, lightly beat the egg white with 2 teaspoons cold water and brush the top of each cookie with the egg wash. Sprinkle each cookie with sparkling white sugar. Bake for 10 to 11 minutes or until the edges are golden brown. Rotate the pans from top to bottom and front to back toward the end of baking time. Let stand for 1 minute, then loosen with a thin metal spatula. Transfer to cooling racks.

STORAGE: Store in an airtight container, layered between strips of wax paper, for up to 3 weeks. These cookies may be frozen.

pecan tassies

MAKES 4 DOZEN 1¾-INCH TASSIES

When I grew up down South, one of my favorite sweet treats was Pecan Tassies. These miniature cookie-like tartlets are reminiscent of the ultimate Southern favorite, pecan pie. The Tassies have a flaky cream cheese pastry with an addictive brown sugar and butter filling with lots of chopped pecans.

Admittedly, Tassies are a time-consuming project—but they can be made ahead and they will freeze beautifully. I guarantee that when you serve them, the oohs and ahhs will more than compensate you for your efforts! As a matter of fact, I wish I had one right now!

AT A GLANCE

PAN: Mini-muffin tins
PAN PREP: Ungreased
OVEN TEMP: 325°
CHILLING TIME: Pastry: 4 hours
BAKING TIME: 20–25 minutes
DIFFICULTY: ●●●

1 recipe Cream Cheese Pastry (page 175), formed into 2 4 × 6-inch rectangles, wrapped in plastic and chilled

FILLING

2 large eggs
2 cups lightly packed *very fresh* dark brown sugar
2 tablespoons unsalted butter, melted and cooled
¼ teaspoon salt
2 teaspoons pure vanilla extract
2 cups coarsely chopped lightly toasted pecans, divided

Cookie Characteristics

Versatile

Moderate shelf life

Travel well

1. Divide each rectangle of pastry into 24 1-inch squares. Roll each square into a ball and place into mini-muffin tins. Mold the dough into each hole, pressing it up the sides (see Tassie Tips, page 73). Chill while preparing the filling.

2. Position the shelves in the upper and lower thirds of the oven. Heat the oven to 325°.

3. Place the eggs, brown sugar, butter, salt, and vanilla in a large bowl. Whisk together until smooth.

4. Distribute 1 cup of the pecans among the pastry-lined muffin cups. Empty the filling into a measuring cup with a spout and pour the mixture into the tins, *filling them no more than two-thirds full*. Sprinkle the tops with the remaining 1 cup nuts.

5. Bake for 20 to 25 minutes or until the pastry is golden brown around the edges. Rotate the pans from top to bottom and front to back toward the end of baking time. Let stand 5 minutes. Using the tip of a paring knife, run the blade carefully around the edges of the muffin cups to loosen the Tassies. When the Tassies are cool enough to handle, remove them from the pan and set on cooling racks. (Note: The Tassies can either be eased out with the tip of the knife or inverted onto the cooling rack.)

Store in an airtight container, layered between strips of wax paper, for up to 5 days. These cookies may be frozen.

"If you are lazy and dump everything together, they won't come out as well as if you add one thing at a time— no shortcuts without compromising quality."

—LIONEL POILÂNE

Tassie Tips

- For best results, use a Tassie or tart tamper to press the dough into the muffin cups (see About Equipment, page 383). If unavailable, use your thumb.

- When lining the muffin cups, be sure to press the dough thinly into the tins, paying special attention to the thickness of the dough that accumulates around the crease of the mold.

- To prevent the filling from leaking through the dough, sprinkle half of the chopped pecans into each of the cups before filling them. This will absorb the syrupy mixture, eliminating the troublesome problem of sticking to the bottom of the muffin tin.

- Mix the batter *briefly* by hand, using a whisk. Do not use an electric mixer, as it creates too many air bubbles.

- Fresh brown sugar is essential because it dissolves better.

- Use a liquid measuring cup with a spout to pour in the filling.

- The Tassie cup should not be filled more than two-thirds full because the filling puffs during baking.

- After baking, the Tassies should be loosened with the tip of a small, thin, sharp knife angled against the side of the pan, and not against the cookie.

- It is best to remove Tassies from the mini-muffin tins while they are still warm.

- Frozen Tassies should be reheated before serving (see Refreshing Cookies, page 400).

coconut lemon-lime tassies

MAKES 4 DOZEN 1¾-INCH TASSIES

Here is a citrusy twist on the classic Tassie recipe. A tangy lemon-lime filling is nestled between layers of flaky coconut. The flavor of the buttery pastry along with the tang of the cream cheese makes the perfect background for these tartlets.

AT A GLANCE

PAN: Mini-muffin tins
PAN PREP: Ungreased
OVEN TEMP: 350°
CHILLING TIME: Pastry: 4 hours
BAKING TIME: 30–32 minutes
DIFFICULTY: ❶❷❸

1 recipe Cream Cheese Pastry (page 175), formed into 2 4 × 6-inch rectangles

FILLING

3 tablespoons all-purpose flour
½ teaspoon baking powder
¼ teaspoon salt
4 large egg yolks
1¼ cups sugar
3 tablespoons fresh lemon juice
3 tablespoons fresh lime juice
2 teaspoons freshly grated lemon zest
2 teaspoons freshly grated lime zest
1 cup chopped sweetened, flaked coconut, divided
1 recipe Vanilla Glaze (page 358)

Cookie Characteristics

Versatile

Moderate shelf life

Travel well

1. Divide each rectangle of pastry into 24 1-inch squares. Roll each into a ball and place into mini-muffin tins. Mold the dough into each hole, pressing it up the sides. Chill while preparing the filling.

2. Position the shelves in the upper and lower thirds of the oven. Heat the oven to 350°.

3. Strain together the flour, baking powder, and salt. Set aside.

4. In a large bowl of an electric mixer fitted with the whip attachment, beat the egg yolks on medium speed until lightened in color. Add the sugar in a steady stream, beating until thickened. On low speed blend in the juices and the zests. Remove the bowl from the machine and fold in the dry ingredients and ½ cup of the coconut.

5. Sprinkle the remaining coconut into the pastry-lined muffin cups. Empty the filling into a measuring cup with a spout and pour the mixture into the tins, *filling them no more than two-thirds full.*

6. Bake for 30 to 32 minutes, or until the pastry is golden brown around the edges. Toward the end of baking time, rotate the pans top to bottom and front to back. Let stand 5 minutes. Using the tip of a paring knife, run the blade carefully around the edges of the muffin cups to loosen the Tassies. When the cups are cool enough to handle, remove them from the pan and set on cooling racks. While they are slightly warm, apply a small amount of Vanilla Glaze to the top of each tassie, spreading it with the bottom of a teaspoon.

STORAGE: Store in the refrigerator in an airtight container, layered between strips of wax paper, for up to 5 days. These cookies may be frozen.

chocolate and vanilla moonstones

MAKES ABOUT 4 DOZEN 3-INCH COOKIES

I began with a vision of a cookie made with chocolate and vanilla dough that would be marbleized. Because this cookie was prepared with a drop cookie dough, I never knew what free-form pattern would emerge. After baking, each cookie came out with different variegated chocolate and vanilla tones reminding me of the surface of the moon. Hence, the name: Chocolate and Vanilla Moonstones. You could also tint the cookie dough with vegetable coloring, making any color combination you wish. Children will love it!

AT A GLANCE

PAN: Cookie sheets
PAN PREP: Moderately buttered
OVEN TEMP: 375°
BAKING TIME: 9–11 minutes
DIFFICULTY: ○

2 ounces unsweetened chocolate, coarsely chopped
2¼ cups all-purpose flour, spooned in and leveled
¼ teaspoon cream of tartar
¼ teaspoon baking soda
¼ teaspoon salt
1 cup (2 sticks) unsalted butter, slightly firm
1 cup superfine sugar
1 large egg
1½ teaspoons pure vanilla extract
3 teaspoons hot water, divided
2 tablespoons granulated sugar, for flattening the cookies

1. Position the shelves in the upper and lower thirds of the oven. Heat the oven to 375°. Moderately butter the cookie sheets.

2. Place the chocolate in a small bowl and melt it over hot water. Keep warm.

3. Strain together the flour, cream of tartar, baking soda, and salt. Set aside.

4. In the large bowl of an electric mixer fitted with the paddle attachment, mix the butter on medium-low speed until smooth, about 1 minute. Add the superfine sugar all at once and mix until well blended, about 1 minute. Scrape down the bowl as needed, then add the egg and vanilla. Mix *just* until blended. Reduce mixer speed to low. Blend in half of the dry ingredients with 2 teaspoons of the hot water. Stop the mixer and scrape down the side of the bowl, then add the remaining dry ingredients, mixing *just* until combined.

5. Transfer one-third (about 1 cup) of the dough to a separate bowl. Using a fork, blend in the remaining 1 teaspoon of hot water. Then add the warm melted chocolate and work the mixture with the

6. Drop the dough from the tip of a teaspoon, making 1¼-inch mounds about the size of walnuts, spaced 2 inches apart onto the cookie sheets. The dough will firm as it stands. After the dough has been portioned, moisten your hands lightly with cold tap water and shape each mound into a ball, remoistening your hands as needed.

7. Place the remaining ¾ cup almonds and the sparkling white sugar in a large shallow dish (a pie plate works well).

8. Dip one side of each ball into the beaten egg white, then into the almond and sugar mixture, pressing to adhere the almonds and sugar to the dough. Place the ball back onto the cookie sheet, nut side up, and press the top gently with the heel of your hand to ½-inch thickness. Repeat with remaining balls.

BAKE THE COOKIES

9. Bake the cookies for 7 minutes. Toward the end of baking time rotate the sheets top to bottom and front to back. Test for doneness by touching the tops of the cookies gently to see if they are set. If not, return to the oven for one minute and check again. *Do not overbake.* The cookies will be soft to the touch, but will firm upon cooling. Let the cookies stand about 5 minutes, then loosen them from the parchment with a thin metal spatula and transfer to cooling racks to air-dry for about 1 hour.

STORAGE: Store in airtight containers layered between sheets of wax paper for up to 5 days. These cookies may be frozen.

Cookie
Characteristics

Versatile

Moderate
shelf life

Travel well

chocolate snowcaps

MAKES ABOUT 4 DOZEN 2-INCH COOKIES

These chocolate shortbread cookies are topped with disks of semi-sweet chocolate nonpareil candies. While nonpareils are available in most supermarkets, those purchased from a specialty candy store will be well worth the investment. Not only are these candies available in assorted flavors of semisweet, milk, and bittersweet chocolate, but some are covered with rainbow nonpareils.

Because these cookies are made with a shortbread-style dough, take care not to overwork the mixture, otherwise the dough will become too soft to handle.

AT A GLANCE

PAN: Cookie sheets

PAN PREP: Well buttered

OVEN TEMP: 350°

CHILLING TIME: 45–60 minutes

BAKING TIME: 11–13 minutes

DIFFICULTY: ◐◐

1¾ cups all-purpose flour, spooned in and leveled

½ cup strained Dutch-processed cocoa powder, spooned in and leveled

¼ teaspoon salt

1 cup (2 sticks) unsalted butter, slightly firm

1 cup strained confectioners' sugar, spooned in and leveled

1 teaspoon pure vanilla extract

3 tablespoons granulated sugar

1½ teaspoons *seedless* raspberry preserves

48 semisweet chocolate nonpareil candies

MAKE THE DOUGH

1. Strain together the flour, cocoa, and salt. Set aside.

2. In the large bowl of an electric mixer fitted with the paddle attachment, mix the butter on low speed until smooth. Add the confectioners' sugar with the vanilla and mix just until blended.

3. Add half of the dry ingredients and mix briefly to incorporate. Using a wooden spoon, stir in the remaining dry ingredients by hand, working the mixture *just* until the dough is smooth. Do not overmix.

4. Scrape the dough onto a strip of plastic wrap, then shape it into a 6 × 8-inch rectangle. Wrap the dough in the plastic and refrigerate until firm, 45 to 60 minutes.

BAKE THE COOKIES

5. Position the racks in the lower and upper thirds of the oven. Heat the oven to 350°. Butter the cookie sheets well.

6. Using a pastry scraper, divide the dough into 48 1-inch squares. Roll each square into a ball and arrange about 2 inches apart on the cookie sheets. Place the granulated sugar in a shallow dish. Dip a flat-bottomed glass into the sugar, then press down on each ball to form a 2-inch disk. Using a small spatula, spread a *dab* of preserves on the bottom of a nonpareil and lightly press the candy, topside up, into the center of each disk.

7. Bake for 11 to 13 minutes or until the cookies feel set on top. Rotate the pans from top to bottom and front to back toward the end of baking time. Remove the cookies from the oven and let stand for 1 to 2 minutes before loosening with a metal spatula. They will harden as they cool. When firm enough to handle, transfer the cookies to cooling racks.

STORAGE: Store in an airtight container, layered between strips of wax paper, for up to 3 weeks. These cookies may be frozen.

Cookie Characteristics

Versatile

Long shelf life

Temperature sensitive

tipsy chocolate date nut gems

MAKES 4 DOZEN

For this cookie, chewy dates and crunchy pecans are nestled in a moist, tasty chocolate cookie batter that is baked in mini-muffin tins. After baking, the cookies are briefly steeped in warm rum syrup. I flatten each cookie with the heel of my hand, transforming it into a chewy chocolate medallion. These cookies are so-o-o good that the effort it takes to make them is worth the reward. Chocolate and dates are a marriage made in heaven—promise you'll try these!

AT A GLANCE **PAN:** Mini-muffin tins

PAN PREP: Nonstick cooking spray

OVEN TEMP: 350°

BAKING TIME: 9–10 minutes

DIFFICULTY: ❍❍❍

RUM SYRUP
- 1½ cups water
- ¾ cup sugar
- 3 to 4 tablespoons dark Jamaican rum

BATTER
- ½ cup all-purpose flour, spooned in and leveled
- ½ cup strained cocoa powder, spooned in and leveled
- ¾ teaspoon salt
- 2 large eggs
- ½ cup lightly packed dark brown sugar
- ½ cup dark corn syrup
- ¼ cup (½ stick) unsalted butter, melted and cooled to tepid
- 1 teaspoon pure vanilla extract
- ½ teaspoon pure almond extract
- 1 cup hand-cut pitted dates (¼-inch dice)
- 1 cup medium chopped pecans
- 2 cups strained confectioners' sugar, spooned in and leveled, divided, for dusting

MAKE THE SYRUP

1. Place the water and sugar in a small saucepan over low heat. Bring to a boil, stirring occasionally to dissolve the sugar, then simmer for 1 minute. Off the heat, stir in the rum and set aside.

MAKE THE COOKIES

2. Position the shelves in the upper and lower thirds of the oven. Heat the oven to 350°. Coat the mini-muffin tins with nonstick cooking spray. Set aside.

3. Strain together the flour, cocoa powder, and salt. Set aside.

4. In the large bowl of an electric mixer fitted with the whip attachment, beat the eggs on medium speed, about 1 minute. Add the dark brown sugar, dark corn syrup, melted butter, and extracts. Mix until well blended, about 1 minute. On low speed, add the dry ingredients and mix *just* until blended. Using an oversize rubber spatula, fold in the dates and pecans.

5. Using a teaspoon, spoon the batter into the mini-muffin tins, filling them about two-thirds full. Bake for 9 to 10 minutes, or until the cookies are *just* set on top.

6. Remove the muffin tins from the oven and let the cookies rest in the pans for 5 minutes, or until the cookies pull away from the sides of the pans. Invert the pans onto wax paper, tapping firmly against the countertop to release the cookies.

7. While the cookies are still warm, using a slotted spoon, dip each cookie into the warm syrup and place on a thin wire cooling rack. The cookies should only be moistened with the syrup, not soaked. (Discard any leftover syrup.) Let the cookies air-dry for 25 to 30 minutes.

8. Place 1 cup of the confectioners' sugar in a large shallow dish, such as a pie plate. Working with one cookie at a time, roll in the sugar, coating thoroughly. While still in the dish, use the heel of your hand to gently flatten the cookie to ⅜- to ½-inch thickness. Return to the rack and air-dry for 30 minutes. Repeat with the remaining cookies.

NOTE: When ready to serve, roll the cookies in the remaining cup of confectioners' sugar. This may be done up to 12 hours ahead. The cookies are best when served at room temperature.

STORAGE: Store the cookies in an airtight container, layered between sheets of wax paper, and refrigerate until ready to use. These cookies will keep for up to 4 weeks in the refrigerator. Freezing is not recommended.

Cookie Characteristics

Versatile

Long shelf life

Temperature sensitive

almondates

MAKES 5 DOZEN 2-INCH COOKIES

Here is an easy no-bake cookie from my recipe archives. I developed it during my catering days to serve at outdoor parties. The combination of crunchy almonds and walnuts, chocolate chips, and chewy dates all rolled in coconut proved irresistible, and I found myself making them more and more frequently! Don't wait for summer to try them. These are wonderful twelve months of the year!

AT A GLANCE

PAN: Cooling racks

PAN PREP: None

DIFFICULTY: ○

½ cup coarsely chopped unblanched
    almonds
½ cup coarsely chopped walnuts
60 whole blanched almonds
1 cup (2 sticks) unsalted butter
¾ cup sugar
1 large egg, lightly beaten
1 pound pitted dates, chopped
2 cups crispy rice cereal
1 tablespoon Amaretto liqueur
¾ cup semisweet chocolate mini-
    morsels, divided
2½ cups sweetened, flaked coconut

1. Heat the oven to 325°. Spread the chopped almonds and walnuts in a shallow baking pan. Bake for 8 to 10 minutes or until lightly toasted. Empty them into a bowl. Then toast the whole blanched almonds for 12 to 15 minutes, or until lightly browned. Set aside.

2. In a heavy, medium saucepan over low heat, melt the butter, then add the sugar, egg, and dates. Bring to a slow boil and cook over low heat for 6 to 7 minutes, or until the mixture is slightly thickened and the dates are cooked. Be sure to stir frequently. Remove from the heat and pour the mixture into a large mixing bowl. Cool for 5 minutes.

3. Fold in the nuts, rice cereal, and Amaretto. When the date mixture is tepid, fold in ½ cup of the mini-morsels. (If the mixture is too hot, the chocolate chips will melt.)

4. Take spoonfuls of the date mixture and form into about 60 1¼-inch balls, moistening your hands with ice water as needed. (The batter will be sticky.)

5. Empty one-third of the coconut into a shallow dish, such as a pie plate. Shape the balls into logs 1 inch wide by 1½ inches long, then roll them in the coconut. Continue shaping the logs and rolling them in the coconut, replenishing the coconut as needed. *Do not empty all of the coconut into the shallow dish at once, as it tends to discolor with use.*

6. Have ready a wire rack set over a jelly roll pan. Place the remaining ¼ cup mini-morsels in a small heat-proof custard cup, and melt on medium setting in a microwave. Using a small offset spatula, spread a dab of the melted chocolate on one side of the toasted almond and press it firmly into the log. Repeat with the remaining logs. Place the logs on the wire rack to air-dry for 1 hour.

STORAGE: Refrigerate in an airtight container, layered between strips of wax paper, for up to 2 weeks. Freezing is not recommended.

Cookie
Characteristics

Versatile

Long shelf life

Temperature
sensitive

3 Big Boys

super sugar sparkles

MAKES 16 5-INCH COOKIES

Bite into one of these monster sugar cookies, and your mouth will be greeted by melting layers of a buttery cookie topped with a generous sprinkling of crackly, crunchy sugar. I like these cookies best when made with coarse sugar, but table sugar is also an option. At holiday time, think about using the coarse rainbow sugar. Package two or three cookies in a cellophane bag tied with a festive ribbon and voilà! What a nice and easy gift!

AT A GLANCE **PAN:** Oversized (14 × 17-inch) cookie sheets

PAN PREP: Well buttered

OVEN TEMP: 375°

BAKING TIME: 13–14 minutes

DIFFICULTY: ◗

3 cups all-purpose flour, spooned in and leveled

½ teaspoon salt

¼ teaspoon baking soda

¼ teaspoon cream of tartar

1 cup (2 sticks) unsalted butter, slightly firm, cut into 1-inch pieces

1¼ cups superfine sugar

2 large eggs, separated

2 teaspoons pure vanilla extract

2 tablespoons milk

2 teaspoons water

⅓ cup sparkling white sugar, for garnish (available in The Baker's Catalogue; see page 403)

1. Position the shelves in the lower and upper thirds of the oven. Heat the oven to 375 °. Butter the cookie sheets well.

2. Strain together the flour, salt, baking soda, and cream of tartar. Set aside.

3. In the large bowl of an electric mixer fitted with the paddle attachment, beat the butter on medium speed until smooth and lightened in color, 1½ to 2 minutes. Add the sugar ¼ cup at a time and beat for 2 minutes longer. Add the egg yolks and the vanilla, mixing for 1 minute longer. Scrape down the bowl as needed.

4. On low speed, add half of the dry ingredients, then add the milk and then the remaining dry ingredients, mixing only to combine.

5. With lightly floured hands, shape about ¼ cup of the dough into a ball. Place six balls of dough about 3 inches apart on each cookie sheet. Using the heel of your hand, press each ball into a 3- to 3½-inch disk. Using a flat-bottomed glass lightly dipped in flour, flatten each disk into a 4-inch circle.

6. Combine the egg whites with the water and beat lightly with a fork. Brush the top of each disk heavily with the egg wash. Sprinkle with ½ to ¾ teaspoon of sparkling white sugar. Bake the cookies for 13 to 14 minutes, or until the edges are lightly browned. To ensure even browning, two-thirds of the way through baking rotate the sheets top to bottom

or ten mini-marshmallows at random onto the tops. Return the cookies to the oven and bake for another 2 minutes or just until the marshmallows start to soften. WATCH CAREFULLY. Do not allow the marshmallows to become too hot or they will melt. These cookies are best slightly underbaked.

6. Let rest on the cookie sheets for 5 minutes or until firm enough to handle before loosening with a large metal spatula. Remove to a wire cooling rack set over a jelly roll pan or a sheet of wax paper.

GLAZE THE COOKIES

7. Combine the chocolate chips and the butter in a medium bowl set over a pan of simmering water. Melt together, stirring occasionally. Add the boiling water, ½ teaspoon at a time, to thin to a pouring consistency. Using a spoon or a fork, drizzle the glaze over each cookie. Let stand on the cooling racks until the glaze sets.

STORAGE: Store in an airtight container, layered between strips of wax paper, for up to 5 days. These cookies may be frozen.

Cookie Characteristics

Homestyle

Moderate shelf life

Temperature sensitive

white chocolate whalers

MAKES 18 4-INCH COOKIES

These delectable cookies are made with a white chocolate and rice cereal dough that is highlighted with orange zest. To give the cookie a bit more crunch, scoops of the cookie dough are rolled in a coating of rice cereal just before baking. If you are a nut fancier, mix in some coarsely chopped toasted almonds. With or without nuts, these Whalers are winners!

AT A GLANCE **PAN:** Oversized (14 × 17-inch) cookie sheets

PAN PREP: Baking parchment

OVEN TEMP: 325°

BAKING TIME: 16–18 minutes

DIFFICULTY: ☻

1 cup (2 sticks) unsalted butter

2 tablespoons grated navel or Valencia orange zest

2¼ cups all-purpose flour, spooned in and leveled

½ teaspoon salt

2 large egg yolks

4 large egg whites

1 cup superfine sugar

1 teaspoon pure vanilla extract

5 cups crispy rice cereal, divided

3 (3.5-ounce) bars high-quality white chocolate, such as Lindt Swiss Classic White, cut in ⅜-inch dice, or 1½ cups white chocolate chips

¾ cup coarsely chopped toasted unblanched almonds (optional)

1. Position the shelves in the upper and lower thirds of the oven. Heat the oven to 325°. Dab the corners of the cookie sheets lightly with butter and line with baking parchment.

2. Melt the butter with the orange zest over low heat. Set aside to cool to tepid.

3. Combine the flour and salt. Set aside.

4. In the large bowl of an electric mixer fitted with the whip attachment, beat the egg yolks and whites on medium speed until thick and lightened in color. Add the sugar 1 tablespoon at a time, then increase the speed to medium-high and beat until well blended, about 1 minute more. Slowly pour in the butter–zest mixture, then add the vanilla. Mix for 1 minute longer to combine, scraping down the bowl as needed. The mixture will thicken as it is beaten.

5. Using an oversized rubber spatula fold in 3 cups of the crispy rice cereal. Strain the dry ingredients over the batter, folding gently with the rubber spatula, until *just* combined. Fold in the chocolate pieces and the almonds, if using.

6. Place the remaining crispy rice cereal in a flat dish (a pie plate works well). Using a #16 ice cream scoop, drop mounds of dough into the cereal and toss lightly to adhere. Place six balls of dough on each cookie sheet, spacing them about 3 inches apart. Using the heel of your hand, flatten into 3-inch disks.

7. Bake 16 to 18 minutes, or until the edges are golden brown. To ensure even browning, two-thirds of the way through baking rotate the sheets top to bottom and front to back. Let rest for 10 minutes, or until firm enough to handle, before loosening with a large metal spatula. Transfer to cooling racks.

STORAGE: Store in an airtight container, layered between strips of wax paper, for up to 2 weeks. These cookies may be frozen.

sam's glazed lavish lemon cookies

One day I took these cookies to my family to critique. I don't know if it was the size of the cookie or the lemon frosting that caught my granddaughter Samantha's eye. "What are these giant cookies?" she asked as she licked away at the icing. I told her they were lemon cookies. "I l-o-o-v-e lemon cookies!" was her perky reply. The cookie has a golden buttery crumb that is richly flavored with lemon, and a lemony frosting, to boot!

When you make these cookies, the dough will be soft, but after chilling it becomes manageable. A pastry scraper (page 379) makes dividing the dough easier, but a sharp knife will do. If lemon is your weakness, beware! The entire—cookie—big as it is! will disappear!

AT A GLANCE

PAN: Oversized (14 × 17-inch) cookie sheets

PAN PREP: Baking parchment

OVEN TEMP: 350°

CHILLING TIME: 1 hour

BAKING TIME: 18–20 minutes

DIFFICULTY: ○○

1¾ cups all-purpose flour, spooned in and leveled

1 cup strained cake flour, spooned in and leveled

1 teaspoon cream of tartar

½ teaspoon baking soda

½ teaspoon salt

1 cup (2 sticks) unsalted butter, slightly firm

2 tablespoons freshly grated lemon zest

1½ cups sugar

4 large egg yolks

¼ cup fresh lemon juice

1 teaspoon pure vanilla extract

1 recipe Lemon Glaze (page 358)

MAKE THE COOKIES

1. Position the shelves in the upper and lower thirds of the oven. Heat the oven to 350 °. Dab the corners of the cookie sheets lightly with butter and line with baking parchment.

2. Strain the all-purpose flour, cake flour, the cream of tartar, baking soda, and salt together 3 times. Set aside.

3. Using an electric mixer fitted with the paddle attachment, mix the butter with the lemon zest on medium-low speed until creamy and lightened in color, about 2 minutes. Add the sugar in a steady stream, mixing again for 1 to 2 minutes. Blend in the egg yolks, mix for 45 to 60 seconds, then pour in the lemon juice and the vanilla, scraping down the bowl as needed.

4. Reduce the mixer speed to low and add the dry ingredients in three additions, mixing *just* until blended. Transfer the dough to a clean bowl, cover with plastic wrap, and chill for 1 hour.

5. Working with one half of the dough at

a time, place it on a floured surface. With lightly floured hands, shape the dough into a disk, coating it with a light dusting of flour. Using a dough scraper or a sharp knife, divide the dough into eight pie-shaped wedges. Flour your hands again and shape each wedge into a ball. (*Note:* This is a soft dough and should not be overworked.) Place the balls on a cookie sheet 3 inches apart (six balls per cookie sheet), and using the heel of your hand, gently flatten into 3- to 3½-inch disks. Repeat with the remaining dough to form eight more disks.

6. Bake the cookies for 18 to 20 minutes, or until the edges are golden brown. To ensure even browning, two-thirds of the way through baking rotate the sheets top to bottom and front to back. Remove the cookies from the oven, let stand for 5 minutes, then carefully loosen with a large, metal spatula. Transfer the cookies to cooling racks set over wax paper.

GLAZE THE COOKIES

7. While the cookies are still warm, spoon 2 to 3 teaspoons of Lemon Glaze on each cookie. Using a small offset spatula or the back of a teaspoon, *immediately* spread the glaze thinly over the top, coating the entire cookie. Set aside and let the cookies air-dry until the frosting has hardened.

STORAGE: Store in an airtight container, layered between strips of wax paper, for up to 10 days. These cookies may be frozen without the glaze.

Cookie Characteristics

Homestyle

Long shelf life

Temperature sensitive

teton trailers

I'm very fond of trail mix, and I wanted the kind of cookie that you would savor outdoors while hiking, picnicking, or sitting around the campfire. Since trail mix can be a hodgepodge of nibbles, this is the combination I came up with. It has the crunch of pretzels and nuts and the chewiness of dried fruit tossed through a cornmeal-textured dough. All of these wonderful ingredients are highlighted with buttery, toasted pepita seeds. If you like chocolate chips or other candy in your trail mix, you can add some as well. The end result of my cookie was a whopping success. I hope you like it as much as my assistants and I did.

AT A GLANCE

PAN: Oversized (14 × 17-inch) cookie sheets

PAN PREP: Well buttered

OVEN TEMP: 350°

BAKING TIME: 20–22 minutes

DIFFICULTY: ○○

1 tablespoon unsalted butter
¾ cup pepitas, divided
Salt to taste
1 cup broken traditional salted pretzel twists (½-inch pieces)
¼ cup coarsely chopped toasted unblanched almonds
½ cup sweetened, flaked coconut
½ cup dried apricots, cut in ½-inch pieces
½ cup dark raisins
2½ cups all-purpose flour, spooned in and leveled
1 teaspoon salt
½ teaspoon baking powder
½ teaspoon baking soda
½ cup stone-ground cornmeal, spooned in and leveled

¾ cup (1½ sticks) unsalted butter, slightly firm
¼ cup vegetable shortening
1 cup light brown sugar
1 cup granulated sugar
2 large eggs
2 teaspoons pure vanilla extract

TOAST THE PEPITAS

1. In a heavy 10-inch sauté pan over medium heat, melt the butter until it begins to sizzle. Add the pepitas and stir to coat with the butter. Reduce the heat to low and sauté the pepitas for 8 to 10 minutes, until they are puffed and very lightly browned. (The pepitas will "pop" as they cook.) Drain on paper toweling and season with salt to taste. Set aside to cool.

MAKE THE COOKIES

2. Position the shelf in the center of the oven. Heat the oven to 350°. Butter the cookie sheets well.

3. Combine one-half of the pepitas with the pretzels, almonds, coconut, apricots, and raisins in a bowl. Set aside.

4. Strain together the flour, salt, baking powder, and baking soda. Stir in the cornmeal and set aside.

5. In an electric mixer fitted with the paddle attachment, mix the butter on medium-low speed for 15 seconds or until smooth and creamy. Add the vegetable shortening and mix for 15 seconds longer, until well blended. Increase the mixer speed to medium and add the brown sugar, then the granulated sugar, and beat for about 2 minutes, scraping down the side of the bowl as needed. Add the eggs one at a time, then the vanilla, and mix for 1 minute longer. Scrape down the side of the bowl again.

6. Reduce the mixer speed to low and add the dry ingredients in three additions, mixing only to blend after each addition. Transfer the dough to a large, wide bowl. Using your hands, work in the pretzel mixture in two additions.

7. Form *scant* balls of dough with a #16 ice cream scoop, placing six mounds of dough about 4 inches apart on each cookie sheet. Sprinkle the top of each with about 1 teaspoon of the remaining pepitas, pressing them gently to adhere.

8. Bake the cookies until the edges are just beginning to brown, 20 to 22 minutes (a bit longer for thicker cookies). It is best to bake these one sheet at a time, but if you wish to bake two sheets adjust the oven shelves to the upper and lower thirds of the oven. To ensure even browning, two-thirds of the way through baking rotate the sheets top to bottom and front to back. Remove from the oven and let cool on the cookie sheet for about 2 minutes before loosening with a thin metal spatula. When the cookies are firm enough to handle, transfer to a wire rack to cool.

STORAGE: Store in an airtight container, layered between strips of wax paper, for up to 2 weeks. These cookies may be frozen.

Cookie
Characteristics

Homestyle

Long shelf life

Travel well

giant ginger spice cookies

MAKES 2 DOZEN 4-INCH COOKIES

Kathleen Sanderson and I have been teaching a diploma series, The Principles of Cooking, together for more years than I would care to admit. I refer to our team as the "Oscar and Felix" of my culinary world. We have such opposite approaches to many things, we often laugh our way through as each of us arrives at home base by a different route.

When I asked Kathleen to share a recipe with me for my book, it was a natural that she, the "Oscar" of the team, should enthusiastically give me a recipe for my Big Boys chapter. I knew that whatever recipe Kathleen recommended would be a winner, and indeed it was. You will love these snappy ginger cookies. They are packed with flavor and crackling crisp, and, in this case, bigger is definitely better! I am sure you will agree that this is an "Oscar"-winning recipe!

AT A GLANCE

PAN: Oversized (14 × 17-inch) cookie sheets

PAN PREP: Baking parchment

OVEN TEMP: 350°

BAKING TIME: 13–15 minutes

DIFFICULTY: ⬡

4½ cups all-purpose flour, spooned in and leveled

1½ tablespoons ground ginger

2 teaspoons baking soda

1 teaspoon ground cinnamon

1 teaspoon ground cloves

½ teaspoon salt

¾ cup (1½ sticks) unsalted butter, slightly firm

¾ cup vegetable shortening, at room temperature

3 cups sugar, divided

2 large eggs

½ cup dark molasses

1. Position the shelves in the upper and lower thirds of the oven. Heat the oven to 350°. Dab the corners of the cookie sheets lightly with butter and line with baking parchment.

2. Strain together the flour, ginger, baking soda, cinnamon, cloves, and salt. Set aside.

3. In the large bowl of an electric mixer fitted with the paddle attachment, mix the butter on medium-low speed until smooth, about 1 minute, then add the shortening and continue to mix until creamy and lightened in color, about 1 minute longer. Add 2 cups of the sugar in four additions and continue to mix for another 2 minutes.

4. Lightly beat the eggs and molasses together. Add to the butter–sugar mixture and mix on medium-low speed until well blended. Reduce the mixer

speed to low and add the dry ingredients in three additions, mixing *just* until combined.

5. Place the reserved 1 cup of sugar in a shallow dish, such as a pie plate. Using a dry ¼-cup measure to portion the dough, form a 3-inch ball by rolling the dough in the palms of your hands. Roll the ball in the sugar and place it on the cookie sheet. Repeat with the remaining dough, placing the balls about 3 inches apart.

6. Bake the cookies for 13 to 15 minutes, until cracked on top but still slightly soft. Rotate the pans from top to bottom and front to back toward the end of the baking time. Let stand for 2 to 3 minutes before loosening from the sheets with a large, metal spatula. Transfer to cooling racks.

STORAGE: Store in an airtight container, layered between strips of wax paper, for up to 3 weeks. These cookies may be frozen.

Cookie Characteristics

Homestyle

Long shelf life

Travel well

butter-nut bonanzas

MAKES 20 4½-INCH COOKIES

Butter! Butter! Butter! That's the name of the game here. After the nuts are roasted in butter, sugar is tossed in the baking pan to absorb the nutty browned butter flavor. I use mixed nuts, and the "deluxe" variety is the way to go. These cookies are rich, but once in a while it's okay to indulge!!

AT A GLANCE

PAN: Oversized (14 × 17-inch) cookie sheets

PAN PREP: Lightly buttered

OVEN TEMP: 350°

BAKING TIME: 14–16 minutes

DIFFICULTY: ◐

1½ cups plus 2 tablespoons (3¼ sticks) unsalted butter, slightly firm, divided

3 cups deluxe salted mixed nuts, coarsely chopped

1½ cups sugar

3 cups all-purpose flour, spooned in and leveled

1½ teaspoons baking powder

½ teaspoon salt

4 large egg yolks

2 teaspoons pure vanilla extract

1 small recipe Quick Chocolate Glaze (page 359)

1. Position the shelves in the upper and lower thirds of the oven. Heat the oven to 350°. Lightly butter the cookie sheets. Set aside.

2. Place 2 tablespoons of the butter on a jelly roll pan and melt it in the oven. Toss the nuts with the melted butter and roast them for about 15 minutes, or until they are a light golden color. Remove the toasted nuts from the pan and set aside to cool. Add the sugar to the pan and use a rubber spatula to mix it with the browned butter drippings, then transfer to a bowl.

3. Strain together the flour, baking powder, and salt. Set aside.

4. In the bowl of an electric mixer fitted with the paddle attachment, mix the remaining 1½ cups butter on medium-low speed until smooth. Scrape down the bowl as needed. Increase the speed to medium and add the flavored sugar, ¼ cup at a time, and mix for 2 minutes. Add the egg yolks one at a time, mixing well after each addition, scraping down the bowl again. Blend in the vanilla. Reduce the mixer speed to low and add the dry ingredients in three additions, mixing *just* to combine. With an oversize rubber spatula, fold in the nuts.

5. With a #16 ice cream scoop or with lightly floured hands, shape the dough into 2-inch balls. Place six balls of dough 3 inches apart on each of the cookie sheets and flatten with the heel of your hand into 3-inch disks.

6. Bake the cookies for 14 to 16 minutes or until the edges are golden brown. To ensure even browning, two-thirds of the way through baking, rotate the sheets top to bottom and front to back. Remove from the oven and let stand for 5 minutes before loosening with a large metal spatula. Transfer to cooling racks. Drizzle with Quick Chocolate Glaze.

STORAGE: Store in an airtight container, layered between strips of wax paper, for up to 3 weeks. These cookies may be frozen.

Cookie Characteristics

Homestyle

Long shelf life

Travel well

black beauties

MAKES 16 4-INCH COOKIES

This killer chocolate cookie, without butter or egg yolks, is made from a chocolate meringue batter generously packed with crunchy walnuts. After a slow bake to give the cookie a chewy texture, it is beautifully glazed with a mirrorlike chocolate icing. If you like chocolate and nuts, this cookie will send your taste buds soaring!

AT A GLANCE

PAN: Oversized (14 × 17-inch) cookie sheets

PAN PREP: Buttered baking parchment

OVEN TEMP: 250°

BAKING TIME: 45–50 minutes

DIFFICULTY: ◐◐

⅔ cup strained Dutch-processed cocoa powder, spooned in and leveled

¼ teaspoon baking soda

¼ teaspoon salt

8 large egg whites, at room temperature

1 cup superfine sugar

2 teaspoons corn syrup

2 teaspoons pure vanilla extract

½ teaspoon fresh lemon juice

12 ounces fine-quality bittersweet or semisweet chocolate, such as Lindt Bittersweet, melted (see page 392) and kept warm

3 tablespoons hot water

2 cups coarsely chopped walnuts

1 large recipe Quick Chocolate Glaze (page 359)

1. Position the oven shelves in the upper and lower thirds of the oven. Heat the oven to 250°. Dab the corners of the cookie sheets lightly with butter and line with baking parchment. Butter the parchment. Set aside.

2. Strain together the cocoa powder, baking soda, and salt. Set aside.

3. In the bowl of an electric mixer fitted with the whip attachment, beat the egg whites on medium speed to firm peaks. Add the sugar gradually, taking about 1 minute to incorporate. Continue to beat for about 2 minutes, until the whites are stiff and glossy. Scrape down the side of the bowl as needed. Add the corn syrup, vanilla, and lemon juice and beat for 30 seconds more.

4. Remove the bowl from the machine. Using a large rubber spatula, blend in the warm chocolate, then the cocoa mixture and the hot water, mixing only to combine. Fold in the nuts.

5. Using a #16 ice cream scoop, drop six mounds of dough about 3 inches apart onto each cookie sheet. Using the back of a spoon, flatten each mound of dough into a 3-inch disk. Bake for 45 to 50 minutes, until the tops of the cookies are set. They will firm as they stand. To ensure even baking, two-thirds of the way through baking rotate the sheets top to bottom and front to back. While the cookies are baking, prepare the glaze.

6. Remove the cookies from the oven and let stand for at least 5 minutes before loosening with a thin metal spatula. Transfer the cookies to a cooling rack set over a sheet pan or wax paper. While the cookies are still slightly warm, use a pastry brush to carefully apply glaze to each cookie, coating the entire top. Let stand until the glaze is dry.

STORAGE: Store in an airtight container, layered between strips of wax paper, for up to 5 days. These cookies may be frozen.

Cookie Characteristics

Homestyle

Moderate shelf life

Temperature sensitive

4 Cold Cuts

old-fashioned icebox cookies

MAKES 9 TO 10 DOZEN 1¾-INCH COOKIES

When you want to make cookies for gift-giving or when festive cookies are in order, this recipe for Old-Fashioned Icebox Cookies is a real bonanza. From this Master Recipe, you can make myriad flavors that are as visually appealing as they are palate-pleasing. There are colorful Confetti Cookies made with glacé cherries, Chocolate Icebox Cookies, Marbled Icebox Cookies, and Cinnamon Nut Swirls. These recipes are just a few of the many varieties you can create.

AT A GLANCE   **PAN:** Cookie sheets

PAN PREP: Ungreased

OVEN TEMP: 375°

CHILLING TIME: 2–3 hours

BAKING TIME: 12–14 minutes

DIFFICULTY: ⊙

1½ cups (3 sticks) unsalted butter, slightly firm

¾ cup sugar

1 large egg

2 teaspoons pure vanilla extract

3 cups all-purpose flour, spooned in and leveled, divided

Coarse sugar, or other trimmings

1 large egg white, lightly beaten with 2 teaspoons water

MAKE THE DOUGH

1. In the large bowl of an electric mixer fitted with the paddle attachment, mix the butter on medium-low speed until smooth and lightened in color. Add the sugar in a steady stream and mix until well blended, about 2 minutes. Mix in the egg and vanilla, scraping down the side of the bowl as needed.

2. Remove 1 cup of the flour and set aside. Reduce the mixer speed to low and add 2 cups of the flour, in three additions, mixing *just* until combined. Knead in the remaining 1 cup flour with your hands. Do not overwork the dough or it will become oily.

3. Divide the dough into sixths. Shape each piece into a cylinder measuring approximately 6 inches by 1¼ inches. Chill for 10 minutes.

4. Place the coarse sugar on a piece of wax paper. Working with one cylinder at a time, brush with the egg white mixture and then roll in the sugar, rotating back and forth until coated.

5. Wrap the log with plastic, twisting the ends tightly to secure. Repeat with the remaining cylinders, adding more sugar each time. Refrigerate for 2 to 3 hours, or until firm. (This dough will keep in the refrigerator for up to 3 days, or may be frozen for up to 1 month.)

BAKE THE COOKIES

6. Position the shelves in the upper and lower thirds of the oven. Heat the oven to 375°.

7. Using a thin, sharp knife, cut the dough into ¼-inch-thick slices, turning the dough every two or three cuts to maintain the shape. Do not make these cookies too thin. Place on the cookie sheets about 2 inches apart. Bake for 12 to 14 minutes, or until lightly golden brown around the edges. To ensure even browning, toward the end of baking time rotate the pans top to bottom and front to back. Remove from the oven and carefully loosen with a thin metal spatula. Cool on wire racks.

STORAGE: Store in an airtight container, layered between strips of wax paper, for up to 3 weeks. These cookies may be frozen.

confetti cookies

MAKES ABOUT 2 DOZEN COOKIES

¾ cup Old-Fashioned Icebox Cookie dough
2 tablespoons chopped red glacé cherries
1 tablespoon chopped green glacé cherries

1. Using your hands, gently knead the chopped cherries into the dough. *Do not overwork.* Shape the dough into a cylinder measuring approximately 7 inches by 1¼ inches. Chill for 10 minutes. Garnish if desired (refer to step 4 of the Master Recipe).
2. Wrap the log with plastic, twisting the ends tightly to secure. Chill for 2 to 3 hours or until firm. (The dough may be frozen for up to 1 month.)
3. When ready to bake the cookies, proceed with step 6 of the Master Recipe.

chocolate icebox cookies

MAKES ABOUT 2 DOZEN COOKIES

¾ cup Old-Fashioned Icebox Cookie dough
1 ounce unsweetened chocolate, melted and kept warm (see page 392)
1 tablespoon sugar

1. Place the cookie dough in a medium bowl. Blend in the warm chocolate and sugar with a spoon, being careful not to overwork the dough. Shape the dough into a cylinder, measuring approximately 6 inches by 1¼ inches. Chill for 10 minutes. Garnish if desired (refer to step 4 of the Master Recipe).
2. Wrap the log with plastic, twisting the ends tightly to secure. Chill for 2 to 3 hours or until firm. (The dough may be frozen for up to 1 month.)
3. When ready to bake the cookies, proceed with step 6 of the Master Recipe.

cinnamon nut swirls

MAKES ABOUT 2 DOZEN COOKIES

¾ cup Old-Fashioned Icebox Cookie dough
1 tablespoon sugar
½ teaspoon ground cinnamon
3 tablespoons finely chopped toasted walnuts (optional)

1. Combine the sugar and the cinnamon. Using your hands, gently knead the mixture into the dough. *Do not overwork.* There should be streaks of cinnamon sugar through the dough. Shape the dough into a cylinder measuring approximately 6 inches by 1¼ inches. Chill for 10 minutes. Garnish if desired (refer to step 4 of the Master Recipe).

Cookie Characteristics

Versatile

Long shelf life

Travel well

2. Wrap the log with plastic, twisting the ends tightly to secure. Chill for 2 to 3 hours or until firm. (The dough may be frozen for up to 1 month.)

3. When ready to bake the cookies, proceed with step 6 of the Master Recipe.

marbled icebox cookies

MAKES ABOUT 4 DOZEN COOKIES

¾ cup Old-Fashioned Icebox Cookie dough (page 114)

1 recipe Chocolate Icebox Cookie dough (page 115)

1. Break each of the doughs into three or four pieces. Knead them gently with your hands only to combine the doughs. (Note: Do not overmix or the marbelization will be lost.) Shape the dough into two cylinders each measuring approximately 6 inches by 1¼ inches. Chill for 10 minutes. Garnish if desired (refer to step 4 of the Master Recipe).

2. Wrap the logs with plastic, twisting the ends tightly to secure. Chill for 2 to 3 hours, or until firm. (The dough may be frozen for up to 1 month.)

3. When ready to bake the cookies, proceed with step 6 of the Master Recipe.

Left to right: Chocolate Fleck Hubcaps; Chocolate Icebox Cookies; Confetti Cookies; Marbled Icebox Cookies; Cinnamon Nut Swirls; Old-Fashioned Icebox Cookies

pinwheel cookies

MAKES ABOUT 8 DOZEN 1¾-INCH COOKIES

This recipe has been part of my cookie repertoire for many years. It was given to me by my friend Eleanor Berg, an excellent baker from Teaneck, New Jersey. From the Master Recipe for Pinwheel dough, you can prepare five eye-catching variations. Harlequins are the easiest to make, followed by Bowties. Next in line are Stripes and Chevrons. Checkerboards are for those of you who welcome a challenge. Think ahead when you want to make this recipe and divide the dough accordingly. Because the different shapes are so attractive, you may want to vary them.

Don't discard the remnants of the dough. Gather them together and pinch off small pieces, form them into a ball, and press them onto a cookie sheet to make marbleized cookies. You may also omit the chocolate in the dough and tint each half with food coloring to create a variety of colors.

"The greatest pleasure in life is doing what people say you can not do."

—WALTER BAGEHOT

PAN: Cookie sheets

PAN PREP: Lightly buttered

OVEN TEMP: 350°

CHILLING TIME: 4–5 hours or overnight

BAKING TIME: 9–11 minutes

DIFFICULTY: ⚫⚫⚫

3 cups all-purpose flour, spooned in and leveled

½ teaspoon baking powder

½ teaspoon salt

1 cup (2 sticks) unsalted butter, slightly firm

1⅓ cups superfine sugar

2 large eggs

2 teaspoons pure vanilla extract

2 ounces unsweetened chocolate, melted and kept warm (see page 392)

MAKE THE DOUGH

1. Strain together the flour, baking powder, and salt. Set aside.

2. In the large bowl of an electric mixer fitted with the paddle attachment, mix the butter on medium-low speed until smooth and creamy. Add the sugar in four additions and mix for 2 minutes longer. Add the eggs one at a time, then the vanilla, mixing again for 1 minute, scraping down the side of the bowl as needed.

3. Reduce the mixer speed to low and add the dry ingredients in three additions, blending *just* until combined. *Do not overmix.*

4. Using a kitchen scale, divide the dough in half. Each half should weigh about 1 pound. If you don't have a scale, measure out about 1⅔ cups of dough. Blend the warm melted chocolate into half of the dough, mixing thoroughly without overworking the dough. Shape each flavor of dough into a 4 × 5-inch

Cookie Characteristics

Versatile

Long shelf life

Travel well

rectangle and wrap each piece in plastic. Refrigerate for 1 hour, or until firm enough to roll.

SHAPE THE PINWHEELS

5. Divide each rectangle into quarters, forming four pieces of chocolate and four pieces of vanilla dough. (Each quarter should weigh about 4 ounces.) With *lightly* floured hands on a *lightly* floured surface, form each piece of dough into a cylinder approximately 4 inches long and 1¼ inches wide. (For longer storage, wrap in plastic, twisting the ends of the wrap tightly to maintain a cylindrical shape, and refrigerate until ready to use. This dough will keep up to 3 days or it may be frozen for up to 3 months.)

6. Place one cylinder of chocolate dough between two 15-inch pieces of wax paper and roll it into a rectangle approximately 6 × 7 inches. Roll one cylinder of the vanilla dough in the same fashion forming a 6 × 6-inch square. Place both pieces of dough, without removing the wax paper, on a cookie sheet and chill until slightly firm, about 10 minutes.

7. Remove the top sheet of wax paper from each flavor. Invert the vanilla dough over the chocolate, aligning it so that ½ inch of chocolate dough shows at the top and bottom. Place a cookie sheet over the two layers of dough and press lightly to seal the layers. Peel off the top layer of wax paper.

8. Using your fingertips and starting at the 6-inch side closest to you, curl the edge of the dough closest to you up and over, shaping it so that there will be no space in the center of the pinwheel. Then, using the wax paper as an aid, lift the paper and continue to turn the dough, making sure it is tightly rolled.

9. Transfer the log to a sheet of plastic wrap, roll it to enclose in the wrap, and twist the ends tightly to secure. Place the log in the refrigerator and chill for 4 to 5 hours or overnight. Turn the log periodically during the first hour to prevent a flat bottom. Repeat with the remaining dough. (The logs may be refrigerated for up to 3 days or frozen for up to 1 month.)

BAKE THE COOKIES

10. Heat the oven to 350°. Position the shelves in the upper and lower thirds of the oven. Lightly butter the cookie sheets.

11. Unwrap one cylinder at a time and place it on a cutting board. Using a thin, sharp knife, cut the roll into 3/16-inch slices. Place the cookies about 1½ inches apart on the cookie sheets and bake for 9 to 11 minutes, or until the edges *just* begin to brown. To ensure even browning, toward the end of baking time, rotate the pans top to bottom and front to back. Remove from the oven, let stand 1 minute, then loosen with a thin metal spatula while the cookies are still hot. Tranfer to cooling racks.

STORAGE: Store in an airtight container, layered between strips of wax paper, for up to 3 weeks. These cookies may be frozen.

harlequins

MAKES 8 DOZEN
1¾-INCH COOKIES

1. Follow the Master Recipe for Pinwheel dough through step 4. Make an egg wash using 1 large egg lightly beaten with 2 teaspoons of water.

2. Divide a chocolate and vanilla cylinder lengthwise into four strips, for a total of eight strips. Place the strips on a piece of plastic wrap. Working with four strips at a time, brush the exposed cut side of the strips lightly with the egg wash, then alternate two chocolate and two vanilla by placing a vanilla strip next to a chocolate, then reverse and place a chocolate *over* the vanilla and then a vanilla *over* the chocolate. Rotate back and forth with your hands to seal the strips together.

3. Roll in plastic wrap, twisting the ends tightly to form a cylinder. Repeat, using the remaining chocolate and vanilla strips. Work the remaining dough in the same manner, for a total of four cylinders. Chill for several hours or up to 3 days, or freeze for up to 1 month. Follow the baking instructions in the Master Recipe beginning with step 10.

bowties

MAKES 8 DOZEN 1¾-INCH COOKIES

1. Follow the directions for Harlequins (above) through step 3. After the dough is sliced and placed on the cookie sheet, gently pinch the opposite sides together. The more you pinch, the greater the definition, but be careful not to separate the dough. Either the chocolate or vanilla side may be pinched, or you may do some of each. Follow the baking instructions in the Master Recipe, beginning with step 10.

checkerboards

**MAKES ABOUT 8 DOZEN 1¾-INCH
COOKIES**

1. Follow the Master Recipe for Pinwheel dough (page 118) through step 3.

2. Divide the dough in half. Blend the
warm chocolate into half the dough.
Shape each flavor of dough into a rectangle approximately 4 × 5 inches, and
wrap each in plastic. Refrigerate for
1 hour, or until firm enough to roll.

3. Place one flavor of dough between
two 18-inch strips of plastic wrap. Using
a tapered rolling pin, roll it into an
8 × 10-inch rectangle, approximately
¼ inch thick. Be sure to roll the dough
as evenly as possible. Place the rolled
dough on a cookie sheet. Using a second
cookie sheet, press gently to even the
surface and then refrigerate. Repeat
with the remaining dough, stacking the
layer on the previous one. Chill for
1 hour or until firm.

4. Remove the dough from the refrigerator. Cut an 18-inch strip of plastic wrap
and place it on a clean cookie sheet.
Starting with the chocolate dough,
remove the top sheet of plastic wrap and
invert the rectangle onto the plastic-
wrap-lined cookie sheet. Peel off the top
piece of plastic wrap. Repeat the procedure with the vanilla dough, placing it
on top of the chocolate.

5. Lay a clean 18-inch strip of plastic
wrap on top of the vanilla dough. Press

gently with a cookie sheet to seal and
even the layers. It's okay if the edges do
not line up exactly. Chill for 1 hour or
until firm.

6. Remove the cookie sheet from the
refrigerator and cut the dough in half
across the 10-inch side, forming two 5 ×
8-inch rectangles. Place one rectangle
over the other aligning the cut sides
together and taking care to place chocolate dough on top of vanilla dough. You
now have a rectangle with four alternating layers. Cover with a clean 18-inch
piece of plastic wrap and gently press
the top with a clean cookie sheet to seal
and even the layers.

7. Chill the stack of dough until it is firm
enough to handle, then tuck the plastic
wrap gently around any exposed dough
to protect it. Refrigerate for at least 6
hours or overnight. (Note: It is best to
chill the dough on the cookie sheet, but
if refrigerator space is at a premium,
you can remove the cookie sheet. Just be
sure to place the dough directly on a
refrigerator shelf.)

8. Unwrap the assembled layers and
place the dough on a cutting board lined
with baking parchment or wax paper.
Using a sharp, thin-bladed knife, trim
the uneven edges from the rectangle.
(These trimmings may be gathered
together, formed into balls, flattened,
and baked as directed in the Pinwheel
recipe.)

9. Have ready a clean cookie sheet lined
with plastic wrap. Working from the
short side of the dough, using a thin-
bladed, sharp knife, cut four slices, 5
inches long and ¼ inch thick. Place the
first slice cut side down on the plastic
wrap. Alternate the next three slices of
dough, reversing the vanilla and the
chocolate with each slice, forming a

checkerboard. Enclose the assembled dough in the plastic wrap, being careful to retain the rectangular shape. Tuck the ends of the wrap gently under the dough and refrigerate. Repeat with the remaining dough.

10. Position the shelves in the upper and lower thirds of the oven. Heat the oven to 350°. Lightly butter the cookie sheets.

11. Using a sharp, thin-bladed knife, cut the cookies into ¼-inch-thick slices. Place 1½ inches apart on the cookie sheets. Bake for 9 to 11 minutes or until the cookies are *just* set on top and barely browned. To ensure even browning, toward the end of baking time rotate the pans top to bottom and front to back. Let stand 1 minute, then carefully remove the cookies using a thin metal spatula. Transfer to cooling racks.

stripes

MAKES 8 DOZEN COOKIES

1. Follow the directions for Checkerboards through step 7. Divide the dough crosswise into quarters. Using a long and thin sharp knife, cut a ⅜-inch strip parallel to the stripes in the dough. Lay the strips flat on the prepared pans.

2. Bake according to the directions for Checkerboards, step 10.

chevrons

MAKES ABOUT 9 DOZEN 2½-INCH COOKIES

1. Follow the directions for Checkerboards through step 7. Make an egg wash using 1 large egg lightly beaten with 2 teaspoons of water. Working from the short side of the dough, use a sharp, thin-bladed knife to cut 3⁄16-inch-thick slices, cutting only two or three slices at a time.

2. Lay each slice down and make a slight indentation in the dough 2 inches from the upper left-hand corner. Then make a slight indentation in the dough 2 inches from the lower right-hand corner. Cut from the upper left indentation to the lower right indentation, dividing the strip in half on an angle. Then turn the right half over and align it with the left half, brushing the overlapping edge lightly with egg wash and forming a *V*. To form the Chevron, arrange the *V* so the point is on the bottom and place it on the prepared cookie sheet. Repeat, making as many Chevrons as you wish.

3. Bake according to the directions for Checkerboards, step 10.

brown sugar cookies

This recipe was inspired by Julia Wolfson, a *grande dame* in every respect of the word. No matter what suggestion Julia proffered, the wise among us always took note. Not only was she a sparkling conversationalist, but she was an extraordinary cook as well. Julia's cookies are richly flavored with dark brown sugar and crunchy with toasted pecans. This recipe has been in her family for years. I am so pleased to be able to share it with you.

AT A GLANCE

PAN: Cookie sheets

PAN PREP: Ungreased

OVEN TEMP: 375°

CHILLING TIME: 2 hours

BAKING TIME: 7–8 minutes

DIFFICULTY: ○

3¼ cups all-purpose flour, spooned in and leveled, divided

1 teaspoon baking soda

½ teaspoon salt

1½ cups toasted pecans, divided

1 cup (2 sticks) unsalted butter, slightly firm

2 cups lightly packed *very fresh* dark brown sugar

2 large eggs

2 teaspoons pure vanilla extract

1 large egg, lightly beaten with 2 teaspoons water

MAKE THE DOUGH

1. Strain together 3 cups of the flour, the baking soda, and salt. Set aside.

2. Place 1 cup of the pecans and the remaining ¼ cup of flour in the work bowl of a food processor fitted with a steel blade. Pulse four to five times, then process for 30 seconds, or until the pecans are finely chopped. Stir the chopped pecans into the dry ingredients. Set aside.

3. In the large bowl of an electric mixer fitted with the paddle attachment, mix the butter on low speed until smooth. Increase the speed to medium and add the brown sugar by handfuls, taking about 1 minute. Beat for 1 minute more. Reduce the mixer speed to medium-low. Add the eggs one at a time and beat for 1 minute longer, then blend in the vanilla. Scrape down the bowl as needed.

4. Reduce the mixer speed to low and add the dry ingredients in three additions, mixing *just* until combined after each addition. Form the dough into three 8-inch logs approximately 1½ inches in diameter. Wrap the logs with plastic, twisting the ends tightly to secure. Refrigerate for 2 hours or until firm. (This dough will keep in the refrigerator for up to 3 days, or may be frozen for 1 month.)

5. Position the shelves in the upper and lower thirds of the oven. Heat the oven to 375°. Chop the remaining ½ cup pecans into small pieces..

6. Using a thin, sharp knife, cut the dough into ³⁄₁₆-inch-thick slices, turning the dough every two or three cuts to maintain the shape. Place 2 inches apart on the cookie sheets. Brush the tops of the cookies with the egg wash and sprinkle with the chopped pecans.

7. Bake for 7 to 8 minutes or until golden brown. To ensure even browning, toward the end of baking time rotate the sheets top to bottom and front to back. Remove from the oven and let rest on the pans for 2 or 3 minutes before loosening with a thin metal spatula. Transfer to cooling racks.

STORAGE: Store in an airtight container, layered between strips of wax paper, for up to 3 weeks. These cookies may be frozen.

Cookie Characteristics

Versatile

Long shelf life

Travel well

Secrets for Making Cold Cuts

- When preparing the textured ingredients for the cookie dough, chop the pieces according to the thickness of the slices. Thinly sliced dough (up to ¼ inch) will require smaller pieces, while thicker slices (about ½ inch) can accommodate larger pieces.
- When forming logs, make them shorter rather than longer. This makes them easier to handle.
- As you roll the log in plastic wrap, pull the dough toward you to ensure a more cylindrical shape. The tighter you twist the ends of the plastic wrap, the more cylindrical the log.
- To maintain the rounded shape of the logs of dough, turn them periodically while chilling.
- When shaping dark-colored doughs, use confectioners' sugar instead of flour. The sugar dissolves during baking and the color of the cookie is retained.
- Cookie logs trimmed with chopped nuts and colored sugars must be brushed with an egg wash before the garnish is applied.
- When brushing cookie logs with egg wash, place the log on a sheet of wax paper. Then lift the paper and roll the log directly into a shallow container filled with the trim.
- Many drop cookie doughs can be converted to refrigerated cookies by shaping the dough into logs and then wrapping, chilling, or freezing them.
- To retain the shape of refrigerated doughs, always slice them when they are well chilled and firm.
- Slicing refrigerator cookies is best done with a thin-bladed knife to avoid tearing the dough.
- Some refrigerator doughs can be sliced while frozen if you use a warm knife. Unused portions can be thoroughly rewrapped and refrozen for later use.

chocolate fleck hubcaps

MAKES ABOUT 4 DOZEN 1¾-INCH COOKIES

Here is a cookie that will absolutely make you look like a pro. It has a dark chocolate "hubcap" that is set off by a circle of vanilla cookie dough. The centers are made with a combination of ground chocolate and nuts heightened with a touch of cinnamon and cloves.

AT A GLANCE

PAN: Cookie sheets
PAN PREP: Ungreased
OVEN TEMP: 375°
CHILLING TIME: 2–3 hours
BAKING TIME: 12–14 minutes
DIFFICULTY: ○○

1½ cups Old-Fashioned Icebox Cookie
   dough, divided (page 114)
1 ounce semisweet chocolate, coarsely
   chopped
½ cup walnuts or pecans
5 tablespoons sugar, divided
½ teaspoon ground cinnamon
Pinch of ground cloves
1 large egg white, lightly beaten with
   2 teaspoons of water

MAKE THE DOUGH

1. In the work bowl of a food processor fitted with the steel blade, finely grind the chocolate. Empty the chocolate onto a strip of wax paper.

2. Place the nuts, 3 tablespoons of sugar, the cinnamon, and cloves in the processor bowl and pulse until the nuts are finely chopped. Empty the mixture into a large bowl. Remove ¼ cup and set aside for trimming. Add the chopped chocolate to the remaining nut mixture along with ½ cup of the cookie dough. Gently knead until the ingredients are *just* combined. *Do not overwork.* Form

into two thin cylinders each about 6 inches long.

3. Roll the remaining 1 cup of dough into a rectangle measuring 10 inches wide by 6 inches long. Cut the rectangle in half, making two strips that are 5 inches wide and 6 inches long.

4. Brush each strip of dough with the beaten egg white. Place a chocolate-nut cylinder in the center of one rectangle, aligning it with the 6-inch side of the rectangle. Wrap the dough around the cylinder, forming a log. The two edges should only slightly overlap. If there is too much excess dough at the seam, remove it with a pastry scraper. Pinch the seam, then roll the cylinder back and forth to seal the seam well. Form another log with the remaining dough and cylinder. Chill the logs 10 minutes.

5. Place the reserved nut mixture on a piece of wax paper and combine with the remaining 2 tablespoons of sugar. Working with one log at a time, brush with the egg white mixture and then roll in the nut mixture, rotating back and forth until coated.

6. Wrap the logs with plastic, twisting the ends tightly to secure. Refrigerate for 2 to 3 hours, or until firm. (This dough will keep in the refrigerator for up to 3 days, or may be frozen for 1 month.)

7. Position the shelves in the upper and lower thirds of the oven. Heat the oven to 375°.

8. Using a thin, sharp knife, cut the dough into ¼-inch slices, turning the dough every two or three cuts to maintain the shape. Do not make these cookies too thin. Place on the cookie sheets about 2 inches apart. Bake for 12 to 14 minutes, or until lightly golden brown around the edges. To ensure even browning, toward the end of baking time, rotate the sheets top to bottom and front to back. Remove from the oven and carefully loosen with a thin, metal spatula. Transfer to cooling racks.

STORAGE: Store in an airtight container, layered between strips of wax paper, for up to 3 weeks. These cookies may be frozen.

Cookie Characteristics

Versatile

Long shelf life

Travel well

"The last dish of a good dinner should be light and elegant and convey the greatest amount of pleasure to the taste, with the least possible nourishment."

—ALYSON KYLE LEOPOLD, *VICTORIAN SWEETS*

tutti-frutti icebox cookies

MAKES 8 DOZEN 2½-INCH COOKIES

James Brackman, who hails from Austin, Texas, and is a graduate of the French Culinary Institute, passed this recipe for his grandmother's Christmas cookies on to me. The cookie dough is made with a jewel-like combination of candied or dried pineapple and glacé cherries with lots of chopped pecans mingled through the dough. Family recipes and grandmothers are true treasures—thank you, James, for sharing both with me.

AT A GLANCE

PAN: Cookie sheets

PAN PREP: Ungreased

OVEN TEMP: 375°

CHILLING TIME: 3 hours

BAKING TIME: 8–9 minutes

DIFFICULTY: ✪

2½ cups all-purpose flour, spooned in and leveled
1½ teaspoons baking soda
½ teaspoon salt
½ cup chopped dried or glacé pineapple
½ cup packed chopped glacé cherries
1 cup (2 sticks) unsalted butter, slightly firm
1 cup sugar
1 large egg
1 cup medium-chopped toasted pecans

MAKE THE DOUGH

1. Strain together the flour, baking soda, and salt in a medium bowl. Combine the glacé pineapple and cherries and toss with 3 tablespoons of the flour mixture, working the flour through the fruit with your fingers to separate the pieces. Set both aside.

2. In the large bowl of an electric mixer fitted with the paddle attachment, mix the butter on medium-low speed until creamy and lightened in color. Add the sugar in a steady stream and mix until well blended, about 2 minutes. Add the egg and mix 1 minute longer, scraping down the side of the bowl as needed.

3. Reduce the mixer speed to low and add the flour mixture in two additions, mixing *only* to blend after each addition. Using a large rubber spatula, fold in the fruits and the pecans.

4. Form the dough into a mound and divide into four equal pieces. Shape each piece into a 6 × 1½-inch log. Wrap each log with plastic, twisting the ends tightly to secure. Refrigerate for 3 hours or until firm. (This dough will keep in the refrigerator for up to 3 days, or may be frozen for 1 month.)

BAKE THE COOKIES

5. Position the shelves in the upper and lower thirds of the oven. Heat the oven to 375°.

6. Using a thin, sharp knife, cut the dough into ¼-inch slices, turning the roll every two or three cuts to maintain the shape. Place the slices 2 inches apart on the cookie sheets. Bake for 8 to 9 minutes or until lightly browned. To ensure even browning, toward the end of baking time, rotate the pans top to bottom and front to back. Remove from the oven and let rest for 1 minute before loosening with a thin metal spatula. Transfer to cooling racks.

STORAGE: Store in an airtight container, layered between strips of wax paper, for up to 3 weeks. These cookies may be frozen.

Cookie
Characteristics

Versatile

Long shelf life

Travel well

Front left: Tutti-Frutti Icebox Cookies; front right: Brown Sugar Cookies

maple walnut icebox cookies

MAKES ABOUT 9 DOZEN 2-INCH COOKIES

These crispy cookies are made with brown sugar, maple extract, and lots of walnuts—a trio of flavors that is absolutely alluring. If you have the willpower to let these cookies "age," the flavor gets even better with time. But when these cookies come out of the oven, my assistants and I race to the cookie sheets to see who will get to savor the first bite.

PAN: Cookie sheets

PAN PREP: Ungreased

CHILLING TIME: 1 hour

OVEN TEMP: 350°

BAKING TIME: 11–12 minutes

DIFFICULTY: ✿

2¼ cups all-purpose flour, spooned in
  and leveled

½ teaspoon baking soda

½ teaspoon salt

¾ cup light brown sugar

¼ cup granulated sugar

2 teaspoons maple extract

¾ cup (1½ sticks) unsalted butter,
  slightly firm

1 large egg

1 large egg yolk

1½ teaspoons pure vanilla extract

2½ cups walnuts, medium chopped,
  divided

1 egg white, lightly beaten with
  2 teaspoons water

MAKE THE DOUGH

1. Strain together the flour, baking soda, and salt. Set aside.

2. In the bowl of a food processor fitted with the steel blade, pulse 5 or 6 times to combine the brown and the granulated sugars. Sprinkle the maple extract onto the sugars and process to incorporate, about 10 seconds. Stop the processor and scrape the bowl to release any extract that may have settled to the bottom. Process again for 8 to 10 seconds.

3. In the large bowl of an electric mixer fitted with the paddle attachment, mix the butter on medium-low speed. Add the sugar mixture in two additions and mix for 2 minutes longer, scraping down the side of the bowl as needed.

4. Add the egg, egg yolk, and vanilla and mix until well blended, about 1 minute longer. On low speed, add 1 cup of the walnuts and the dry ingredients in two additions, mixing *just* until combined. *Do not overmix.*

5. Form the dough into a ball and shape into quarters. Have ready a 15-inch sheet of wax paper. On a lightly floured surface, shape each piece of dough into a 6 × 1½-inch log and place on the wax paper. Place the remaining walnuts in a shallow pan or pie plate. Working with one log at a time, brush with the egg white and roll in the walnuts, pressing to adhere. Wrap the log with plastic, twisting the ends tightly to seal securely. Refrigerate for 1 hour or until firm.

(This dough will keep in the refrigerator for up to 3 days or may be frozen for 1 month.)

BAKE THE COOKIES

6. Position the shelves in the upper and lower thirds of the oven. Heat the oven to 350°.

7. Using a thin, sharp knife, cut the dough into ¼-inch-thick slices, turning the dough after two or three cuts to maintain the shape. Place the slices 2 inches apart on the cookie sheets.

Bake for 11 to 12 minutes, until the edges start to brown. To ensure even browning, toward the end of baking time, rotate the pans top to bottom and front to back. Remove from the oven and let rest for 1 minute before loosening with a thin metal spatula. Transfer to cooling racks.

STORAGE: Store in an airtight container, layered between strips of wax paper, for up to 3 weeks. These cookies may be frozen.

Cookie Characteristics

Versatile

Long shelf life

Travel well

Broken

Coarsely Chopped

Medium Chopped

Finely Chopped

Nut Meal

coconut apricot icebox cookies

MAKES ABOUT 6 DOZEN 2-INCH COOKIES

Sweet coconut and bits of tangy dried apricot are blended together in these chewy macaroon-like cookies. An egg-yolk glaze brushed on before baking gives them a delicate golden hue. These cookies benefit from being moist, so be careful not to overbake them.

AT A GLANCE

PAN: Cookie sheets

PAN PREP: Ungreased

OVEN TEMP: 325°

CHILLING TIME: I hour

BAKING TIME: 12–15 minutes

DIFFICULTY: ⊙

1 (10-ounce) package sweetened, flaked coconut

2¼ cups all-purpose flour, spooned in and leveled

½ teaspoon baking soda

¼ teaspoon salt

½ cup (6 ounces) plumped dried apricots, chopped in ⅛-inch pieces (see page 391)

1 cup (2 sticks) unsalted butter, slightly firm

¾ cup sugar

1 large egg

1½ teaspoons pure vanilla extract

½ teaspoon imitation coconut extract

1 large egg white, lightly beaten with 2 teaspoons water, for brushing the logs

1 large egg yolk

1 teaspoon half-and-half or milk

MAKE THE DOUGH

1. Place the coconut in the work bowl of a food processor fitted with the steel blade. Pulse five or six times, then process until finely chopped. Set aside.

2. Strain together the flour, baking soda, and salt. Remove 2 tablespoons of the dry ingredients and toss with the apricots. Set aside.

3. In the large bowl of an electric mixer fitted with the paddle attachment, mix the butter on medium-low speed. Pour in the sugar in a steady stream, and mix for 1 to 2 minutes. Add the egg and mix for 1 minute longer, scraping down the bowl as needed. Mix in the extracts.

4. Reduce the mixer speed to low and blend in 1¾ cups of the coconut. Add the dry ingredients in two additions, mixing only to combine after each addition. Using a large rubber spatula, mix in the apricots. Shape the dough into three logs, each measuring about 8 × 1½ inches.

5. Place the remaining coconut on a 15-inch sheet of wax paper. Brush each log with the egg wash and place on the coconut, positioning it so that the length of the log is parallel to the short sides of the wax paper. Grasp each side of the wax paper, lift the paper off the counter, and, moving your hands up and down, roll the log to coat it with the coconut.

6. Wrap the log with plastic, twisting the ends of the wrap tightly to secure. Refrigerate for at least 1 hour or until firm. (This dough will keep in the refrigerator for up to 3 days or may be frozen for 1 month.)

7. Position the shelves in the upper and lower thirds of the oven. Heat the oven to 325°.

8. Using a sharp knife with a thin blade, cut the dough into ⅜-inch-thick slices, turning the dough every two or three cuts to maintain the shape, and place on the cookie sheets about 2 inches apart. If the dough tears when slicing, press it back together.

9. Using a fork, mix the egg yolk and the half-and-half in a shallow bowl, then lightly brush the tops of the cookies with the glaze. Bake for 12 to 15 minutes or until *lightly* browned around the edges. To ensure even browning, toward the end of baking time rotate the pans top to bottom and front to back. *Do not overbake.* Remove from the oven. Let stand for 1 minute before loosening with a thin metal spatula. Transfer to cooling racks.

STORAGE: Store in an airtight container, layered between strips of wax paper, for up to 2 weeks. These cookies may be frozen.

Cookie
Characteristics

Versatile

Long shelf life

Travel well

chocolate–peanut butter yo-yo's

MAKES ABOUT 3 DOZEN 1¾-INCH SANDWICH COOKIES

If you want a little whimsy in your cookie-baking projects, try these Chocolate–Peanut Butter Yo-Yo's. Marbleized cookies made with chocolate and peanut butter dough are sandwiched with chocolate glaze and then rolled in crunchy chopped peanuts.

To have some fun with children, simulate a yo-yo by placing a string between the cookies before they are sandwiched. As the icing dries, it will hold the string in place. If your little people don't fancy nuts, you're sure to win them over with a trimming of chocolate jimmies!

AT A GLANCE

PAN: Cookie sheets

PAN PREP: Lightly buttered

OVEN TEMP: 350°

CHILLING TIME: 1 hour

BAKING TIME: 8–9 minutes

DIFFICULTY: ◐◐

1 cup all-purpose flour, spooned in and leveled

¼ teaspoon baking soda

¼ teaspoon salt

¼ cup (½ stick) unsalted butter, at room temperature

¼ cup smooth peanut butter

6 tablespoons granulated sugar

¼ cup lightly packed light brown sugar

1 large egg

¾ teaspoon pure vanilla extract

½ teaspoon hot water

1 ounce unsweetened chocolate, melted and kept warm (see page 392)

1 large recipe Quick Chocolate Glaze (page 359)

¾ cup medium-chopped salted peanuts

MAKE THE DOUGH

1. Strain together the flour, baking soda, and salt. Set aside.

2. In the large bowl of an electric mixer fitted with the paddle attachment, mix the butter on medium-low speed. When the butter is smooth and creamy, add the peanut butter and mix to thoroughly combine. Add the granulated sugar, then the light brown sugar and mix for 1 minute to incorporate. Mix in the egg for 1 minute, scraping down the side of the bowl as needed. Mix in the vanilla.

3. Reduce the mixer speed to low and add the dry ingredients in three additions, mixing *just* to combine after each addition.

4. Remove ½ cup of dough and place in a wide, medium bowl. Using a wooden spoon, mix in the hot water, then blend in the warm melted chocolate. Drop tablespoons of chocolate dough onto the peanut butter dough, being careful to distribute the chocolate dough evenly around the bowl. With a table knife, cut through the two doughs about six times to marbleize them. *Do not overmix* or the marbleization will be lost. Form into

two 1¼-inch-diameter logs, being careful not to disturb the marbleization. Wrap the logs with plastic, twisting the ends tightly to secure. Refrigerate for 1 hour or until firm. (This dough will keep in the refrigerator for up to 3 days or may be frozen for 1 month.)

BAKE THE COOKIES

5. Position the shelves in the upper and lower thirds of the oven. Heat the oven to 350°. Lightly butter the cookie sheets.

6. Using a thin, sharp knife, slice the dough into ³⁄₁₆-inch-thick rounds, turning every two or three cuts to maintain the shape. Place on the cookie sheets about 2 inches apart.

7. Bake for 8 to 9 minutes or until *lightly* browned. To ensure even browning, toward the end of baking time rotate the sheets top to bottom and front to back. Let stand for 1 or 2 minutes before loosening with a thin metal spatula. Transfer to cooling racks.

ASSEMBLE THE YO-YO'S

8. While the cookies are cooling, prepare the glaze. Using a small offset spatula, sandwich each cookie with about ½ teaspoon of the chocolate glaze, then coat the side. Place the chopped peanuts in a low, flat dish and roll the side of each cookie through the peanuts, pressing the nuts into the glaze. Place on a rack and let the glaze set.

STORAGE: Store in an airtight container, layered between strips of wax paper, for up to 2 weeks. These cookies may be frozen.

Cookie Characteristics

Versatile

Long shelf life

Travel well

hot chocolate wafers

MAKES ABOUT 4 DOZEN 2½-INCH COOKIES

Imagine a dark chocolate cookie sparked with the zing of black pepper, and that's what Hot Chocolate Wafers are about. These cookies benefit from fine-quality chocolate, so take the time to ferret it out. I prefer to use freshly ground pepper, but if you don't have a peppermill, use preground and reduce the amount by half. If you're not a pepper fan, the pepper may be omitted. When you make these cookies, take out the vanilla ice cream—the combination of the Hot Chocolate Wafer and the coolness of the ice cream is dynamite!

AT A GLANCE

PAN: Cookie sheets

PAN PREP: Ungreased

OVEN TEMP: 350°

CHILLING TIME: 3 hours

BAKING TIME: 10–11 minutes

DIFFICULTY: ○

½ cup (1 stick) unsalted butter

3 ounces fine-quality bittersweet or semisweet chocolate, such as Lindt Bittersweet, coarsely chopped

½ teaspoon instant espresso powder

1¼ cups all-purpose flour, spooned in and leveled

6 tablespoons strained Dutch-processed cocoa powder

1 teaspoon freshly ground black pepper

¼ teaspoon baking soda

⅛ teaspoon salt

¾ cup superfine sugar

1 large egg, lightly beaten

1 teaspoon pure vanilla extract

MAKE THE DOUGH

1. In a heavy 3-quart saucepan, melt the butter over low heat, then add the chocolate. When the chocolate is almost melted, turn off the heat and let the mixture stand, stirring occasionally until the chocolate is completely melted. Blend in the espresso powder. Set aside.

2. Strain together the flour, cocoa powder, black pepper, baking soda, and salt. Set aside.

3. Stir the sugar into the chocolate mixture, blending until smooth. Stir in the egg and the vanilla. Add the dry ingredients in two additions, mixing *only* to combine. The dough will be oily.

4. Have ready two 12-inch strips of plastic wrap. Shape the dough into two 5 × 1¾-inch logs. Wrap each log with plastic, twisting the ends tightly to secure. Refrigerate for 3 hours or until firm. (This dough will keep in the refrigerator for up to 3 days or may be frozen for 1 month.)

BAKE THE COOKIES

5. Position the shelves in the upper and lower thirds of the oven. Heat the oven to 350°.

6. Using a thin, sharp knife, cut the dough into ³⁄₁₆-inch slices. After two or

PAN: Cookie sheets

PAN PREP: Ungreased

EQUIPMENT: Pastry bag

OVEN TEMP: 350°

BAKING TIME: 12–14 minutes

DIFFICULTY: ◐

1 recipe Chocolate Espresso Spritz
  Cookie dough (page 145)
8 ounces coarsely chopped, fine-quality
  white chocolate, such as Lindt Swiss
  Classic White
½ cup finely chopped pistachios,
  preferably unsalted

MAKE THE COOKIES

1. Position the shelves in the upper and lower thirds of the oven. Heat the oven to 350°.

2. Fit a pastry bag with a large #4 star tip. Place a 10-inch strip of plastic wrap on a flat surface. Put the dough in the center of the strip and wrap the plastic around the dough, leaving an opening at the bottom. Fill the pastry bag with the plastic-wrapped dough. Twist the top of the bag securely, and holding the pastry bag at a 45-degree angle to the cookie sheet, pipe strips approximately 2 inches long, spacing them 1½ inches apart.

3. Bake for 12 to 14 minutes, or until the tops are set. To ensure even baking, toward the end of baking time, rotate the sheets top to bottom and front to back. Let rest on the cookie sheets for 2 or 3 minutes before loosening with a thin metal spatula. Cool on wire racks.

GARNISH THE COOKIES

4. Warm the white chocolate in a double boiler over low heat, *just* until it is almost melted, stirring occasionally. Watch carefully; it should not get too hot. When the chocolate is almost melted, remove the double boiler from the heat and set the chocolate aside to complete the melting process. While dipping, the chocolate should remain over the hot water to keep it fluid.

5. Place the pistachios in a small bowl. Dip the end of each cookie into the melted chocolate, then into the pistachios. Let stand on a cooling rack until the chocolate is set; this can take 1 hour or longer (see page 399).

STORAGE: Store in an airtight container, layered between strips of wax paper, for up to 3 weeks. These cookies may be frozen.

Cookie
Characteristics

Festive

Long shelf life

Temperature
sensitive

> "Tis an ill cook that cannot lick his own fingers."
>
> —WILLIAM SHAKESPEARE

buttery crispy spritz

MAKES 4 DOZEN 2-INCH COOKIES

This recipe comes from my computer tutor, Lorette Cheswick, a woman who excels not only in the world of "dot coms" but in the kitchen as well. Her husband's aunt was known for her outstanding spritz cookies. Not only do these have the lovely buttery flavor of spritz but they have a pleasant crispy texture as well.

AT A GLANCE

PAN: Cookie sheets

PAN PREP: Ungreased

EQUIPMENT: Cookie press

OVEN TEMP: 350°

BAKING TIME: 8–10 minutes

DIFFICULTY: ○

2 cups all-purpose flour, spooned in
    and leveled
1 teaspoon baking powder
⅛ teaspoon salt
1 cup (2 sticks) unsalted butter, slightly
    firm
¾ cup sugar
1 egg yolk
1 teaspoon pure almond extract

1. Position the shelves in the upper and lower thirds of the oven. Heat the oven to 350°.

2. Strain together the flour, baking powder, and salt. Set aside.

3. In a large bowl of an electric mixer fitted with the paddle attachment, mix the butter on medium-low speed until creamy and lightened in color. Add the sugar in a steady stream, mixing for 2 minutes. Add the egg yolk and mix to combine, about 30 seconds. Scrape down the side of the bowl as needed. Mix in the almond extract.

4. Reduce the mixer speed to low and add the dry ingredients in two additions, mixing *only* to combine after each addition.

5. Place desired forming plate into the cookie press. Following the manufacturer's instructions, fill the press with the dough and press the cookies onto the cookie sheets, spacing them about 1 inch apart.

6. Bake the cookies for 8 to 10 minutes, or until the bottoms are *very* lightly browned. To ensure even browning, toward the end of baking time rotate the pans top to bottom and front to back. Let rest for 2 or 3 minutes before loosening with a thin metal spatula. Cool on wire racks.

STORAGE: Store in an airtight container, layered between strips of wax paper, for up to 3 weeks. These cookies may be frozen.

Cookie
Characteristics

Versatile

Long shelf life

Travel well

almond spritz

MAKES 4 DOZEN 2-INCH COOKIES

Traditional spritz cookies are made with ground almonds, and that's what we have here. The toasted almonds add terrific flavor and texture to the delicate buttery cookies. If you want the cookie to have a beautiful golden hue, be sure to use blanched almonds.

AT A GLANCE

PAN: Cookie sheets
PAN PREP: Ungreased
EQUIPMENT: Cookie press
OVEN TEMP: 375°
BAKING TIME: 9–11 minutes
DIFFICULTY: ⊙

1 cup toasted blanched almonds
2 cups all-purpose flour, spooned in and leveled
¼ teaspoon salt
1 cup (2 sticks) unsalted butter, slightly firm
4 ounces almond paste, finely shredded, at room temperature
⅔ cup sugar
2 large egg yolks
1½ teaspoons pure vanilla extract
½ teaspoon almond extract

Cookie Characteristics

Versatile

Long shelf life

Travel well

1. Position the shelves in the upper and lower thirds of the oven. Heat the oven to 375°.
2. In the work bowl of a food processor fitted with a steel blade, pulse the almonds five to six times until they are coarsely chopped. Add ½ cup of the flour and process until the mixture develops a sandy texture and holds together when pressed gently in your hand, about 30 seconds. Add the remaining flour and salt and pulse to combine.

3. In the standing bowl of an electric mixer fitted with the paddle attachment, mix the butter on medium-low speed until creamy and lightened in color, about 2 minutes. Add the almond paste and mix 30 seconds to combine. Pour in the sugar in a steady stream, then add the egg yolks one at a time, scraping down the side of the bowl as needed. Beat in the extracts.
4. Reduce the mixer speed to low and add the dry ingredients in three additions, mixing *only* to combine after each addition.
5. Place the desired forming plate into the cookie press. Following the manufacturer's instructions, fill the press with the dough and press the cookies onto the cookie sheets, spacing them about 1 inch apart.
6. Bake the cookies for 9 to 11 minutes, or until the bottoms are very lightly browned. To ensure even browning, toward the end of baking time, rotate the cookie sheets top to bottom and front to back. Let rest for 2 or 3 minutes before loosening with a thin metal spatula. Cool on wire racks.

STORAGE: Store in an airtight container, layered between strips of wax paper, for up to 3 weeks. These cookies may be frozen.

spiced rickrack wafers

MAKES 7 DOZEN 2-INCH COOKIES

Spiced Rickracks are wafer-thin cookies flavored with a zesty combination of ground cloves, ginger, and cinnamon. The dough is thinly pressed through the cookie gun and lightly trimmed with finely chopped sugared toasted pecans. These delicate cookies are a perfect accompaniment to your favorite ice cream or sorbet.

AT A GLANCE

PAN: Cookie sheets

PAN PREP: Ungreased

EQUIPMENT: Cookie press

OVEN TEMP: 350°

BAKING TIME: 7 minutes

DIFFICULTY: ✪

¼ cup finely chopped toasted pecans

¾ cup plus 1 tablespoon sugar, divided

2½ cups all-purpose flour, spooned in and leveled

1½ teaspoons ground ginger

1 teaspoon ground cinnamon

½ teaspoon ground cloves

½ teaspoon baking soda

½ teaspoon salt

1 cup (2 sticks) unsalted butter, slightly firm

1 large egg

2 tablespoons dark unsulfured molasses

1 teaspoon pure vanilla extract

1. Place the pecans and 1 tablespoon of the sugar in the bowl of a food processor and pulse until finely chopped. Set aside.

2. Strain together the flour, ginger, cinnamon, cloves, baking soda, and salt. Set aside.

3. In the large bowl of an electric mixer fitted with the paddle attachment, mix the butter on medium-low speed until creamy and lightened in color, about 2 minutes. Add the remaining ¾ cup sugar and mix for another 2 minutes to combine. Mix in the egg, molasses, and vanilla, scraping down the side of the bowl as needed.

4. Reduce the mixer speed to low and add the dry ingredients in two additions, mixing *only* to combine after each addition.

5. Place the ridged bar forming plate (this is the plate with "teeth" on the top and a flat surface on the bottom) into the cookie press. Following the manufacturer's instructions, fill the press with the dough.

6. Holding the cookie press at a 45-degree angle, form a straight line of dough 10 to 12 inches long along the length of the cookie sheet. (Note: The ridges should be on top.) Using a thin, sharp knife, cut the strips of dough every 2 inches. You do not have to separate them. Sprinkle lightly with the pecan–sugar mixture.

7. Bake the cookies for 7 minutes or until the edges *begin* to color. To ensure even baking, toward the end of baking time rotate the sheets top to bottom and front to back. Do not overbake. Cut

classic sugar cookies

MAKES ABOUT 4 DOZEN 2-INCH COOKIES

There is no doubt that a great sugar cookie recipe is worth its weight in gold! This beloved cookie, whether decorated with sparkling sugars, colorful sprinkles, or glazes, is always on the list of everyone's favorites. This Master Recipe, with its variations, will provide you with a delectable assortment of cookies for any occasion.

AT A GLANCE

PAN: Cookie sheets
PAN PREP: Ungreased
OVEN TEMP: 350°
CHILLING TIME: 15 minutes
BAKING TIME: 12–14 minutes
DIFFICULTY: ✪

3 cups sifted cake flour, spooned in and leveled
¼ teaspoon baking powder
½ teaspoon salt
1 cup (2 sticks) unsalted butter, slightly firm
¾ cup superfine sugar
1 large egg
1½ teaspoons pure vanilla extract
1 large egg white, lightly beaten with 2 teaspoons of water
Sparkling white sugar, pearl sugar, or sanding sugar, for sprinkling (available from The Baker's Catalogue; see page 403)

1. Strain together the flour, baking powder, and salt. Set aside.

2. In the large bowl of an electric mixer fitted with the paddle attachment, mix the butter and sugar on medium-low speed.

3. Using a fork, beat the egg and vanilla together and mix into the butter–sugar mixture. Add the dry ingredients one-half at a time, mixing *only* until mixture begins to form a mass. Empty the dough onto a lightly floured surface and knead four or five times, or just until smooth. Divide the dough into quarters. Using lightly floured hands, shape the dough into four disks. Dust lightly with flour and wrap each with plastic. Chill for at least 15 minutes.

4. Position the racks in the upper and lower thirds of the oven. Heat the oven to 350°.

5. On a lightly floured pastry cloth or board, working with one-fourth of the dough at a time, roll the dough to a ³⁄₁₆-inch thickness. Cut into desired shapes with cookie cutters. After cutting, transfer the cookies to a sheet of wax paper. Brush the tops lightly with egg wash and sprinkle evenly with sparkling white sugar, pearl sugar, or sanding sugar. Carefully place on cookie sheets.

6. Bake the cookies for 12 to 14 minutes, or until the edges begin to brown. To ensure even browning, toward the end of baking time rotate the sheets from top to bottom and front to back. Let stand on pans for 1 or 2 minutes. With a thin metal spatula, remove to cooling racks. Let cool before decorating.

Store in an airtight container, layered between strips of wax paper, for up to 3 weeks. These cookies may be frozen.

nutty sugar cookies

Using one-fourth of the dough, knead in ¼ cup finely chopped pecans before chilling. Do not overwork.

cinnamon swirl sugar cookies

Combine ¾ teaspoon ground cinnamon with 2 teaspoons sugar. Add to one-fourth of the dough. Lightly knead the mixture three or four times into the dough to create a marbled effect. Do not overwork.

chocolate fleck sugar cookies

Using one-fourth of the dough, knead in ¼ cup finely shaved semisweet or bittersweet chocolate before chilling. Do not overwork.

Cookie
Characteristics

Versatile

Long shelf life

Travel well

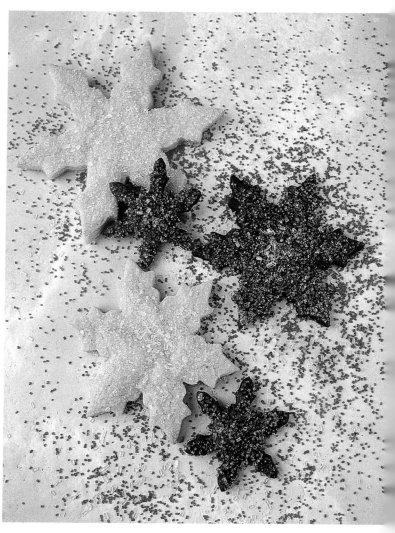

cookie-cutter chocolate cookies

MAKES 5 DOZEN 2-INCH COOKIES

With a nod to the chocoholics in your crowd, chocolate cutouts are a "must have" to pair with sugar cookies in any holiday assortment. Feel free to go to town when you have all of your decorative trimmings at hand. And don't forget to use one of the chocolate glazes (page 359). Chocolate-on-chocolate—need I say more?

AT A GLANCE

PAN: Cookie sheets

PAN PREP: Baking parchment

OVEN TEMP: 350°

CHILLING TIME: 2 hours

BAKING TIME: 9–11 minutes

DIFFICULTY: ⊘

1½ cups all-purpose flour, spooned in and leveled

2 tablespoons strained Dutch-processed cocoa powder

½ teaspoon baking powder

¼ teaspoon baking soda

½ teaspoon salt

½ cup (1 stick) unsalted butter, slightly firm

1 cup superfine sugar

1 large egg

1 teaspoon pure vanilla extract

1 teaspoon instant espresso powder, dissolved in ½ teaspoon boiling water

3 ounces unsweetened chocolate, melted (see page 392)

Strained confectioners' sugar, for rolling

MAKE THE DOUGH

1. Strain together the flour, cocoa powder, baking powder, baking soda, and salt. Set aside.

2. In the large bowl of an electric mixer fitted with the paddle attachment, mix the butter on medium-low speed until it is creamy and lightened in color. Add the sugar in a steady stream, mixing for 2 minutes to combine. Mix in the egg, vanilla, and espresso mixture. Scrape down the side of the bowl as needed, then mix in the melted chocolate.

3. Reduce the mixer speed to low and blend in the dry ingredients in two additions, mixing *only* to combine after each addition. Remove the dough from the bowl and divide in half. Form into two 3 by 4-inch rectangles and wrap in plastic. Refrigerate for 2 hours or until firm. (The dough may be frozen at this point for up to 1 month.)

BAKE THE COOKIES

4. Position the shelves in the upper and lower thirds of the oven. Heat the oven to 350°. Dab the corners of the cookie sheets lightly with butter and line with baking parchment.

5. Sprinkle a pastry cloth and rolling pin with confectioners' sugar, rubbing it well into the weave. Working with one piece of dough at a time, roll it into a rectangle ³⁄₁₆ inch thick. Cut into desired shapes. Place the cutouts on the cookie sheets.

6. Bake for 9 to 11 minutes, or until the cookies feel set on top. To ensure even baking, toward the end of baking time rotate the sheets from top to bottom and front to back. Let cookies rest on the sheet for 2 minutes before loosening with a thin metal spatula. Cool on wire racks.

Store in an airtight container, layered between strips of wax paper, for up to 3 weeks. These cookies may be frozen.

Cookie Characteristics

Versatile

Long shelf life

Travel well

Nutty Sugar Cookies, Chocolate Fleck Sugar Cookies, Cinnamon Swirl, and Cookie-Cutter Chocolate Cookies.

chocolate-glazed pecan leaves

MAKES 5 DOZEN 3-INCH OVAL COOKIES

These buttery cookies are glazed with a thin layer of chocolate ganache and then dipped in chopped toasted pecans. The tender crumb of the cookie, the crunch of the pecans, and the mellow chocolate is a combination that I adore.

AT A GLANCE

PAN: Cookie sheets

PAN PREP: Ungreased

EQUIPMENT: 3-inch fluted-edge oval cookie cutter

OVEN TEMP: 350°

CHILLING TIME: 15 minutes

BAKING TIME: 12–14 minutes

DIFFICULTY: ○

3 cups sifted cake flour, spooned in and leveled

¼ teaspoon baking powder

½ teaspoon salt

1 cup (2 sticks) unsalted butter, slightly firm

¾ cup superfine sugar

1 large egg

1½ teaspoons pure vanilla extract

1 recipe Ganache Glaze (page 360)

1 cup chopped toasted pecans, in ⅛-inch pieces, preferably hand-chopped

MAKE THE DOUGH

1. Strain together the flour, baking powder, and salt. Set aside.

2. In the large bowl of an electric mixer fitted with the paddle attachment, mix the butter and sugar on medium-low speed.

3. Using a fork, beat the egg and vanilla together and mix into the butter–sugar mixture. Add the dry ingredients, one-half at a time, mixing *only* until mixture begins to form a mass. Turn the dough out onto a lightly floured surface and knead four or five times, or just until smooth. Divide the dough into quarters. Using lightly floured hands, shape the dough into four disks. Dust lightly with flour and wrap each with plastic. Chill for at least 15 minutes.

BAKE THE COOKIES

4. Position the shelves in the upper and lower thirds of the oven. Heat the oven to 350°.

5. On a lightly floured pastry cloth or board roll out the dough to a ³⁄₁₆-inch thickness. Cut into leaf shapes using a 3-inch oval cookie cutter with a fluted edge.

6. Place on the cookie sheets and bake for 12 to 14 minutes, or until the edges begin to brown. To ensure even browning, toward the end of baking time rotate the sheets from top to bottom and front to back. Let stand on the pans for 1 minute, then remove to wire racks using a thin metal spatula.

GLAZE THE COOKIES

7. When the cookies are cool, using a small offset spatula, spread a thin layer

may be refrigerated at this point for up to 3 days or frozen for 1 month.)

BAKE THE COOKIES

5. Position the shelves in the upper and lower thirds of the oven. Heat the oven to 350°. Dab the corners of the cookie sheets lightly with butter and line with baking parchment.

6. Lightly flour a pastry cloth or flat surface. Working with one disk at a time, roll the dough until ⅛ inch thick and cut into desired shapes. Place on the cookie sheets.

7. Bake for 9 to 11 minutes for small cookies or 10 to 12 minutes for large cookies, until lightly browned around the edges. To ensure even baking, toward the end of baking time rotate the sheets from top to bottom and front to back. Let rest on the cookie sheets for 2 or 3 minutes before loosening with a thin metal spatula. Transfer to wire racks. The cookies will firm as they cool.

When the cookies have thoroughly cooled, prepare the vanilla glaze. Partially fill a plastic squeeze bottle with the glaze and have fun decorating! Be sure to snip or cut the decorating tip to the appropriate size and test the consistency of the glaze before you start.

STORAGE: Store in an airtight container, layered between strips of wax paper, for up to 4 weeks. These cookies may be frozen.

Cookie
Characteristics

Festive

Long shelf life

Travel well

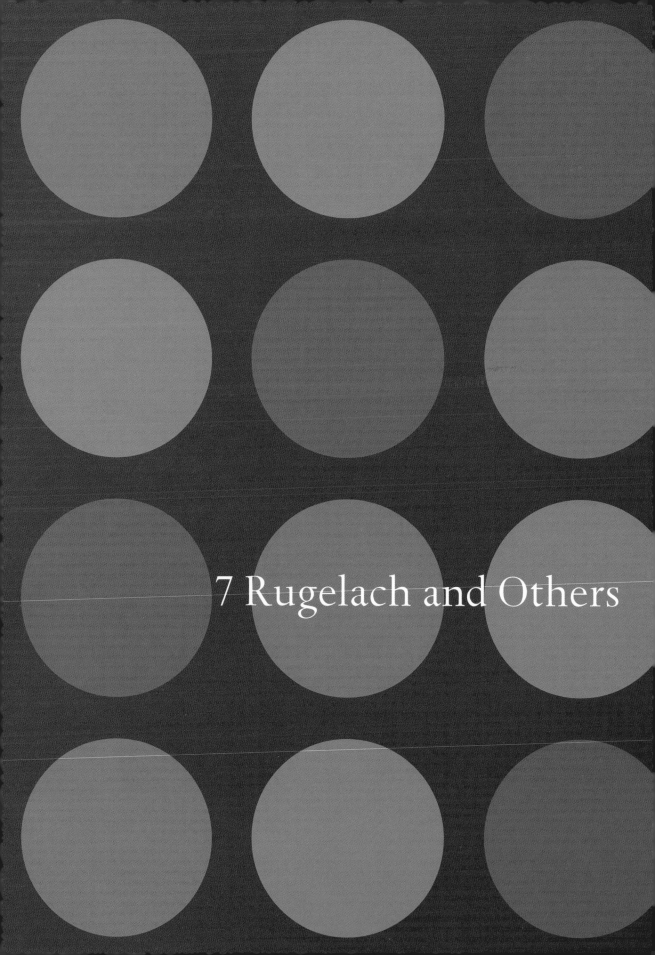

7 Rugelach and Others

rugelach

MAKES 7 DOZEN 1¾-INCH COOKIES

Rugelach wears many guises. These petite pastries can be made with any one of a variety of doughs. They include yeast-style doughs and doughs made with cream cheese or sour cream. Sometimes the doughs contain eggs and other accent ingredients. The tasty fillings include nuts, sugar, cinnamon, raisins or currants, and sometimes preserves, chocolate chips, or cocoa. While they are most commonly formed in crescent shapes, the dough can also be rolled in logs and sliced.

Of all of the many "takes" on rugelach, this recipe remains my favorite. My pastry of choice is a simple cream cheese dough. The sweetness of the butter contrasted with the tang of the cheese imparts a pleasing flavor that is unique. I take extra care to avoid overworking the dough. When rolled in a mixture of confectioners' sugar and flour, the crust forms many delicate layers and becomes

extra-special. I fill the dough with lots of chopped nuts, cinnamon, sugar, and moist, golden raisins. No, I do not include preserves because I shape the dough into crescents, and if the preserves are not unusually thick, they tend to run because of the many exposed edges. I believe that preserves can be used more successfully in pastries such as Strudelettes (page 177), or other similar cookies within this section.

PAN: Cookie sheets

PAN PREP: Ungreased

OVEN TEMP: 350° (see Note)

CHILLING TIME: 4 hours before shaping, ½ hour after shaping

BAKING TIME: 20–25 minutes (see Note)

DIFFICULTY: ◐◐

CREAM CHEESE
PASTRY

1 cup (2 sticks) unsalted butter, at room temperature

8 ounces cream cheese, at room temperature

2¼ cups all-purpose flour, spooned in and leveled, divided

¼ teaspoon salt

¼ cup strained confectioners' sugar, spooned and leveled

FILLING

¾ cup granulated sugar

1 tablespoon ground cinnamon

1½ cups finely chopped walnuts

1 cup golden raisins, plumped (see page 391)

Strained confectioners' sugar, for dusting

MAKE THE PASTRY

1. In a large bowl, using a wooden spoon, mix together the butter and cream cheese until smooth and thoroughly blended.

2. Mix in 1 cup of the flour and the salt, working until almost incorporated. Cut in another ½ cup flour with the spoon, again working it until the flour is almost incorporated. Complete the process by kneading in another ½ cup flour. *Do not overwork.* (Note: The remaining ¼ cup of flour is used for rolling.)

3. With lightly floured hands, shape dough into a mound, then divide in half and form two 5-inch disks. Dust the disks lightly with a little flour, score with the side of your hand to even the tops, and wrap with plastic. Chill for at least 4 hours or up to 3 days.

SHAPE AND FILL THE RUGELACH

This procedure will be used each time you roll a portion of the dough.

4. Remove the dough from the refrigerator and let stand at room temperature for 30 minutes before rolling. It is ready to roll when you can leave a slight imprint in the dough when you press it with your fingers. Combine the remaining ¼ cup flour and the confectioners' sugar. Dust a pastry board or other flat surface with this mixture. Have cookie sheets ready.

5. Divide 1 disk of the dough into thirds, coat each third lightly with the flour–sugar mixture, and form into cylinders. Working with one cylinder at a time, tap it about six times with a rolling pin to flatten. Then roll the cylinder into a long rectangle approximately 5 inches wide and 18 inches long, about 1/16 inch thick.

6. Combine the granulated sugar and cinnamon. Sprinkle the strip of dough with 2 tablespoons of this mixture, along with ¼ cup of the chopped walnuts. Run the rolling pin gently over the walnuts to press them into the dough.

7. With a fluted pastry wheel, cut triangles at 2-inch intervals. Place six or seven raisins on the widest side of each triangle and roll up loosely, tucking the end underneath. It's okay if some of the filling falls out; just sprinkle it back on. Place on the cookie sheets. Repeat with the remaining dough. Chill for ½ hour before baking. (The rugelach may be frozen at this point for up to 1 month.)

BAKE THE RUGELACH

8. Position the shelves in the upper and lower thirds of the oven. Heat the oven to 350°.

9. Bake the rugelach for 20 to 25 minutes, or until golden brown. To ensure

Cookie
Characteristics

Versatile

Moderate
shelf life

Travel well

even browning, toward the end of baking time rotate the sheets top to bottom and front to back. Remove from the oven and let rest for 1 minute, then loosen with a thin metal spatula. Transfer to cooling racks. When cool, sprinkle with confectioners' sugar.

NOTE: If the rugelach are frozen, do not defrost them before baking. Reduce the oven temperature to 325° and add 4 or 5 minutes to the baking time.

STORAGE: Store in an airtight container, layered between strips of wax paper, for up to 1 week. These cookies may be frozen.

chocolate chip rugelach

¾ cup granulated sugar
2 tablespoons strained unsweetened
   cocoa powder
½ to 1 teaspoon ground cinnamon
1½ cups finely chopped walnuts
About ¾ cup mini-chocolate chips
Strained confectioners' sugar, for
   dusting

Follow the directions through step 5 of the Master Recipe. In a medium bowl, whisk together the granulated sugar, cocoa powder, and cinnamon. Sprinkle each strip of pastry generously with this mixture. Top with a layer of chopped walnuts and press the rolling pin lightly over the surface to press the topping into the dough.

With a pastry wheel, cut triangles at 2-inch intervals. Place about ½ teaspoon of chocolate chips on the wide end of the triangles. Starting with the widest side, loosely roll the triangles of dough and place them on the ungreased cookie sheets, with the end underneath. Chill for ½ hour before baking as directed in the Master Recipe. When cool, sprinkle with confectioners' sugar.

The Perfect Cream Cheese Pastry

- It is essential for rugelach that the butter and cream cheese be at room temperature and of equal consistency. Depending on the ambient temperature, this can take 3 to 4 hours.
- If the consistency of the butter and cream cheese is not the same, cream the firmer one first until it softens to the same consistency as the other.
- If making the dough with a stand mixer, reserve half of the flour to incorporate by hand.
- When adding the flour, cut it into the butter–cream cheese mixture using a wooden spoon. When the mixture becomes too difficult to work with the spoon before all of the flour has been added, knead in the remaining amount with your hands.

strudelettes

The recipe for these chewy little pastries comes from my cousin, Peggy Berg. Made with a flaky sour cream dough, they are filled with a mixture of fruit preserves, nuts, coconut, and raisins. Try your own combination of preserves, but use discretion when adding the sugar. The sweetness of the preserves will vary.

AT A GLANCE

PAN: Cookie sheets

PAN PREP: Baking parchment

OVEN TEMP: 350°

CHILLING TIME: 3 to 4 hours

BAKING TIME: 35–40 minutes

DIFFICULTY: ◕◕

SOUR CREAM PASTRY

1½ cups all-purpose flour, spooned in and leveled

1 tablespoon granulated sugar

¼ teaspoon salt

¾ cup (1½ sticks) cold unsalted butter, cut into ½-inch cubes

⅓ cup sour cream

1 large egg yolk

½ teaspoon pure vanilla extract

FILLING

1¼ cups walnuts, medium-chopped

1 cup sweetened, flaked coconut, chopped

1 cup golden raisins, plumped (see page 391)

½ cup blanched hazelnuts, toasted and coarsely chopped

¼ to ⅓ cup granulated sugar

1 teaspoon ground cinnamon

⅔ cup thick strawberry preserves

⅓ cup orange marmalade

¾ teaspoon freshly grated orange zest

Cornstarch, for rolling

½ cup strained confectioners' sugar, for garnish

MAKE THE SOUR CREAM PASTRY

1. Combine the flour, sugar, and salt in the work bowl of a food processor fitted with the steel blade and pulse two or three times to combine. Add the butter, pulse three or four times, then process for 8 to 10 seconds, or until the mixture resembles fine meal.

2. Empty the mixture into a large bowl and form a well in the center. In a small bowl, blend the sour cream with the egg yolk and vanilla. Pour the mixture into the well and work in with a mixing spoon, drawing the crumbs in from the center and working toward the outside. Empty the mixture onto a lightly floured surface and, with floured hands, gently knead 4 to 5 times or until a smooth dough is formed. Divide in half and shape into 2 flat rectangles measuring 3 × 4 inches. Cover with plastic wrap and chill for 3 to 4 hours or overnight. (This dough will keep for up to 3 days or frozen for up to 1 month.)

MAKE THE FILLING

3. Combine the walnuts, coconut, raisins, hazelnuts, sugar, and cinnamon in a large bowl. Blend in the preserves, marmalade, and zest. This filling can be refrigerated, covered, for up to 1 week.

4. Heat the oven to 350°. Place the racks in the upper and lower thirds of the oven. Dab the corners of the cookie sheets with butter and line with baking parchment.

5. Lightly dust a rolling surface with cornstarch. Working one rectangle of the dough at a time, divide the piece into four 1-inch strips. Shape each strip into a 3- to 4-inch cylinder by rolling the dough back and forth with your hand on the rolling surface. Sprinkle the rolling surface with additional cornstarch as necessary. Lay a piece of plastic wrap loosely over the cylinders to prevent them from drying out.

6. Roll one cylinder into a rectangle measuring approximately 4 × 10 inches. Using approximately 6 tablespoons of the filling, make a 1¼-inch strip down the center of the pastry.

7. Moisten the far edge of the strip with ice water. Fold the edge of the dough closest to you over the filling, then roll the strip over the moistened edge to adhere the dough. Roll the log back to expose the seam, then pinch the dough at the seam to seal. *Be sure to seal the seam well to prevent the filling from leaking.* Push the filling in at the ends of the strip with a dough scraper.

8. Place the roll seam side down off center on the cookie sheet. (You will bake 3 to 4 rolls per sheet.) Using the dough scraper, angle the ends, then slash the strip slightly with the point of the dough scraper at 1-inch intervals to make air vents. Repeat using the remaining dough and filling.

9. Bake for 35 to 40 minutes or until golden brown. (It's okay if the filling runs a bit.) To ensure even browning, toward the end of baking time rotate the sheets top to bottom and front to back. Let stand 5 minutes, then loosen the rolls from the baking parchment while still hot. When cool, using a dough scraper or a thin-bladed sharp knife, cut on an angle into 1-inch slices. Place the confectioners' sugar in a medium-gauge strainer and sprinkle the tops of the Strudelettes. Air-dry for several hours on a cooling rack.

STORAGE: Store in an airtight container, layered between strips of wax paper, for up to 1 week. These cookies may be frozen.

raspberry apricot strudelettes

Substitute ½ cup raspberry preserves and ½ cup apricot preserves for the strawberry preserves and orange marmalade and reduce the sugar from ¼ to ⅓ cup to 3 to 4 tablespoons. The remaining ingredients are not changed. Proceed as directed in the Master Recipe.

Cookie
Characteristics

Versatile

Long shelf life

Travel well

"A raisin is a worried-
looking grape."

—ANONYMOUS

Mix and Match Menu for Flaky Pastries

You can create cookies to please your own taste buds from the array of doughs and fillings found in this book. They are interchangeable, so mix and match as you please. For example: If you like the sweet taste of the Ice Cream Pastry, pair it with the tangy Apricot Filling; if the Cream Cheese Pastry is the easiest for you to roll, it can be used with any filling in this chapter. There may be slight differences in baking times; however, my constant rule is, "Let your nose be your guide." When you detect a pleasant aroma coming from the oven, it's time to take a peek. The cookies are ready when they are golden brown.

Pastries
Cream Cheese Pastry (page 175)

Sour Cream Pastry (page 177)

Yeast Cookie Pastry (page 182)

Ricotta Cheese Pastry (page 192)

Ice Cream Pastry (page 190)

Buttery Baking Powder Pastry (page 184)

Fillings
Apricot Filling (page 245)

Prune Filling (page 244)

Chocolate Prune Filling (page 244)

Poppy Seed Filling (page 245)

Cheese Filling (page 180)

Cherry Raisin Filling (page 188)

Thyme-Scented Fig and Port Filling (page 186)

Walnut Filling (page 278)

cheese cracklies

MAKES ABOUT 5 DOZEN 1½-INCH COOKIES

Throughout my years of teaching baking, many of my students have requested a cheese filling that didn't run for rugalah-style pastries. And that's what we have here. Flaky sour cream pastry enrobes a mixture of lightly sweetened farmer and cream cheeses.

After filling, the log is cut into bite-size pieces, dipped in egg white, and then rolled in sugar. As the cookie bakes, the surface develops an appealing crackly glaze. Don't be concerned if the sugary coating caramelizes slightly around the edges of some of the cookies. You can trim it off, but, quite frankly, I like to eat it!

AT A GLANCE

PAN: Cookie sheets

PAN PREP: Baking parchment

OVEN TEMP: 350°

CHILLING TIME: 3–4 hours (pastry); 1 hour (cookies)

BAKING TIME: 20–25 minutes

DIFFICULTY: ◐◐

1 recipe Sour Cream Pastry (page 177)

CHEESE FILLING

8 ounces farmer cheese, at room temperature

1 (3-ounce) package cream cheese, at room temperature

1 cup sugar, divided

1 tablespoon unsifted flour

½ teaspoon freshly grated orange zest, or to taste

½ teaspoon freshly grated lemon zest, or to taste

1 large egg yolk

¾ teaspoon pure vanilla extract

⅛ teaspoon salt

2 large egg whites, lightly beaten with 2 teaspoons water

SHAPE AND FILL THE PASTRIES

1. Pass the farmer cheese and the cream cheese through a food mill or a medium-gauge strainer into a large bowl. Blend in 2 tablespoons of the sugar, the flour, zests, egg yolk, vanilla, and salt. Chill for 3 to 4 hours or overnight, or up to 3 days.

2. Lightly dab the corners of the cookie sheets with butter. Line the sheets with baking parchment.

3. Working with one rectangle of the sour cream pastry dough at a time, divide it into four pieces. With floured hands, roll each piece into a strip measuring 3 × 14 inches. Roll a 2-ounce piece of the cheese mixture, about ¼ cup, into a rope ½ to ¾ inch wide and 14 inches long, and place it lengthwise down the center of the rectangle. Brush the far side of the strip with the beaten egg white.

4. Using a dough scraper, lift the edge of the dough closest to you up and over the cheese filling. Then turn the roll over again so the filling is completely enclosed and the seam is on the bottom. Using the dough scraper or a thin-bladed sharp knife, slice into 1-inch pieces.

5. Place the remaining sugar in another shallow dish. Dip each piece of dough into the beaten egg white, turning it to completely coat with egg wash. Then roll in the sugar and place on the parchment-lined cookie sheet seam side down. Chill at least 1 hour before baking or freeze for up to 1 month.

BAKE THE PASTRIES

6. Position the shelves in the upper and lower thirds of the oven. Heat the oven to 350°.

7. Carefully slide the parchment off the cookie sheets onto the countertop. Dab the corners of the cookie sheets with butter and *reline with clean baking parchment*. Then replace the pastries on the clean parchment.

8. Bake for 20 to 25 minutes, or until golden brown. (It's okay if the sugar coating runs a bit.) To ensure even browning, toward the end of baking time rotate the sheets top to bottom and front to back. Remove the Cracklies from the oven, let stand for 2 or 3 minutes, then use a thin metal spatula to transfer them to cooling racks. When cool, use a paring knife to trim any excessive crusty edges from the bottom of the Cracklies.

STORAGE: Store in an airtight container, layered between strips of wax paper, for up to 5 weeks. These cookies may be frozen.

Cookie Characteristics

Versatile

Moderate shelf life

Temperature sensitive

apricot melt-o-ways

MAKES 4 DOZEN 2½-INCH COOKIES

This pastry has been in my repertoire for years. At one time I sold a line of baked goods to a specialty store in northern New Jersey. These Apricot Melt-o-Ways were at the top of the list in popularity. Unlike bread dough, this yeast-style cookie dough does not require rising. I like to prepare my own apricot filling because it is fruitier; however, thick apricot preserves will work nicely. For more filling ideas, refer to the chart on page 179.

AT A GLANCE

PAN: Jelly roll pans

PAN PREP: Baking parchment

OVEN TEMP: 350°

CHILLING TIME: 1 hour (dough); 15 minutes (cookies)

BAKING TIME: 13–14 minutes

DIFFICULTY: ◐◐

YEAST COOKIE PASTRY

1 tablespoon sugar

½ cup milk, scalded and cooled to 110°–115°

1 package active dry yeast

3 cups all-purpose flour, spooned in and leveled

½ teaspoon salt

1 cup (2 sticks) cold, unsalted butter, cut into ½-inch pieces

1 large egg, lightly beaten

½ teaspoon pure vanilla extract

FILLING AND FINISH

¾ to 1 cup strained confectioners' sugar, for rolling and garnish

1 recipe Apricot Filling (page 245) or ½ cup thick apricot preserves

MAKE THE YEAST COOKIE PASTRY

1. Stir the sugar into the warm milk, then sprinkle the yeast over the top. Cover with a saucer and let stand 5 minutes or until the yeast is dissolved.

2. Place the flour and salt in the work bowl of a food processor fitted with the steel blade. Pulse two to three times to blend. Add the butter and pulse five times, then process for 6 to 8 seconds, or until the mixture resembles fine meal. Empty into a large bowl and make a well in the center.

3. Stir the milk–yeast mixture, then blend in the egg and vanilla. Pour the mixture into the well and, using a wooden spoon, work the liquid and dry ingredients together starting in the center and working outward. Complete the blending by using your hands to knead four to five times, or until a smooth dough is formed.

4. On a lightly floured surface, divide the dough into four parts, flatten, and shape into rectangles. Wrap each with plastic and chill for 1 hour or up to 3 days.

MAKE THE COOKIES

5. Position the shelves to the upper and lower thirds of the oven. Heat the oven to 350°. Line the pans with baking parchment.

6. Sprinkle a wooden board and rolling pin well with confectioners' sugar. Working one piece of dough at a time, roll into an 8 × 11-inch rectangle. Trim the edges with a pastry wheel and divide into twelve 2½-inch squares.

7. Drop 1 scant teaspoon of the apricot filling or preserves into the center of each square. Do not overfill. If using homemade filling, remember that any remaining filling can be saved and used at a later time. (Refrigerate leftover filling in a glass jar for up to 4 months.)

8. Moisten the opposite ends with ice water, bring together, and pinch to seal. Place the cookies on the prepared pans and chill for 15 minutes.

BAKE THE COOKIES

9. Bake the Melt-o-Ways for 10 minutes or until *just* starting to brown. To ensure even browning, toward the end of baking time rotate the sheets top to bottom and front to back. Remove from the oven and, being careful not to touch the hot filling, carefully pinch any cookies together that have spread apart. Return to the oven and continue to bake until golden brown, about 3 to 4 minutes, rotating the pans again top to bottom and front to back. Let cool 5 minutes before loosening with a thin metal spatula. Transfer to cooling racks. Dust with confectioners' sugar before serving.

STORAGE: Store in an airtight container, layered between strips of wax paper, for up to 3 weeks. These cookies may be frozen.

Cookie Characteristics

Versatile

Long shelf life

Travel well

pineapple walnut rolls

MAKES 45 3½-INCH SLICES

A few years ago, before the inception of this book, my feisty friend Selma Yagoda came to my home to show me how she made her famous pineapple roll-ups. She whisked out her recipe and began to make a dough. As she measured the flour, I said to her, "Uh . . . how much flour are you putting in?" Her reply was "As much as it takes!" I bit my lip (hard) and let her "do her thing." The result was a most delicious pastry, and I knew I wanted to duplicate it.

These chewy pastries are generously filled with pineapple preserves and crunchy walnuts. Be sure the rolls are well baked so the spiraled pastry bakes thoroughly in the center. At times, the rolls may split on top because they are generously filled, but upon cooling, this adds to the character of the cookie. Just dust the surface with confectioners' sugar, sip a cup of tea, and savor each slice!

AT A GLANCE

PAN: Cookie sheets

PAN PREP: Baking parchment

OVEN TEMP: 350°

CHILLING TIME: 1 hour

BAKING TIME: 45–50 minutes

DIFFICULTY: ◐◐

BUTTERY BAKING POWDER PASTRY

3 cups all-purpose flour, spooned in and leveled

2 tablespoons sugar

1¼ teaspoons baking powder

½ teaspoon salt

1 cup (2 sticks) cold, unsalted butter, cut into ½-inch cubes

¼ cup milk

1 large egg

1 large egg yolk

1 teaspoon pure vanilla extract

FILLING AND GLAZE

2 cups pineapple preserves (2–2½ jars)

2 cups medium-chopped walnuts

1 large egg white, lightly beaten with 2 teaspoons water

2 to 3 tablespoons sugar

MAKE THE PASTRY

1. Place the flour, sugar, baking powder, and salt in the work bowl of a food processor fitted with the steel blade. Pulse two or three times to combine. Add the butter and pulse five times, then pulse again for 8 to 10 seconds, or until the mixture resembles fine meal. Empty the contents into a large bowl and make a well in the center.

2. In a small bowl, combine the milk, egg, egg yolk, and vanilla. Pour the mixture into the well and, using a fork, gradually draw the crumb mixture into the center. Then, using your fingertips, work the mixture until all the flour is absorbed. Turn the dough out onto a floured surface and knead briefly until smooth, six to eight turns. Shape into three flat rectangles measuring about 3 × 5 inches. Dust the rectangles lightly with flour, wrap with plastic, and chill for 1 hour.

SHAPE THE PASTRY

3. Position the shelves in the lower and upper thirds of the oven. Heat the oven to 350°. Dab the corners of the cookie sheets with butter and line with baking parchment.

4. In a medium bowl, mix the pineapple preserves with the walnuts.

5. On a lightly floured surface, roll one piece of dough at a time into a 10-inch square approximately 3/16 inch thick. Spread the dough with one-third of the pineapple and nut mixture, leaving a 1-inch border on the far side of the pastry.

6. Starting at the side closest to you and using a dough scraper to help lift the pastry, loosely roll the filled dough into a log. Carefully place the roll off-center on the cookie sheet, arranging it seam side down. Repeat with the remaining dough and filling. Brush the surface of the rolls with the egg white mixture, and sprinkle heavily with the sugar.

7. Bake the logs for 45 to 50 minutes, or until golden brown. To ensure even browning, toward the end of baking time rotate the sheets top to bottom and front to back. The rolls should be well baked so the pastry cooks thoroughly in

the center. It's okay if some of the filling runs from the bottom and the rolls split on top. Let cool for 5 minutes, then loosen with a thin metal spatula. Let rest on the cookie sheet until firm enough to handle, then transfer to a cooling rack. On a cutting board, slice each log on an angle into 15 pieces.

STORAGE: Store in an airtight container, layered between strips of wax paper, for up to 5 days. These cookies may be frozen.

Cookie Characteristics

Versatile

Moderate shelf life

Travel well

"Cooking is like love. It should be entered into with abandon or not at all." —HARRIET VAN HORN

fig bars

Here is a bar cookie made with dried figs simmered in a syrup of honey and orange, accented by fresh thyme and a splash of port. The mixture is puréed and the filling nestled in flaky pastry. A sprinkling of sugar and toasted almonds tops them off.

AT A GLANCE

PAN: Cookie sheets
PAN PREP: Baking parchment
OVEN TEMP: 350°
CHILLING TIME: 1 hour (pastry)
BAKING TIME: 20–25 minutes
DIFFICULTY: ◐◐

1 recipe Buttery Baking Powder Pastry (page 184)

THYME-SCENTED FIG AND PORT FILLING

1½ cups (9 ounces) cubed Calimyrna figs
1½ cups water
2 slices of orange, with rind, slightly less than ¼-inch thick
3 tablespoons honey
3 tablespoons light brown sugar
3 thyme sprigs
3 tablespoons port wine or Madeira

GLAZE

1 large egg, lightly beaten with 2 teaspoons water
6 tablespoons crushed toasted almonds
2 tablespoons sugar

1. Place the figs, water, orange slice, honey, brown sugar, and thyme in a medium, heavy-bottomed saucepan, cover, and bring to a boil over medium heat. Lower the heat and simmer for 20 minutes, or until the figs are barely tender and the liquid is almost evaporated. Remove the thyme and slip off any remaining leaves back into the fig mixture.

2. Add the port and continue to simmer, uncovered, for 1 to 2 more minutes, or until the liquid evaporates. Watch carefully to avoid burning. While the fig mixture is still warm, place it in the work bowl of a food processor fitted with the steel blade and pulse four or five times, or until the texture of fruit preserves. Let cool before using. (The filling may be stored in the refrigerator for up to 3 months.)

BAKE THE COOKIES

3. Position the shelves in the upper and lower thirds of the oven. Heat the oven to 350°. Dab the corners of the cookie sheets lightly with butter and line with baking parchment.

4. Lightly flour a pastry board or other flat surface and a rolling pin. Working with one piece at a time, roll the dough into an 8 × 12-inch rectangle. Divide the rectangle in half lengthwise. You should have two 4 × 12-inch rectangles.

5. Place about ⅓ cup of the filling down the center of one rectangle of dough. Brush the far end of the strip with the egg wash. Fold the edge of the dough closest to you over the fig filling using a dough scraper to guide you. Then turn the log over to completely enclose the

carole's best brownies

MAKES 32 1½ X 2-INCH BROWNIES

Buttery, chewy, chocolatey brownies bursting with crunchy walnuts, along with a glass of ice-cold milk, send me over the top. When I get a midnight craving, I will bake brownies right then and there. The day I came home from the hospital after giving birth to each of my children, I made a beeline to the kitchen and immediately made a batch of brownies. They are my comfort food!!

As with chocolate chip cookies, it seems that every family has a sacred brownie recipe. And my family is no different. Every time I introduce a new brownie to them, I get comments like "Gee, Mom, what did you do to the brownies now? We like your old recipe the best!" And so I share with you my family's all-time favorite brownie.

each addition. Pour the batter into the prepared pan.

5. Bake for 10 to 12 minutes, or until the top is *just* set. The brownies should barely be pulling away from the sides of the pan. Remove from the oven and sprinkle the cashew brittle over the top. Do *not* press the brittle into the surface. Return to the oven for 8 to 9 minutes, or until the brittle *just* begins to melt.

(The brittle should remain glossy and not melt into the brownies.) The brownie bar may seem underdone, but will firm up as it cools. Let stand for 3 to 4 hours before cutting into bars.

STORAGE: Store in a container with the cover or lid ajar, layered between strips of wax paper, for up to 5 days. These bars may be frozen.

Cookie Characteristics

Versatile

Moderate shelf life

Humidity sensitive

stephen schmidt's white chocolate macadamia squares

MAKES 40 1½ X 1¾-INCH SQUARES

One year, at a covered-dish supper held by the New York Association of Cooking Professionals, the buzz at dessert time was about a fantastic bar cookie brought by cookbook author and teacher Stephen Schmidt. The cookie was made with a mountain of salty macadamia nuts, lots of flaked, sweet coconut, and generous chunks of white chocolate, all bound with a mixture of heavy cream and sugar. This decadent bar cookie was so good that it's no wonder it was the hit of the evening. These squares will be the hit of your cookie platter, as well. Thanks, Stephen!

PAN: 9 × 13 × 2-inch metal baking pan

PAN PREP: Buttered heavy-duty aluminum foil

OVEN TEMP: 350°, 325°

BAKING TIME: 25 minutes, crust; 40–50 minutes, topping

DIFFICULTY: ○

CRUST 2⅓ cups all-purpose flour, spooned in and leveled

⅔ cup strained confectioners' sugar, spooned in and leveled

½ teaspoon salt

¾ cup (1½ sticks) unsalted butter, cold, cut into ½-inch dice

TOPPING 1 cup plus 2 tablespoons granulated sugar

1 cup heavy cream

¼ cup (½ stick) unsalted butter, melted

1 tablespoon strained fresh lemon juice

1½ teaspoons pure vanilla extract

½ teaspoon salt

3 cups (about 9 ounces) lightly packed sweetened, flaked coconut

2½ cups salted macadamia nuts, halved and toasted

8 to 9 ounces fine-quality white chocolate, such as Lindt Swiss Classic White Chocolate, cut into ¼- to ½-inch chunks

1. Position the rack in the center of the oven. Heat the oven to 350°. Lightly butter a 9 × 13-inch metal pan. Tear an 18 × 16-inch sheet of heavy-duty aluminum foil. Invert the pan and center the foil over the pan, pressing it across the bottom and down the sides. Remove the foil, turn the pan right side up, and place the foil shell into the pan, shaping it smoothly across the bottom and snugly against the sides of the pan. Thoroughly butter the foil, taking care not to tear it.

Cookie Characteristics

Homestyle

Moderate shelf life

Temperature sensitive

MAKE THE CRUST

2. Combine the flour, confectioners' sugar, and salt in the work bowl of a food processor and pulse several times to blend. Add the butter and process until a smooth dough forms. Divide the dough into eight pieces and arrange it in two rows in the pan. Using a bâtarde or the bottom of a glass, press the dough evenly into the pan. Bake the crust until golden, about 25 minutes.

MAKE THE TOPPING

3. Combine the granulated sugar, heavy cream, melted butter, lemon juice, vanilla, and salt in a large bowl, mixing well. Add the coconut, nuts, and chocolate chunks, then stir until the ingredients are coated with the sugar–cream mixture. Empty the topping over the hot crust and smooth it with an offset spatula or the back of a spoon.

4. Reduce the oven temperature to 325°. Place the pan in the oven and bake for 40 to 50 minutes, or until the topping has flattened, stopped bubbling, and is browned lightly. (Initially it will puff up.) Set the pan on a rack and cool to room temperature, then cover the pan with aluminum foil and refrigerate until cold. This will take several hours.

5. To release the bar from the pan, place the pan on top of the stove and over low heat, rotate it until it is warm. Then, using the foil to grip the bar, lift it out of the pan. While the bar is still chilled, using a sharp, heavy knife, trim the hard edges, then cut the bar crosswise into eight strips. Divide each strip into five pieces.

STORAGE: Refrigerate in an airtight container, layered between strips of wax paper, for up to 5 days.

chocolate cream cheese brownies

MAKES 25 1¾-INCH BROWNIES

Since brownies and cheesecakes are among our most favorite desserts, marrying the two is a sure winner. The dark chocolate batter is marbled with swirls of velvety cream cheese. For a contrast of texture, I added some toasted walnuts. When you marble the two batters together, be sure to keep your knife in the upper portion of the batters and do not overmix or the marble effect will be lost. Granted, these are sinfully rich, but once in a while a little indulgence is good for the soul.

AT A GLANCE

PAN: 9-inch square baking pan
PAN PREP: Buttered heavy-duty aluminum foil
OVEN TEMP: 350°
BAKING TIME: 45–50 minutes
DIFFICULTY: ○

CREAM CHEESE BATTER

6 ounces (2 3-ounce packages) cream
   cheese, at room temperature
¼ cup sugar
1 tablespoon flour
1 large egg
2 tablespoons sour cream
½ teaspoon pure vanilla extract
2 teaspoons fresh lemon juice

BROWNIE BATTER

½ cup all-purpose flour, spooned in
   and leveled
¼ teaspoon baking powder
¼ teaspoon salt
6 tablespoons (¾ stick) unsalted butter
5 ounces fine-quality bittersweet or
   semisweet chocolate, such as Lindt
   Bittersweet, chopped
2 ounces unsweetened chocolate,
   chopped
3 large eggs
1¼ cups sugar

1½ teaspoons pure vanilla extract
¾ cup broken walnut pieces, toasted

MAKE THE CREAM CHEESE BATTER

1. Place the cream cheese and sugar in a medium bowl and stir with a wooden spoon until smooth. Stir in the flour.
2. Whisk together the egg, sour cream, vanilla, and lemon juice and gradually add to the cream cheese mixture. Whisk until smooth. Set aside.

MAKE THE BROWNIE BATTER

3. Position the shelf in the center of the oven. Heat the oven to 350°. Cut a 15-inch square sheet of heavy-duty aluminum foil. Invert the baking pan and center the sheet of foil over the pan, pressing the foil across the bottom and down the sides. Remove the foil, invert the pan, and place the foil shell into the pan, shaping it smoothly across the bottom and snugly against the sides of the pan. Carefully and thoroughly butter the foil, taking care not to tear it. Set the pan aside.
4. Strain together the flour, baking powder, and salt. Set aside.

page 396.) Bake the dough for 14 to 15 minutes, or until firm to the touch. *Do not overbake.* Let the dough rest for 5 minutes.

MAKE THE CENTER LAYER

4. While the crust is baking, place the butter and chocolates in a large bowl (about 3-quart) set over a saucepan filled with 1 inch of simmering water. (The bottom of the bowl should not touch the water.) Melt the butter and the chocolates, stirring occasionally. When only a few pieces of chocolate remain, remove the bowl from the heat and let stand, stirring occasionally, until the chocolate is melted.

5. Using a large wooden spoon or rubber spatula, stir the peppermint schnapps and sugar into the warm chocolate mixture. Add the eggs one-third at a time. Then beat with a wooden spoon until shiny, taking approximately 25 to 30 strokes. Mix in the vanilla, then fold in the flour, stirring just until blended.

6. Pour the batter over the warm crust and, using a small offset spatula, spread it evenly. Bake for 10 to 11 minutes, or until just set on top. *Do not overbake.* A toothpick inserted should come out clean. Let stand for 15 to 20 minutes.

MAKE THE TOP LAYER

7. Gently stir the peppermint schnapps and extract into the ganache, stirring only to combine. Pour the ganache over the warm cake and spread it evenly with an offset spatula. To achieve a mirror-like glaze, the ganache should be some-what fluid. Let stand until the ganache is set before cutting into bars.

STORAGE: Store in an airtight container, layered between strips of wax paper, for up to 5 days. These bars may be frozen, although the glaze will lose its gloss.

Cookie Characteristics

Versatile

Moderate shelf life

Temperature sensitive

ebony and ivory tiles

MAKES 64 1¼ X 1¾-INCH BARS

For these bar cookies, melted semisweet or bittersweet chocolate is sandwiched between a bottom layer of butter cookie dough and a nutty chocolate meringue top. Before baking, I sprinkle the meringue with sparkling white or ganulated sugar, which creates a beautiful sparkle against the deep chocolate topping. Be sure to use a fine-quality chocolate here, as it really counts.

AT A GLANCE

PAN: 10½ × 15½ × 1-inch jelly roll pan

PAN PREP: Buttered heavy-duty aluminum foil

OVEN TEMP: 350°

BAKING TIME: 16–18 minutes, crust; 20–22 minutes, topping

DIFFICULTY: ◐◐

CRUST

1 cup (2 sticks) unsalted butter, softened

¾ cup sugar

2 large egg yolks

1 teaspoon vanilla extract

2 cups all-purpose flour, spooned in and leveled

4 ounces fine-quality bittersweet or semisweet chocolate, such as Lindt Bittersweet, melted and kept warm

TOPPING

2 cups walnuts

¼ cup strained Dutch-processed cocoa powder

2 large egg whites, at room temperature

¼ teaspoon salt

⅔ cup sugar

2 tablespoons unsalted butter, melted and cooled until tepid

1 teaspoon pure vanilla extract

2 tablespoons sparkling white sugar (available in The Baker's Catalogue; see page 403) or granulated sugar

MAKE THE CRUST

1. Position the shelf in the center of the oven. Heat the oven to 350°. Tear a 15 × 18-inch sheet of heavy-duty aluminum foil. Invert the pan and center the foil over the pan, pressing it across the bottom and down the sides. Turn the pan right side up, and place the foil into the pan, shaping it smoothly. Using a pastry brush, butter the bottom and sides well.

2. In the bowl of an electric mixer fitted with the paddle attachment, mix the butter with the sugar on medium-low speed until smooth and lightened in color. Add the yolks one at a time, then the vanilla, mixing to blend. Scrape down the bowl as needed.

3. Reduce the mixer speed to low and mix in half of the flour. Remove the bowl from the machine and work in the remaining flour by hand, kneading to form a smooth dough. Shape into a 6 × 8-inch rectangle, then, using a dough scraper, divide the dough into 12 pieces.

4. Place the pieces of dough in the pan, making rows of three pieces across and four pieces down. Place a strip of plastic wrap over the pan. Using a bâtarde or

5. Bake for 16 to 18 minutes, or until the top is set and starting to brown. Remove from the oven, let stand 1 minute, then spread with the melted chocolate. Let stand for 20 minutes to cool, then refrigerate for 10 minutes or until the chocolate is set.

MAKE THE TOPPING

6. Place the nuts and cocoa powder into the bowl of a food processor and pulse six to eight times, then process until very finely chopped. Stop the processor every three or four seconds and pulse, then return to processing.

7. In the bowl of an electric mixer fitted with the whip attachment, beat the egg whites and salt on medium speed until frothy. Increase the speed to medium-high, add the sugar 1 tablespoon at a time, and beat until stiff and shiny.

8. On low speed, add the cocoa–nut mixture, the tepid melted butter, then the vanilla and mix 1 minute longer. Spread the meringue over the chocolate layer, smoothing with an offset spatula. Sprinkle evenly with sparkling white or granulated sugar.

9. Bake for 20 to 22 minutes, or until the top is set and starting to brown. Remove from the oven and cool completely. Using a thin-bladed knife, cut into sixty-four 1¼ × 1¾-inch bars, making eight strips down and eight strips across.

STORAGE: Store in an airtight container, layered between strips of wax paper, for up to 5 days. These cookies may be frozen.

Cookie Characteristics

Versatile

Moderate shelf life

Travel well

blondies

MAKES 4 DOZEN 1¾ X 2½-INCH BARS

I suspect that Blondies were born when a harried baker didn't have the patience to make individual chocolate chip cookies. Instead of making the drop cookies the traditional way, the batter was baked as a bar cookie. And why not? Baking the batter in this manner results in a thicker, moister, chewier cookie than its drop-cookie cousin. However, as with chocolate chip cookies, care must be taken not to overbake. They can quickly lose their addictive chewiness, which is what Blondies are all about.

Instead of using chocolate chips, I much prefer to dice high-quality chocolate bars, such as Lindt. When you use specialty chocolates such as this, ordinary Blondies are elevated into an extraordinary treat.

AT A GLANCE
PAN: 10½ × 15½ × 1-inch jelly roll pan
PAN PREP: Well buttered
OVEN TEMP: 350°
BAKING TIME: 28–30 minutes
DIFFICULTY: ◑

2½ cups all-purpose flour, spooned in and leveled
½ teaspoon baking soda
½ teaspoon salt
1 cup (2 sticks) unsalted butter, divided
¾ cup lightly packed light brown sugar
¾ cup granulated sugar
2 large eggs
1½ teaspoons pure vanilla extract
1 cup walnuts, chopped and divided
5 ounces high-quality bittersweet or semisweet chocolate, such as Lindt Bittersweet, cut into ¼-inch dice

1. Position the shelf in the center of the oven. Heat the oven to 350°. Butter the jelly roll pan well.

2. Strain together the flour, baking soda, and salt. Set aside.

3. In a heavy-bottomed saucepan, warm ½ cup (1 stick) of the butter over medium-low heat until it is *almost* melted, but some solid pieces still remain. Remove from the heat and add the brown sugar, mixing well.

4. In the bowl of an electric mixer fitted with the paddle attachment, beat the remaining ½ cup (1 stick) of butter on medium speed. Add the granulated sugar in a steady stream and mix until lightened in color. Add the eggs one at a time, mixing well after each addition. Blend in the tepid melted butter and brown sugar. (If the mixture has solidified, warm briefly over low heat to melt.) Beat on medium speed until thick and creamy, about 1 minute, scraping down

the side of the bowl as needed. Beat in the vanilla.

5. Reduce the mixer speed to low and add the dry ingredients in two additions, mixing *only* to combine. Remove the bowl from the machine and, using a large wooden spoon or rubber spatula, fold in ¾ cup of the chopped walnuts and all of the diced chocolate. Scrape the batter into the pan, using the back of a large spoon to spread it evenly. Sprinkle with the remaining walnuts.

6. Bake for 28 to 30 minutes, or until the top is golden brown and the edges *just* begin to pull away from the sides of the pan. *Do not overbake.* Remove from the oven and place on a cooling rack. Let stand 1 hour, then cut into 1¾ × 2½-inch bars.

STORAGE: Store in an airtight container, layered between strips of wax paper, for up to 5 days. These blondies may be frozen.

Cookie Characteristics

Versatile

Moderate shelf life

Travel well

"Everybody has some special food that makes them feel taken care of, a culinary escape from danger."

—JANE AND MICHAEL STERN, *SQUARE MEALS*

toffee nut squares

MAKES 5 DOZEN 1¾ X 2-INCH SQUARES

This recipe has been part of my baking repertoire for years. It was inspired by Blondies (page 218), but is a thinner version made only with brown sugar. Because I prefer to make these with light brown sugar, instead of dark brown, the cookie has a wonderful caramel flavor that complements the taste of the butter. It is essential that the brown sugar be very fresh, so this is the time to break open a new box. To retain the chewiness of the cookie, underbake them slightly.

AT A GLANCE

PAN: 10½ × 15½ × 1-inch jelly roll pan
PAN PREP: Well buttered
OVEN TEMP: 350°
BAKING TIME: 16–18 minutes
DIFFICULTY: ✪

2 cups all-purpose flour, spooned in and leveled
½ teaspoon baking soda
½ teaspoon salt
⅔ cup (1⅓ sticks) unsalted butter, slightly firm
2 cups lightly packed *very fresh* light brown sugar
2 large eggs
2 teaspoons pure vanilla extract
1 cup plus 2 tablespoons medium-fine chopped walnuts, divided
1 cup semisweet chocolate chips

Cookie Characteristics

Versatile

Moderate shelf life

Travel well

1. Position the shelf in the center of the oven. Heat the oven to 350°. Butter the jelly roll pan well.

2. Strain together the flour, baking soda, and salt. Set aside.

3. In the bowl of an electric mixer on medium speed, beat the butter until lightened in color. Add the brown sugar, about ¼ cup at a time, and beat well until light in color, about 2 minutes. Scrape down the side of the bowl as needed. Beat in the eggs one at a time, then the vanilla. Reduce the mixer speed to low and add the dry ingredients in three additions, mixing *just* to incorporate.

4. Remove the bowl from the mixer and, using a large rubber spatula, fold in 1 cup of the walnuts and the chocolate chips. Spread the mixture in the pan, smoothing the top with a small offset spatula. Sprinkle with the remaining 2 tablespoons of walnuts.

5. Bake for 16 to 18 minutes, or until the sides are lightly browned. *Do not over-bake.* A toothpick inserted in the center should still show signs of moistness. Place on a cooling rack for 1 hour, then cut into 1¾ × 2-inch bars.

STORAGE: Store in an airtight container, layered between strips of wax paper, for up to 5 days. These squares may be frozen.

mississippi bayou bars

MAKES 64 1¼ X 2-INCH BARS

These nutty bars bring back memories of my childhood in Tennessee. The flavor and textures of the coconut and pecans combined with brown sugar are the flavors I grew up with, so reminiscent of the Deep South. They make a chewy cookie that is irresistible and one that your family and friends are sure to love.

AT A GLANCE
PAN: 10½ × 15½ × 1-inch jelly roll pan
PAN PREP: Buttered heavy-duty aluminum foil
OVEN TEMP: 350°
BAKING TIME: 20 minutes, crust; 22–25 minutes, topping
DIFFICULTY: ◑◑

CRUST

1 cup (2 sticks) unsalted butter
3 cups all-purpose flour, spooned in and leveled
½ cup granulated sugar
½ cup firmly packed light brown sugar

TOPPING

1 (10-ounce) package sweetened, flaked coconut (3¾ cups)
2 tablespoons all-purpose flour
½ teaspoon baking soda
4 large eggs
½ cup dark corn syrup
1¼ cups firmly packed light brown sugar
2 tablespoons (¼ stick) unsalted butter, melted
2 teaspoons pure vanilla extract
1½ cups broken pecans, lightly toasted

MAKE THE CRUST

1. Position the shelf in the center of the oven. Heat the oven to 350°. Tear a 15 × 18-inch sheet of heavy-duty aluminum foil. Invert the pan and center the foil over the pan, pressing it across the bottom and down the sides. Turn the pan right side up, and place the foil into the pan, shaping it smoothly. Using a pastry brush, butter the bottom and sides well.

2. In a medium saucepan, melt the butter. Set aside to cool to tepid. Add the flour and sugars, blending with a fork until the mixture forms large crumbs.

3. Distribute the crumbs evenly over the bottom of the pan, pressing firmly. Lay a strip of plastic wrap over the surface, then smooth the crumbs with a flat-bottomed glass or a bâtarde. Remove the plastic wrap and use a small offset spatula to reach into the corners and even the surface. Test for evenness by inserting the tip of a knife or toothpick into the dough.

4. Bake the crust for 20 minutes, or until the top is set and the edges begin to brown. While the crust is baking, make the topping.

MAKE THE TOPPING

5. Place the coconut in the work bowl of a food processor fitted with a steel blade, then process for 10 to 15 seconds, or until finely chopped. Set aside.

6. Strain together the flour and baking soda. Set aside.

7. Place the eggs in a large mixing bowl

BAKE THE COOKIES

8. Bake for 22 to 25 minutes, or until the edges begin to brown and the top feels set. Place on a cooling rack and let stand for 15 minutes. Run a knife around the sides of the pan to loosen the crusty edges. Let stand for another 15 minutes.

9. Using a sharp knife, make seven cuts across the narrow side and seven cuts across the wide side to cut into 64 bars. Let the bars air-dry on a cooling rack before storing.

STORAGE: Store in an airtight container, layered between strips of wax paper, for up to 3 weeks. These bars may be frozen.

Cookie Characteristics:

Versatile

Long shelf life

Travel well

rainbow cookies

MAKES 80 1¼ X ⅝-INCH SLICES

Rainbow Cookies are popular at Christmas, when they are called Neapolitan or Venetian cookies, perhaps to denote the colors of the flag of Italy. They are sometimes associated with the Passover holidays (when made with matzo cake meal instead of flour). The classic Rainbow Cookie is made with tinted layers of an almond-paste flavored cookie dough that, after baking, is spread with seedless raspberry preserves and then weighted to seal the layers. The cookies are then divided into long strips, coated with melted dark chocolate, and and cut into slices.

Because this recipe requires three oblong shallow baking pans, I suggest using disposable aluminum baking pans. Although these cookies are somewhat labor intensive, there are many pluses: they have a long shelf life, they are beloved by adults and children alike, the recipe makes many servings, and best of all, they are a showstopper on any dessert table.

AT A GLANCE

PAN: 3 12¼ × 8¼ × 1-inch disposable aluminum pans
PAN PREP: Buttered baking parchment
OVEN TEMP: 350°
RESTING TIME: 24 hours
BAKING TIME: 10–12 minutes
DIFFICULTY: ❍❍❍

12 ounces (1½ 8-ounce cans) almond paste
1 cup (2 sticks) unsalted butter, slightly firm
1 cup sugar
4 large eggs, separated
1 teaspoon pure vanilla extract
2 cups all-purpose flour, spooned in and leveled

or 1½ cups sifted matzo cake meal, spooned in and leveled
½ teaspoon salt
6 to 8 drops green food color
8 to 10 drops red food color
¼ cup seedless raspberry preserves
1 cup apricot preserves
10 ounces semisweet chocolate, coarsely chopped

1. Position the shelves in the upper and lower thirds of the oven. Heat oven to 350°. Lightly butter the bottom of the baking pans. Line the bottoms with the baking parchment, then butter the parchment and the sides of each pan.
2. Break the almond paste into pieces

and place it in the work bowl of a food processor fitted with the steel blade. Process for 10 to 15 seconds, or until finely chopped. Alternatively, shred the almond paste on a box grater.

3. In the bowl of an electric mixer fitted with the paddle attachment, mix the butter on medium-low speed just until smooth. Increase the speed to medium, add the grated almond paste, and beat until lightened in color, about 2 minutes. Pour in the sugar in a steady stream, beating for 1 minute longer. Then add the egg yolks and the vanilla, beating well to combine. Scrape down the bowl as needed.

4. Combine salt and flour, and at low speed blend in three additions, just until incorporated.

5. In a clean mixer bowl, using the whip attachment, beat the egg whites on medium speed until frothy. Increase the speed to medium-high and continue beating until firm peaks form. Using a large rubber spatula, gently fold one-third of the egg whites into the batter to lighten the mixture, then fold in the remaining egg whites in two more additions.

6. Divide the batter into thirds (each measuring approximately 1⅔ cups) and place into three separate bowls. Tint one portion with the green food coloring, blending until evenly colored. Tint another portion with the red food coloring, again blending until evenly colored. The remaining batter is not colored. Spread the batters in the pans, smoothing the tops with a small offset spatula. *Be sure the batter is evenly distributed, especially into the corners of the pans.*

7. Bake for 10 to 12 minutes, or until the tops are firm to the touch and slightly

brown. Let stand on wire racks until cool enough to handle, then invert each pan and peel off the parchment.

ASSEMBLE THE LAYERS

8. Have ready a large sheet of plastic wrap placed on a cookie sheet. Invert the green layer onto the plastic, top side down. Using a small offset spatula, spread the surface evenly with 2 tablespoons of the raspberry preserves. Place the plain layer, again top side down, on top of the raspberry preserves. Align the two layers and press them together. Spread 2 tablespoons of the raspberry preserves over the plain layer, again using a small offset spatula. Then place the pink layer, *top side up,* on top of the raspberry preserves. Be sure that the three layers are evenly aligned, then press them together again.

9. Wrap the layered stack tightly with plastic, sealing the ends securely, and place it on a clean cookie sheet. Place another cookie sheet on top of the wrapped stack and weight it with two or three heavy cookbooks to compress the layers. Let the stack rest at room temperature for at least 24 hours, turning it over once or twice during the weighting period.

GLAZE THE LAYERS

10. Unwrap the stack and set it on a cutting board. Using a large serrated knife, trim ¼ inch from all sides. Then cut the stack into five equal strips, each measuring approximately 1¼ inches wide. Separate the strips and place them on a large wire rack set over a cookie sheet.

11. Make the apricot glaze: Place the apricot preserves and 2 tablespoons water in a small saucepan. Bring to a

Cookie Characteristics

Festive

Long shelf life

Temperature sensitive

boil, then simmer for 1 minute. Pass through a fine strainer into a bowl and discard the pulp. This can be made ahead and reheated just before using. Brush a thin layer of the warm glaze on the top and sides of each strip to seal the surface. Let stand for ½ hour or longer.

12. When ready to coat the strips, fill a medium pot with 1 inch of water and bring it to a simmer. Place the chocolate in a large bowl and set it over the simmering water to melt, gently stirring occasionally with a rubber spatula. *Watch carefully! The chocolate should not become too hot.* When the chocolate is almost melted, remove it from the heat and allow it to stand until it is com-

pletely melted. Gently stir occasionally. It is ready to apply when it is smooth, tepid, and the consistency of chocolate syrup. (Note: If the chocolate becomes too thick, warm it over simmering water until it reaches the correct consistency.)

13. Working one strip at a time, spoon about one-fifth of the melted chocolate down the length of the strip. Using a small offset spatula, spread the chocolate evenly over the top and sides, taking care to smooth all surfaces. Repeat with the remaining strips. Let the strips stand at room temperature until the chocolate hardens. This can take several hours depending on the temperature of the room and climate conditions. Cut each strip into ⅝-inch slices.

STORAGE: Store in an airtight container, layered between strips of wax paper, for up to 3 weeks. (Note: These cookies may be frozen, preferably before slicing.) This cookie improves with age.

date 'n nut fingers

If you like a cookie with lots of texture, these Date 'n Nut Fingers will be at the top of your list. Enrobed in sugar, these slender bars are full of chewy dates and crunchy walnuts. Easy to make, delicious to taste, quick to disappear!

AT A GLANCE

PAN: 9-inch square baking pan

PAN PREP: Buttered heavy-duty aluminum foil

OVEN TEMP: 375°

BAKING TIME: 20–25 minutes

DIFFICULTY: ✪

¾ cup all-purpose flour, spooned in and leveled

¼ teaspoon baking powder

¼ cup (½ stick) unsalted butter

1 cup granulated sugar

½ teaspoon pure vanilla extract

2 large eggs, well beaten

1 cup medium-chopped walnuts

1 cup chopped dates (¼-inch pieces)

1 cup strained confectioners' sugar, spooned in and leveled

Cookie Characteristics

Versatile

Moderate shelf life

Travel well

1. Position the shelf in the center of the oven. Heat the oven to 375°. Tear a 15-inch square sheet of heavy-duty aluminum foil. Invert the pan and center the foil over the pan, pressing it across the bottom and down the sides. Remove the foil, turn the pan right side up, and place the foil shell into the pan, shaping it smoothly across the bottom and snugly against the sides of the pan. Thoroughly butter the foil, taking care not to tear it.

2. Strain together the flour and baking powder. Set aside.

3. Place the butter in a 3-quart saucepan and heat until almost melted. A few small pieces should still remain. Remove from the heat and cool until tepid.

4. Using a large wooden spoon, add the sugar to the butter and mix well. Thoroughly blend in the vanilla and eggs. Blend in the dry ingredients, then fold in the nuts and dates.

5. Spread the batter in the pan and bake for 20 to 25 minutes, or until firm on top and the sides begin to release. Allow to rest in the pan for 15 minutes.

6. While still warm, remove the bar from the pan by lifting the sides of the aluminum foil. Place on a cutting board, and using a thin-bladed, sharp knife, cut into 1 × 2-inch bars. Roll each bar in the confectioners' sugar, then place on cooling racks to cool completely.

STORAGE: Store in an airtight container, layered between strips of wax paper, for up to 5 days. These cookies may be frozen.

apple pie bars

MAKES 32 1½ X 2-INCH BARS

The recipe for these Apple Pie Bars was created by my talented assistant, Kathie Finn Redden. Kathie, one of my teaching peers at Kings Cooking Studio, has keen taste buds and a wonderful way with food. When testing recipes for an upcoming class, she told me of a terrific apple bar cookie that I might want to include in my book. And she was so right.

Kathie's cookies are made with sliced apples sautéed with brown sugar and honey. She places them on top of a buttery crust, then covers the apples with a cinnamon-scented pecan streusel. Not only am I lucky to have this spunky gal as my assistant, when it comes to creating great recipes, Kathie's a winner.

AT A GLANCE

PAN: 9 × 13 × 2-inch baking pan

PAN PREP: Buttered heavy-duty aluminum foil

OVEN TEMP: 375°, 350°

BAKING TIME: 15–18 minutes, crust; 20–25 minutes, bar cookie

DIFFICULTY: ○○

APPLES

6 Granny Smith or Golden Delicious apples, peeled, cored, and sliced ¼ inch thick (see Note)

⅓ cup firmly packed light brown sugar

2 tablespoons fresh lemon juice

1 tablespoon honey

CRUST

2¼ cups all-purpose flour, spooned in and leveled

½ teaspoon baking powder

½ teaspoon salt

1 cup (2 sticks) unsalted butter, slightly firm

½ cup lightly packed light brown sugar

1 large egg

THE STREUSEL TOPPING

1 cup all-purpose flour, spooned in and leveled

¼ cup granulated sugar

¼ cup lightly packed light brown sugar

1 teaspoon ground cinnamon

¼ teaspoon salt

½ cup (1 stick) cold unsalted butter, cubed

1 cup medium-chopped toasted pecans

COOK THE APPLES

1. In a large skillet over medium heat, combine the apples with the brown sugar, lemon juice, and honey. Cover the pan for 2 to 3 minutes. Uncover when the apples have released their juices and cook, stirring occasionally, until the apples have turned a golden brown and there is no liquid left in the pan, about 15 minutes. Set aside to cool.

MAKE THE CRUST

2. Position the shelf in the center of the oven. Heat the oven to 375°. Tear an 18 × 16-inch sheet of heavy-duty aluminum foil. Invert the pan and center the foil over the pan, pressing it across the bottom and down the sides. Remove the foil, turn the pan right side up, and place the foil shell in the pan, shaping it smoothly across the bottom and snugly against the sides. Using a pastry brush, grease the bottom and sides with softened butter, taking care not to tear the foil.

3. Strain together the flour, baking powder, and salt. Set aside.

4. In the large bowl of an electric mixer fitted with the paddle attachment, mix the butter with the brown sugar on medium-low speed until smooth and creamy, about 2 minutes. Add the egg and mix to blend. On low speed, add the dry ingredients in two additions, mixing only to combine after each addition. Divide the mixture into eight parts and place them in two rows down the length of the pan. With lightly floured hands, press the mixture evenly into the pan. (See "Spreading Batters and Doughs," page 396.) Bake for 15 to 18 minutes, or until the crust has turned golden brown and begins to release from the sides of the pan. While the crust is baking, prepare the streusel topping.

MAKE THE TOPPING

5. In the large bowl of an electric mixer fitted with the paddle attachment, combine the flour, granulated and brown sugars, cinnamon, and salt. Mix briefly on low speed. Add the butter and mix on medium-low speed until the mixture is crumbly and barely holds together when squeezed gently. Stir in the pecans with a large rubber spatula or a large wooden spoon. Set aside.

BAKE THE BAR

6. When the crust is done, immediately spread the cooked apples evenly over the hot crust. Sprinkle the streusel topping over the apples, pressing gently to help it adhere.

7. Reduce the oven temperature to 350°. Return the pan to the oven and bake for 20 to 25 minutes, or until the topping is lightly browned and crisp. Let rest in the pan for 2 to 3 hours before removing and slicing with a long, sharp knife. (Note: These slice better if they are chilled.)

NOTE: The apples can be sliced in a food processor using a #4 slicing disk.

STORAGE: Refrigerate the bars in a cookie tin, layered between strips of wax paper, for up to 5 days. Bring to room temperature before serving.

Cookie Characteristics

Homestyle

Moderate shelf life

Temperature sensitive

minna's apricot squares

MAKES 25 1¾-INCH SQUARES

A few years ago, I was visiting my friend Minna Berger, from Elizabeth, New Jersey, a gracious hostess and terrific baker. Minna had lots of practice baking because she had an audience of her husband and four sons who not only appreciated fine food but possessed a passion for fine sweets as well. On this occasion, she set a small platter of homemade cookies down for me to enjoy with my tea. My eye was instantly caught by a deep golden-brown bar cookie with pecans on top. Ooh! With my first bite, I thought, "Oh! I must have this recipe!" Minna generously shared it with me and now I happily share it with you.

AT A GLANCE **PAN:** 9-inch square baking pan

PAN PREP: Buttered heavy-duty aluminum foil

OVEN TEMP: 350°

BAKING TIME: 20 minutes, crust; 40 minutes, topping

DIFFICULTY: ○

4 ounces (⅔ cup packed) dried apricots

1½ cups water

CRUST   1 cup all-purpose flour, spooned in and leveled

¼ cup strained confectioners' sugar, spooned in and leveled

½ cup (1 stick) unsalted butter, slightly firm and cut in 1-inch pieces

TOPPING   ⅓ cup all-purpose flour, spooned in and leveled

½ teaspoon baking powder

¼ teaspoon salt

2 large eggs

1 cup lightly packed dark brown sugar

½ teaspoon pure vanilla extract

¾ cup coarsely chopped walnuts, divided

1. Place the apricots and water in a small saucepan, cover, and bring to a boil. Reduce the heat to low and simmer for 20 minutes. Drain the apricots, rinse with cold water, then blot dry on paper toweling. When cool, place the apricots in the work bowl of a food processor fitted with the steel blade and pulse four or five times to coarsely chop. You should have about ¾ cup.

MAKE THE CRUST

2. Position the shelf in the lower third of the oven. Heat the oven to 350°. Tear a 15-inch square of heavy-duty aluminum foil. Invert the pan and center the foil over the pan, pressing it across the bottom and down the sides. Remove the foil, turn the pan right side up, and place the foil shell into the pan, shaping it smoothly across the bottom and snugly against the sides. Using a pastry brush, grease the bottom and sides with softened butter, taking care not to tear the foil.

3. Strain together the flour and confec-

Cookie
Characteristics

Versatile

Moderate
shelf life

Travel well

tioners' sugar. Place the dry ingredients in the bowl of an electric mixer fitted with the paddle attachment. Add the butter and mix on medium speed until the texture of coarse crumbs. Press the crumbs evenly into the pan, forming a smooth layer of dough. Bake for 20 minutes or until golden brown.

MAKE THE TOPPING

4. Strain together the flour, baking powder, and salt. Set aside.

5. In the bowl of an electric mixer fitted with the whip attachment, mix the eggs with the brown sugar on medium-low speed until lightened, about 2 minutes. Do not overbeat. Blend in the vanilla.

6. Reduce the mixer speed to low and add the dry ingredients. Stir in the chopped apricots and ½ cup of the walnuts. Pour the batter over the crust. Sprinkle with the remaining ¼ cup of chopped nuts.

BAKE THE COOKIES

7. Bake for 40 minutes, or until firm and just starting to pull away from the edges of the pan. Let cool in the pan before removing and cutting into bars.

STORAGE: Store loosely covered in a container, layered between strips of wax paper, for up to 5 days. These squares may be frozen.

"Eggs of an hour, bread of a day, wine of a year, a friend of thirty years." —ITALIAN PROVERB

cherry-pecan meringue bars

MAKES 32 1½ X 2-INCH BARS

A brown-sugar shortbread crust is topped with a blend of pureed dried cherries, cherry preserves, spices, and cherry liqueur. This tasty layer is finished with a nutty meringue topping, then generously sprinkled with more chopped pecans. While this unusual bar cookie is wonderful when first made, you will find it even more delicious a few days after baking.

AT A GLANCE

PAN: 9 × 13 × 2-inch baking pan

PAN PREP: Buttered heavy-duty aluminum foil

OVEN TEMP: 350°

BAKING TIME: 15–17 minutes, crust; 35–40 minutes, topping

DIFFICULTY: ◐◐

FILLING
1 cup dried cherries
½ cup water
1 cup cherry preserves
1 teaspoon freshly grated lemon zest
½ teaspoon ground cinnamon
Pinch of ground cloves
Pinch of salt
2 tablespoons Cherry Heering

CRUST
¾ cup (1½ sticks) unsalted butter
⅓ cup lightly packed light brown sugar
1 teaspoon freshly grated lemon zest
1¾ cups all-purpose flour, spooned in and leveled
½ teaspoon salt

MERINGUE NUT TOPPING
8 ounces pecans, or enough to yield 2 cups chopped, divided
¾ cup superfine sugar
3 large egg whites, at room temperature
⅛ teaspoon salt
1 teaspoon pure vanilla extract

1. Position the shelf in the center of the oven. Heat the oven to 350°. Invert the pan, then tear an 18 × 16-inch sheet of heavy-duty aluminum foil and center it over the top, smooth the surface, then press it down the sides. Remove the foil, turn the pan right side up, and place the foil shell into the pan, shaping it smoothly across the bottom and snugly against the sides of the pan. Using a pastry brush, grease the bottom and sides with softened butter, taking care not to tear the foil.

MAKE THE FILLING

2. Place the cherries and water in a small saucepan. Cook, covered, over medium-low heat for 5 to 7 minutes, or until the cherries are tender and almost all of the liquid has evaporated.

3. Add the preserves, lemon zest, cinnamon, cloves, and salt. Bring to a boil, stirring to combine. Off the heat, add the Cherry Heering.

4. Place the mixture in the work bowl of a food processor fitted with the steel blade. Pulse five or six times or until chopped medium-fine. The mixture should still have some texture. Chill for 30 minutes or up to 1 week.

crumbs. Bake for 7 to 8 minutes, or until just set. While the crust is baking, prepare the filling.

MAKE THE FILLING

4. In the bowl of an electric mixer fitted with the whip attachment, beat the egg yolks on medium-high speed until slightly thickened and lightened in color, 3 to 4 minutes. Slowly add the condensed milk and beat 4 to 5 minutes longer. Reduce the mixer speed to medium-low and mix in the lime juice and zest.

5. Let the crust rest for 2 or 3 minutes before pouring half of the filling (approximately 1 cup) over it, spreading with the back of a tablespoon. Give the pan several firm taps on a hard surface to spread the filling evenly. Return to the oven and bake for 9 to 10 minutes, until set on top. (It's okay if a little sticks to your finger.)

6. Sprinkle the remaining crumbs over the warm filling, spreading them carefully. Press gently with the bottom of a glass to even the crumbs. Bake for 8 to 9 minutes, or until set. Let rest for 2 or 3 minutes.

7. Pour the remaining filling mixture over the crust, spreading evenly with the back of a tablespoon. Tap the pan on the counter to even the filling. Bake for 10 minutes, or until set.

8. Let stand for 2 or 3 minutes, then sprinkle with approximately half of the toasted coconut, pressing it in gently. Then top with the remaining coconut. Refrigerate for 4 to 5 hours before removing from the pan. Using a long, thin-bladed knife dipped in warm water as needed, cut into 25 squares.

STORAGE: Store in the refrigerator in an airtight container, layered between strips of wax paper, for up to 5 days. These cookies may be frozen.

Cookie
Characteristics

Versatile

Moderate
shelf life

Temperature
sensitive

9 Around the World

hamantaschen

Every spring, Hamantaschen—fruit-filled triangular pastries—pop up in bakeries around the country. They herald the joyous celebration of Purim, the Jewish festival that commemorates the deliverance of the Jews from annihilation in the fifth century B.C.

The pastries can be made with yeast dough, cookie dough, or pie dough. While they are commonly filled with a cooked prune purée known as *lekvar,* they can also be made with apricot lekvar or poppy seed filling. These fillings are sometimes mixed with chopped nuts and spices, while more contemporary versions are made with fine-quality chocolate candy or chocolate chips. No matter what filling you chose, this cookie will fly off the plate.

Shirley Lynch, my good friend from Greensboro, North Carolina, kindly shared this recipe with me. Shirley is known for her superb baking, and my cookbook would not be complete without including a recipe from her vast collection.

AT A GLANCE

PAN: Cookie sheets

PAN PREP: Baking parchment

EQUIPMENT: 3-inch round cookie cutter

OVEN TEMP: 350°

CHILLING TIME: 1 hour

BAKING TIME: 15–18 minutes

DIFFICULTY: ◐◐

DOUGH

3 cups all-purpose flour, spooned in and leveled

1 cup sugar

2 teaspoons baking powder

¼ teaspoon salt

⅔ cup (1⅓ sticks) cold, unsalted butter or margarine, cut into ½-inch cubes

2 large eggs

2 large egg yolks

1 teaspoon pure vanilla extract

1 recipe Hamantaschen filling (see pages 244–245)

2 large egg whites, lightly beaten with 2 teaspoons of sugar

MAKE THE DOUGH

1. Place the flour, sugar, baking powder, and salt in the work bowl of a food processor fitted with a steel blade and pulse two or three times to combine. Add the butter and pulse five times, then process 5 seconds to form meallike crumbs.

2. Place the eggs, egg yolks, and vanilla in a small bowl and mix with a fork to combine. Pour the mixture into the processor and pulse four or five times, then process for 1 minute, or until the

basler brunsli

I first heard of this from a Swiss gentleman who lived in the United States and missed indulging in his country's favorite cookie, Basler Brunsli. He described it to me from his taste buds' memory, and after my curiosity got the best of me, I went to work to provide him with a "taste of home."

Brunsli are flourless cookies, made primarily with almond flour, ground chocolate, cocoa, cinnamon, and cloves folded into a sugary meringue. Although the cookies are traditionally made with spices, they are equally good without them. When baked, Brunsli have a chewy, macaroon-like texture. The dough is rolled more thickly than most, making it easy to handle, so you can really have fun with your cookie cutters! Sparkling white sugar contrasts beautifully against the deep chocolate background.

Although this cookie requires a special almond flour, it is available through The Baker's Catalogue (as is the sparkling white sugar; see page 403) and the extra effort will be time well spent.

AT A GLANCE

PAN: Cookie sheets
PAN PREP: Baking parchment
EQUIPMENT: 2-inch cookie cutters
OVEN TEMP: 250°
COMBINED RESTING TIME: 1½ hours
BAKING TIME: 9–10 minutes
DIFFICULTY: ☉

8 ounces fine-quality bittersweet or semisweet chocolate, such as Lindt Bittersweet, coarsely chopped
6 tablespoons strained Dutch-processed cocoa powder
2 teaspoons ground cinnamon (optional)
¼ teaspoon ground cloves (optional)
2 large egg whites
¾ cup superfine sugar

3 tablespoons Kirschwasser
¾ pound almond flour (3 cups lightly packed and leveled; see headnote)
¼ cup granulated sugar, for rolling
2 tablespoons sparkling white sugar

MAKE THE DOUGH

1. In the work bowl of a food processor fitted with the steel blade, combine the chopped chocolate with the cocoa powder and the spices, if using. Process for 45 to 60 seconds, until the chocolate is very finely ground, stopping occasionally to scrape any accumulated chocolate from the bottom and the edges of the work bowl. Remove the chocolate mixture from the work bowl and set aside.

2. In the large bowl of an electric mixer

fitted with the whip attachment, beat the egg whites on medium speed until soft peaks form. Increase the speed to medium-high and add the sugar 1 tablespoon at a time, taking about 2 minutes to form a stiff meringue. Transfer the meringue to a large, wide mixing bowl.

3. Using a large rubber spatula or wooden spoon, fold in the Kirschwasser, then fold in the chocolate mixture and the almond flour. Shape into two rectangles, wrap each with plastic, and refrigerate for 30 minutes.

SHAPE THE DOUGH

4. Dab the corners of the cookie sheets lightly with butter and line with baking parchment.

5. Lightly coat a flat surface, such as a countertop or cutting board, with 2 tablespoons of the granulated sugar. Working one piece of dough at a time, place on the surface, turn two or three times to coat with the sugar, and roll out until ⅜ inch thick. Cut with small cookie cutters, no larger than 2 inches, and place them on a piece of wax paper, then sprinkle with sparkling white sugar. Place cookies on the pans and let air-dry for 1 hour before baking.

BAKE THE COOKIES

6. Position the shelves in the upper and lower thirds of the oven. Heat the oven to 250°. Bake for 9 to 10 minutes, or until *just* set on top. To ensure even browning, toward the end of the baking time rotate the sheets top to bottom and front to back. *Do not overbake.* The cookies will firm as they cool. Let rest on the cookie sheets for 2 to 3 minutes, then transfer to cooling racks.

STORAGE: Store in an airtight container, layered between strips of wax paper, for up to 3 weeks. These cookies may be frozen.

"Once in a young lifetime one should be allowed to have as much sweetness as one can possibly want and hold."

—JUDITH OLNEY

pfeffernüsse

MAKES 9 DOZEN 1½-INCH COOKIES

Pfeffernüsse, one of the oldest of German cookies, is a classic Christmas treat. The "bite" of this cookie is very firm, and therefore it is best when dunked in your coffee, tea, mulled cider, or hot chocolate. The crumb of the cookie softens and the spicy flavors burst when they hit the warmth of a hot beverage.

Recipes for this spice cookie vary in size from very small drop cookies to those that are rolled and hung as Christmas tree ornaments. Classically, the cookie is made without fat. More modern recipes use butter to make the cookie more flavorful and appealing. While one would think that the German name *Pfeffernüsse* would denote a "peppery" cookie, it is believed that the name refers not to pepper itself but to the variety of spices that were imported from the East, where spices were abundant.

AT A GLANCE
PAN: Cookie sheets
PAN PREP: Buttered baking parchment
OVEN TEMP: 350°
BAKING TIME: 14–15 minutes
DIFFICULTY: ✪

COOKIES
½ cup toasted unblanched sliced almonds
3 cups all-purpose flour, spooned in and leveled
1 teaspoon ground cinnamon
½ teaspoon baking soda
½ teaspoon baking powder
½ teaspoon salt
½ teaspoon ground nutmeg
½ teaspoon ground ginger
¼ teaspoon ground allspice
¼ teaspoon freshly ground black pepper
½ cup (1 stick) unsalted butter, slightly firm

2 teaspoons freshly grated navel orange zest
2 teaspoons freshly grated lemon zest
1 cup lightly packed dark brown sugar
1 large egg
¾ cup honey
2 tablespoons finely chopped candied orange peel
2 tablespoons finely chopped candied lemon peel

THE SPICED SUGAR
1 cup strained confectioners' sugar, spooned in and leveled
1 teaspoon ground cinnamon
1 teaspoon ground ginger
½ teaspoon ground nutmeg
¼ teaspoon ground allspice

Cookie
Characteristics

Homestyle

Long shelf life

Travel well

MAKE THE COOKIES

1. Position the shelves in the upper and lower thirds of the oven. Heat the oven to 350°. Lightly dab the corners of the cookie sheets with butter and line with baking parchment. Lightly butter the parchment.

2. Place the almonds in the work bowl of a food processor fitted with the steel blade and process until finely chopped, 25 to 30 seconds. Set aside.

3. Strain together the flour, cinnamon, baking soda, baking powder, salt, nutmeg, ginger, allspice, and pepper. Stir in the almonds and set aside.

4. In the bowl of an electric mixer fitted with the paddle attachment, beat the butter with the zests on medium speed until soft. Add the brown sugar and mix until well blended, then add the egg, scraping down the side of the bowl as needed. Blend in the honey and the candied orange and lemon peel.

5. Reduce the mixer speed to low and add the dry ingredients in three additions, mixing just until blended. It is important not to overmix the batter.

6. Roll the batter into ¾-inch balls and place 1½ inches apart on the cookie sheets. Bake for 14 minutes, or until the cookies are very lightly browned around the edges. To ensure even browning, toward the end of baking time rotate the sheets from top to bottom and front to back. The tops will be soft, but will firm up as the cookies stand. Let rest on the cookie sheets for 3 minutes.

MAKE THE SPICED SUGAR

7. Strain the confectioners' sugar, cinnamon, ginger, nutmeg, and allspice into a large bowl. While the cookies are still warm, roll them in the sugar mixture, then place on cooling racks set over sheets of wax paper to cool completely.

STORAGE: Store cookies in an airtight container, layered between strips of wax paper, for up to 3 weeks. These cookies may be frozen before rolling in the spiced sugar.

"Where would we be without spices? Everything would be plain vanilla."

—CLAUDIA FLEMING

speculaas

This spicy Christmas cookie, a specialty of Holland, is also popular in Germany and Austria, where it is known as *spekulatius*. The translation of the Dutch word *Speculaa* is "mirror," which in this context is thought to reflect various images of the world. On the other hand, Spekulatius represent Saint Nicholas and are baked to celebrate December 6, Saint Nicholas Day.

The cookie dough is made with ground almonds and is highlighted with a blend of cinnamon, cardamom, cloves, and ginger. Like Springerle (page 257), the dough is pressed into handsome wooden molds. The recipe yield varies depending on the size of the molds chosen. Whether served with mulled cider or eggnog, spicy Speculaas will disappear in a flash.

AT A GLANCE

PAN: Jelly roll pans

PAN PREP: Baking parchment

EQUIPMENT: Speculaas molds

OVEN TEMP: 350°

CHILLING TIME: 1 hour

BAKING TIME: 10–15 minutes, depending on size of cookies

DIFFICULTY: ❍❍❍

⅓ cup ground blanched almonds

2¼ cups all-purpose flour, spooned in and leveled, divided

½ teaspoon baking soda

⅔ cup sugar

1 teaspoon ground cinnamon

½ teaspoon ground cardamom

½ teaspoon ground cloves

½ teaspoon ground ginger

1 large egg

⅔ cup (1⅓ sticks) unsalted butter, softened

MAKE THE DOUGH

1. Place the ground almonds and ¼ cup of the flour in the work bowl of a food processor fitted with the steel blade. Pulse two or three times to combine, then process for 15 seconds, stop the processor to scrape around the bowl, then process for 10 seconds longer or until the mixture becomes cakey and clumps when pressed in your hand.

2. Strain the remaining 2 cups flour with the baking soda, sugar, cinnamon, cardamom, cloves, and ginger onto a flat surface or cutting board. Make a well in the center of the mound. In a small bowl, lightly beat the egg with a fork and pour it into the well. Using the fork, incorporate the egg into the flour as best you can. Then take a handful of the flour mixture and rub it gently between the palms of your hands. Do this several times to thoroughly incorporate the egg. The mixture will be dry.

3. Place the almond mixture in a bowl and add the butter. Work in the butter with your fingertips until the mixture comes together and forms a mass.

4. Form the flour–egg mixture into a mound and make a large well in the center. Place the almond–butter mixture in the well and use the fraisage method of kneading (see page 396) to form a dough. The almond–butter mixture should be thoroughly incorporated into the flour–egg crumbs.

5. Divide the dough in half. Shape each half into a disk, lightly flour, and wrap with plastic. Chill about 1 hour or freeze for up to 3 months.

6. To shape the Speculaas, see below, "How to Shape Springerle and Speculaas."

BAKE THE COOKIES

7. Position the shelves in the upper and lower thirds of the oven. Heat the oven to 350°. Line the pans with baking parchment. Bake the Speculaas for 10 to 15 minutes, or until the edges *just* begin to brown. (The baking time will depend upon the size of the cookies.) For even doneness, rotate the pans top to bottom and front to back toward the end of the baking time.

8. Remove the cookies from the oven. When firm enough to handle, transfer to cooling racks.

STORAGE: Store in an airtight container, layered between strips of wax paper, for up to 2 weeks. These cookies may be frozen.

Cookie Characteristics

Festive

Long shelf life

Fragile

How to Shape Springerle and Speculaas

Making Springerle and Speculaas is a lot of fun. From Springerle you can create charming decorations for Christmas trees by simply making a small hole in the top of each cookie before baking. A #802 plain, round cake-decorating tube makes the perfect size hole, but a sturdy drinking straw will do. To continue this centuries-old tradition, try your hand at making these artistic cookies.

- The first one or two cookies may not come out well, but as the mold becomes "seasoned," they will improve.
- Be sure the mold is well floured after each use.
- Pinch off the appropriate-size piece of dough, and, with floured hands, form it into the shape of the mold (e.g., square, circle, oval, etc.). Note: As an example, a 3-inch mold will use about 1½ ounces of dough. A kitchen scale is helpful here.
- Flour the dough and, using your hand, gently flatten it to about a ³⁄₁₆-inch thickness.
- Press the dough into the floured mold, pressing it gently but firmly with your thumb. It is helpful to study the mold to observe where the definitions are. Even the tiniest grooves will make a difference in the finished cookie.
- Run a rolling pin gently over the dough to smooth the surface, taking care not to roll the dough to the edge of the mold, in order to retain its shape.
- Tap the far side of the mold against a jelly roll pan lined with baking parchment to release the cookie. Do not brush off any excess flour; doing so will ruin the definition you have worked so hard to achieve.
- After all the Springerle are shaped, air-dry them overnight, uncovered, at room temperature.

BAKE THE COOKIES

5. Position the shelves in the lower and upper thirds of the oven. Heat the oven to 325°.

6. Bake the cookies for 5 to 7 minutes or until *set* on top. These cookies should not brown. To ensure even baking, toward the end of baking time, rotate the sheets top to bottom and front to back. Let cool for 2 minutes on the pans before transferring to cooling racks.

STORAGE: Store in an airtight container, layered between strips of wax paper, for up to 4 weeks. These cookies may be frozen.

Cookie
Characteristics

Versatile

Long shelf life

Travel well

raspberry linzer bars

MAKES 4½ DOZEN 2¼-INCH BARS

This Middle European cookie, made with a linzer-style dough, is reminiscent of the renowned linzertorte, a classic pastry created in Linz, Austria. The dough is commonly made with finely ground almonds, sieved hard-boiled egg yolks, spices, lemon zest, and raspberry preserves. The hard-boiled egg yolks and ground nuts give the dough a unique texture and outstanding flavor.

While many linzer cookies are sandwiched with the jam in the middle, I find it easier to form the dough into logs, make troughs down the centers, and fill them with raspberry preserves. Take care not to make the wells too deep, or the jam will leak through. The logs are sliced on the diagonal, creating beautiful ribbonlike strips with ruby-red centers. Raspberry preserves with seeds make the prettiest cookie, but seedless preserves may be used if you wish.

AT A GLANCE
PAN: Cookie sheets
PAN PREP: Lightly buttered
OVEN TEMP: 325°
CHILLING TIME: 30 minutes
BAKING TIME: 18 to 20 minutes
DIFFICULTY: ○○

DOUGH
4 ounces (about ¾ cup) whole almonds, with skins
2 cups all-purpose flour, spooned in and leveled, divided
½ teaspoon baking powder
½ teaspoon ground cinnamon
½ teaspoon salt
⅛ teaspoon ground cloves
1 cup (2 sticks) unsalted butter, slightly softened
½ teaspoon freshly grated lemon zest
½ teaspoon freshly grated orange zest
⅓ cup sugar
4 hard-boiled egg yolks, finely sieved
1½ teaspoons pure vanilla extract

TO ASSEMBLE THE COOKIES
¼ cup all-purpose flour, spooned in and leveled
¼ cup strained confectioners' sugar, spooned in and leveled
About ½ cup raspberry preserves

MAKE THE DOUGH
1. In the work bowl of a food processor fitted with the steel blade, pulse the almonds and ¼ cup of the flour four or five times, then process 45 to 50 seconds, or until the mixture is the consistency of fine meal. Add the remaining flour, baking powder, cinnamon, salt, and cloves and pulse to combine.

2. In the bowl of an electric mixer fitted with the paddle attachment, cream the butter and the zests on medium-low speed until smooth. Add the sugar in a steady stream, then blend in the sieved yolks and the vanilla, mixing just until blended. Scrape down the side of the bowl as needed.

3. Reduce the mixer speed to low and add 1 cup of the flour–almond mixture, then remove the bowl from the machine, scrape the paddle clean, and work in the remaining flour mixture one-third at a time, using a wooden spoon. Divide the dough into thirds and wrap each piece in plastic, then chill for 30 minutes.

SHAPE THE COOKIES

4. Position the shelves in the upper and lower thirds of the oven. Heat the oven to 325°. Lightly butter the cookie sheets.

5. Divide the dough into six equal pieces. Combine the flour and confectioners' sugar and stir to blend. Lightly dust a pastry board or other flat surface with the mixture. Working with one piece of dough at a time, roll the pastry back and forth until it forms a cylinder 10 inches long × ¾ inch wide. Repeat with remaining pieces.

6. Place each cylinder on a cookie sheet and flatten with the heel of your hand until it is approximately 1¼ inches wide. Depress the center of the strip with the rounded handle of a kitchen knife or wooden spoon to form a trough running the entire length of the cylinder. Do not make the trough too deep. Hold the sides of the roll as you press to keep it from spreading too much. Each roll should measure 10 inches by 1¼ inches.

7. Prick the inside of the trough with a fork. Using a dough scraper or thin-bladed knife, *partially* cut each strip on a slight angle, dividing it into eight 1-inch-wide pieces. *Do not cut all the way through.*

BAKE THE COOKIES

8. Bake the strips for 10 minutes. Remove from the oven, depress the centers gently with the handle of a wooden spoon, and fill with about 2 tablespoons of the raspberry preserves, dropping the jam from the tip of a teaspoon. Do not overfill. Continue baking for 8 to 10 minutes longer, or until the preserves start to bubble and the bars are lightly browned. To ensure even browning, toward the end of baking time rotate the sheets from top to bottom and front to back. Remove from the oven and let stand for 15 minutes. Cut through each bar where there is an indentation. When cool enough to handle, transfer the cookies to cooling racks.

STORAGE: Store in an airtight container, layered between strips of wax paper, for up to 3 weeks. These cookies may be frozen.

Cookie
Characteristics

Versatile

Long shelf life

Fragile

lacy lemon ginger cones

MAKES 2½ DOZEN 3-INCH CONES

Here is a twist on a classic French lace cookie. The batter is made with zesty crystallized ginger, which never fails to perk up the palate! For added zing, the little cones are filled with a flavorful Gingery Mascarpone Cream. The cones can be made ahead, but they must be filled just before serving. While lace cookies may seem intimidating at first, the technique is easy to master. If you want to dazzle your guests with your baking prowess, this is the way to go!

AT A GLANCE

PAN: Cookie sheets

PAN PREP: Silpat or nonstick baking mats or well-buttered and floured cookie sheet

EQUIPMENT: Large (2-inch) pastry tube for molding

OVEN TEMP: 350°

BAKING TIME: 9–10 minutes

DIFFICULTY: ○○○

¼ cup all-purpose flour, spooned in and leveled

¼ cup sliced unblanched almonds (about ¾ ounce)

½ teaspoon ground ginger

⅛ teaspoon salt

¼ cup (½ stick) unsalted butter

¼ cup superfine sugar

1 tablespoon heavy cream

1 tablespoon corn syrup

½ teaspoon freshly grated lemon zest

2 tablespoons minced crystallized ginger

1 recipe Gingery Mascarpone Cream (page 357)

MAKE THE COOKIES

1. Position the shelves in the upper and lower thirds of the oven. Heat the oven to 350°. Place the Silpat mats on the cookie sheets. Alternatively, butter the cookie sheets well and, using a flour shaker, dust with flour and tap firmly over the sink to remove any excess.

2. Place the flour, almonds, ground ginger, and salt in the work bowl of a food processor fitted with the steel blade. Pulse four to five times, then process for 15 seconds, or until the mixture is the consistency of coarse meal.

3. Place the butter, sugar, cream, corn syrup, and zest in a heavy-bottomed 2-quart saucepan and bring to a full boil over medium heat. The mixture will bubble up. Reduce the heat and let simmer for 15 to 20 seconds, then remove from the heat and add the crystallized ginger, stirring to blend. Using a whisk, stir in the dry ingredients. Let stand 5 minutes.

4. Shape the batter into ½-inch balls and place no more than five at a time on the cookie sheet. These will spread during baking. Baking one sheet at a time, bake for 9 to 10 minutes, or until the cookies

have stopped bubbling and are golden brown. To ensure even browning, toward the end of baking time rotate the sheet top to bottom and front to back.

SHAPE AND FILL THE CONES

5. Remove cookies from the oven and let rest for about 2 minutes or until firm enough to mold. Using a small blade spatula, remove one cookie at a time and place it upside down on a paper towel. Using the paper towel as an aid, mold the cookie into a cone by rolling the cookie around a large 2-inch round pastry tube, such as a #802, pressing down gently on the seam to seal the cone. Transfer to a cooling rack and proceed to shape the remaining cookies. If the cookies become too firm to mold, return to the oven for a few seconds to soften. Since only one sheet of cookies is baked at a time, to facilitate the baking, as one sheet is removed from the oven, another should be put in to bake. You can be shaping the cones while one pan is baking.

6. Fit a 16-inch pastry bag with a #825 large star tube. Spoon the Gingery Mascarpone Cream into the bag. Shortly before serving, pipe the filling into the cones. (Note: These cookies will soften after they are filled. However, once the filling is made, the pastry bag can be filled and ready to go. Since piping only takes a few minutes, it can be done just before serving.)

STORAGE: Store the unfilled cones in an airtight container, layered between strips of wax paper, for up to 3 weeks. The unfilled cookies may be frozen.

Cookie
Characteristics

Festive

Long shelf life
(unfilled)

Fragile

french lace what-nots

Wait until you hear the raves when you serve these charming French Lace What-Nots! These buttery lace cookies literally melt in your mouth. Instead of molding the cookies into uniform shapes, I push the edges of the hot cookies toward their centers, and I get a variety of whimsical shapes. For a finishing touch, I web the tops with thin lines of melted chocolate.

AT A GLANCE

PAN: Cookie sheet

PAN PREP: Silpat or other nonstick baking mat or well-buttered and floured cookie sheet

OVEN TEMP: 350°

STANDING TIME: 1 hour

BAKING TIME: 5–7 minutes

DIFFICULTY: ○○

COOKIES

½ cup cake flour, spooned in and leveled

3 ounces (about ½ cup) whole blanched almonds

Pinch of salt

½ cup (1 stick) unsalted butter

⅓ cup lightly packed light brown sugar

¼ cup light corn syrup

½ teaspoon pure vanilla extract

GLAZE

2 ounces fine-quality bittersweet or semisweet chocolate, such as Lindt Bittersweet, chopped

½ teaspoon vegetable oil

MAKE THE BATTER

1. Combine the flour, almonds, and salt in the work bowl of a food processor fitted with the steel blade. Pulse five or six times, then process for 40 to 50 seconds, until the mixture has a fine, meallike consistency. Stop occasionally to scrape around the side of the work bowl. Set aside.

2. Combine the butter, brown sugar, and corn syrup in a small, heavy saucepan. Bring to a slow boil over low heat, and simmer for 20 to 30 seconds. Remove from the heat and stir in the vanilla and the flour–nut mixture. Scrape the batter into a bowl and let stand for about 1 hour. The batter will thicken as it cools and will be somewhat oily.

BAKE THE COOKIES

3. Position the shelf in the center of the oven. Heat the oven to 350°. Line a cookie sheet with a Silpat or other nonstick baking mat. Alternatively, generously butter the cookie sheet and, using a flour shaker, dust evenly with flour. Tap firmly over the sink to remove any excess flour.

4. Shape the batter into marble-size ½- to ¾-inch balls, placing no more than six on the cookie sheet at a time, spacing them evenly apart. *Do not crowd.* The batter will spread. Bake the cookies for 5 to 7 minutes, or until they are golden brown and no longer bubbling. Watch carefully! They overbake quickly.

5. Remove from the oven and let cool 1 minute. Loosen one cookie at a time from the sheet and place top side up on a double sheet of paper towels. While still soft and pliable, push the edge of the cookie to the center, first pushing in from the right and left sides, then from the top and bottom. Use another piece of paper towel or more as needed to *protect your fingers while molding the hot cookie.* Repeat with the remaining cookies. If the cookies become too brittle to shape, return them to the oven for a few seconds to soften. Place the formed cookies on a cooling rack set over a sheet of wax paper.

GLAZE THE COOKIES

6. When all the cookies are baked, melt the chocolate over a water bath (see page 393). When the chocolate is almost melted, stir in the vegetable oil. Do not let the chocolate mixture get too hot; the chocolate is ready when it is warm and runny. Dip the tines of a fork into the melted chocolate and zigzag the glaze over the tops of the cookies. Let the cookies rest at room temperature until the chocolate is set. This could take several hours, depending on the humidity and the season of the year.

STORAGE: The cookies may be stored in an airtight container, carefully layered between strips of wax paper, for up to 3 weeks.

Cookie
Characteristics

Festive

Long shelf life

Fragile

curled butter wafers

MAKES ABOUT 5 DOZEN 3-INCH COOKIES

These light-as-a-feather Curled Butter Wafers were inspired by the classic French cookies called *langues-de-chat,* or cat's tongues. They are thin and crisp cookies, golden in the center with warm brown edges, that marry beautifully with cool, creamy desserts, especially ice cream.

Because these cookies are so thin, while they are still hot, they can be formed into a variety of shapes. For this book, I curl the long cookies using a round wooden spoon handle. The cookies cool in a matter of seconds, and when the handle is removed, the cookies remain in charming corkscrew shapes. As an alternative to curling the cookies, you may lay the handle of the spoon on top of the hot cookies and gently press them to create an arched effect. A folded paper towel will protect your hand from the heat of the cookies.

While patience is a virtue here, making these cookies is well worth your time. Their twists and turns make a tasty impression, but alas, they will disappear in the blink of an eye.

PAN: Cookie sheets

PAN PREP: Silpat or nonstick baking mats or well-buttered cookie sheets

OVEN TEMP: 400°

BAKING TIME: 7–8 minutes

DIFFICULTY: ○○

⅔ cup (1⅓ sticks) unsalted butter, slightly firm

½ cup sugar

3 large egg whites, at room temperature

1½ teaspoons pure vanilla extract

1 cup all-purpose flour, spooned in and leveled

Pinch of salt

1. Position the shelf in the middle of the oven. Heat the oven to 400°. If not using Silpat or a nonstick baking mat, butter the cookie sheets well.

2. In the bowl of an electric mixer fitted with the paddle attachment, cream the butter on medium speed until smooth and lightened in color. Add the sugar 1 tablespoon at a time, taking about 2 minutes. Gradually add the egg whites and the vanilla, scraping down the side of the bowl as needed. (The mixture may appear to separate.) Reduce the mixer speed to low and mix in the flour and salt, mixing about 5 seconds longer. *Do not overmix.*

3. Fit a 14-inch pastry bag with a #802 or #803 large round tube. Fill the bag one-third full with the cookie batter. Pipe six 4-inch lines of batter spaced about 2 inches apart onto one cookie sheet.

4. Bake the cookies for 7 to 8 minutes, or until lightly browned. *Do not overbake.* While the cookies are baking, pipe another six cookies on the second cookie sheet to have ready to bake when the first is removed.

5. Have ready two wooden spoons with ⅜- to ½-inch-thick round handles. Remove the cookies from the oven and, if not using a baking mat, loosen *at once* with a thin metal spatula. Holding a paper towel in your hand, place one cookie on the towel *top side down.* Then wrap it around the handle of a wooden spoon using the paper towel to protect you. Squeeze your hand gently to curl the cookie.

6. Repeat until all the cookies are molded. If the cookies become too firm to curl, return them briefly to the oven to soften. Repeat the baking and shaping with the remaining cookie dough. These cookies are very fragile. Handle carefully.

STORAGE: Store in an airtight container, layered between strips of wax paper, for up to 3 weeks. These cookies may be frozen.

Cookie Characteristics

Festive

Long shelf life

Fragile

"Nothing wins you friends faster than a full cookie jar—accessible to raiders, big and little." —MARY HUNT ALTFILLISCH

giant almond wafers

MAKES 16 TO 18 6-INCH COOKIES

Several years ago, I was privileged to work in the kitchen of Restaurant Troisgros in Roanne, France. At dessert time, in the center of their petit-four platter stood enormous wafer-thin cookies that caught the eye because of their size. Not only were they great to look at, but they tasted fantastic. This is my improvisation on these sensational cookies. No need to take out your electric mixer for this; the batter is easy to make by hand. When you prepare your almonds, be sure they are very finely ground.

AT A GLANCE

PAN: Oversized (14 × 17-inch) cookie sheets

PAN PREP: Silpat or nonstick baking mats or well-buttered cookie sheets

OVEN TEMP: 400°

BAKING TIME: 5–6 minutes

DIFFICULTY: ◐◐

¾ cup finely ground slivered blanched almonds

¼ cup strained cake flour, spooned in and leveled

3 tablespoons unsalted butter, at room temperature

⅓ cup sugar

⅓ cup egg whites (about 2 extra-large)

1 teaspoon pure vanilla extract

⅓ cup sliced unblanched almonds

1. Position the shelf in the middle of the oven. Heat the oven to 400°. If not using Silpat or a nonstick baking mat, butter the cookie sheets well.

2. Combine the ground almonds and the cake flour. Set aside.

3. In a large bowl, mix the butter with a wooden spoon or large rubber spatula. Gradually add the sugar, stirring well. Whisk the egg whites lightly with a fork and slowly add them to the butter–sugar mixture, then beat in the vanilla. Blend in the dry ingredients, mixing *just* until combined. Do not overmix.

4. Spoon about 1½ tablespoons of the batter for each cookie onto a cookie sheet. Spread the batter into a 4-inch circle by tapping it with a fork dipped in ice water. Keep dipping the fork in the water as you spread the batter. Sprinkle each wafer with 1 teaspoon of sliced almonds. Use the tapping motion to press the almonds into the wafers.

5. Bake the cookies, one sheet at a time, for about 5 minutes or until lightly browned. Watch carefully, as they brown quickly. As soon as the cookies are baked, remove them from the pans with a very thin spatula. Immediately invert the cookies into *a French bread pan, almond side down.* (The rounded shape of the pan makes the perfect implement for working several wafers at once.) Alterna-

tively, without inverting the cookies, lay each one over a barrel rolling pin and press gently, using a piece of paper towel to protect your hand. They will harden as they cool, retaining their shape.

STORAGE: Store in an airtight container, layered between strips of wax paper, for up to 5 days. These cookies may be frozen.

Cookie Characteristics

Festive

Moderate shelf life

Fragile

Working with Lace and Curled Cookies

- These are best baked on a cookie sheet without sides, or on an inverted jelly roll pan, so the cookies are easier to release.
- The cookie sheet must be well buttered and floured, if not using a Silpat or a nonstick baking mat.
- Once you have buttered and floured the cookie sheet, you don't have to do it again.
- Baking parchment is not recommended because it slides on the cookie sheet.
- Use a flour shaker for dusting because the flour distributes more evenly.
- Do not bake more than four or five cookies at one time.
- Watch carefully during the final minutes of baking, as browning occurs quickly.
- Because lace cookies are so thin, they continue to brown on the cookie sheet when out of the oven.
- Remove cookies with an offset spatula made of thin metal because spatulas with thick edges will break the cookies.
- If the cookies become too hard, return them to the oven to soften.
- Invert the baked cookie onto paper toweling and use the paper towel to facilitate molding or shaping the cookie.
- Shapes can be changed as desired—that is, for *cigarettes,* use the handle of a wooden spoon; for *cones,* use a large 2-inch pastry tube; for *cups,* use an ungreased mini-muffin pan.
- Batter will keep in the refrigerator up to 5 days and can be baked as needed.

palmiers

MAKES 3 DOZEN 2½-INCH COOKIES

Palmiers, named for their fan-shaped resemblance to palm leaves, are classic fare in French pâtisseries. They are made with sugared layers of buttery puff pastry and are absolutely addictive.

These Palmiers are made with a quicker version of puff pastry that I have adapted for the food processor. The dough is rolled on a bed of sugar instead of flour, and don't skimp on the sugar here! It's important for the finished result. The sugar will caramelize during baking, forming an irresistible candylike surface.

Be sure to look at the cinnamon palmiers variation that follows. It's also a winner. Whether you make those or the plain sugared variety, every time these cookies are served, you'll see how quickly they are devoured!

AT A GLANCE

PAN: Jelly roll pans
PAN PREP: Baking parchment
OVEN TEMP: 400°, 350°
CHILLING TIME: 45 minutes
BAKING TIME: 18–22 minutes
DIFFICULTY: ●●●

⅓ to ½ cup granulated sugar, for rolling
1 recipe Processor Puff Pastry
    (page 275)
1 large egg, lightly beaten with
    2 teaspoons water
Sparkling white sugar, for garnish
    (optional; available in The Baker's
    Catalogue, see page 403)

SHAPE THE PALMIERS

1. Sprinkle the work surface heavily with the granulated sugar. Place the pastry on top, then sprinkle the top of the dough well with additional granulated sugar. Roll the dough into a rectangle measuring about 12 inches from top to bottom and 16 inches wide, turning the pastry over as needed and sprinkling generously with sugar each time it is turned. When the dough is rolled to the correct size, prick it with a fork at 1-inch intervals to prevent shrinking. Using the dough scraper, trim the right and left edges to even the dough. Make a slight indentation in the pastry with the dough scraper at the exact center, measuring from right to left.

2. Fold 2 inches of the dough over on the right and left sides, then brush the dough along the edges of the folds with the egg wash. Fold the dough over two more times on each side, brushing the edges of the folded dough with egg wash each time the dough is turned, leaving a ¼-inch space in the middle. (*Note: When folding the dough, it is important that it be folded loosely and not be stretched, because the dough needs room to expand during baking.*)

3. Run the rolling pin from the bottom to the top of the strip to seal the layers of dough and elongate the strip to 13 inches. Make a slight depression with the rolling pin in the center, between the right and left sides. This will make the dough easier to turn for the final fold. Brush the strip down the center with the egg wash, then fold the right side of the strip over the left side, making a total of six layers of dough. It should measure about 12 to 13 inches from top to bottom and about 2 inches wide.

4. Place a tapered rolling pin or the handle of a long wooden spoon lengthwise on top of the strip and press gently to seal the layers. Turn the strip over and press the opposite side. Place the strip on a parchment- or wax-paper-lined cookie sheet, cover loosely, and chill for 30 minutes. (For longer storage, wrap the strip with wax paper and then aluminum foil for up to 3 days. Do not use plastic wrap because it will cause too much condensation. The uncut Palmiers may be frozen, *well wrapped,* for up to

Cookie
Characteristics

Festive

Moderate
shelf life

Travel well

4 months. Thaw in the refrigerator before slicing.)

BAKE THE PALMIERS

5. Have ready the jelly roll pans lined with parchment, and sprinkle lightly with cold water. While the pastry is still cold, using a dough scraper or sharp knife, slice the strip into ¼-inch pieces. The cookies widen during baking so space the slices 2 inches apart in the pans. The rows can be spaced more closely, about 1 inch apart, because the cookies do not spread lengthwise.

6. To allow the Palmiers to fan, spread the open end apart (about ¾ inch), then place the pans in the refrigerator or freezer to chill for 15 minutes.

7. Position the shelves in the upper and lower thirds of the oven. Heat the oven to 400°. Place the Palmiers in the oven and bake for 12 to 14 minutes, or until they are golden brown on the bottom. Remove the Palmiers from the oven, then *reduce the oven to 350°.* Using a small spatula, turn the Palmiers over, sprinkle lightly with sparkling white sugar, and bake again for 6 to 8 minutes or until nicely caramelized. To ensure even browning, rotate the pans top to bottom and front to back. Watch carefully as the cookies can quickly overbake. Remove from the oven, let stand for 5 minutes, then carefully remove from the pans while still warm. Cool on wire racks. (Note: If not serving immediately, re-crisp the cookies in a 325° oven for 3 to 5 minutes.)

STORAGE: Store in an airtight container, layered between strips of wax paper, for up to 5 days. These cookies may be frozen. Re-crisp frozen cookies in a 325° oven for 5 to 7 minutes.

caramel-glazed cinnamon palmiers

Follow the Master Recipe for Palmiers, blending 1½ to 2 teaspoons of cinnamon into the sugar when ready to roll the dough.

processor puff pastry

MAKES 3 DOZEN PALMIERS

1 cup all-purpose flour, spooned in and
   leveled
⅓ cup cake flour, spooned in and leveled
½ teaspoon salt
12 tablespoons (1½ sticks) unsalted
   butter, cut into ½-inch dice, divided
1 teaspoon fresh lemon juice
⅓ cup ice water

1. Place the flours and salt in the work bowl of a food processor fitted with the steel blade. Pulse four or five times to combine, then process for 5 to 7 seconds. Remove 2 tablespoons of the dry ingredients and toss with 8 table-spoons of the cubed butter. (A plastic zippered bag works well for this.) Place in the refrigerator to chill. Chill the remaining dry ingredients in the work bowl for 30 minutes. Keep the remaining 4 tablespoons of butter at room temperature; it should become very soft.

2. Place the work bowl back on the processor and add the 4 tablespoons of butter. Pulse four or five times, then process for 6 to 8 seconds, or until the mixture resembles fine meal. Add the flour-coated butter to the work bowl and pulse four or five times. Stir the lemon juice into the ice water and add to the processor bowl. Pulse three or four times. The mixture should be rough textured

and some of the butter should still be in large pieces. *Do not let it form a ball.*

3. Empty the mixture onto a well-floured surface. Press it into a rectangle, as best you can, measuring about 4 × 5 inches. With a heavy rolling pin, roll into a rectangle measuring 14 inches from top to bottom and 7 inches wide. (See "Rolling and Shaping Puff Pastry," page 276.) Even the edges of the dough with a dough scraper from time to time. Using the dough scraper or the dull side of a knife, make a slight indentation across the center of the dough. Then bring the top and bottom ends of the dough to the center where the indentation was made and press gently with the rolling pin to seal the ends. This indentation will make it easier to fold the dough. Fold over again, like a book, making four layers of pastry. Give the dough a quarter-turn so the seam, or open side, is on your right. (Each time you roll and fold the pastry, it is called a turn.)

4. Roll the dough again into a slightly larger rectangle measuring about 7 × 16 inches, turning it over, lightly flouring as needed. Use the dough scraper to make the edges as even as you can. Fold the dough, bringing the ends to the center, then fold again. Press the top of the dough gently with your hand to flatten slightly. Be sure to square off the edges of the pastry. You have now made a second turn. Wrap with wax paper and chill for 10 to 15 minutes, or until the dough feels cool and slightly firm but not hard.

5. Roll the dough again on a well-floured surface, enlarging it to a 7 × 18-inch rectangle. Fold the ends to the middle, then fold again. Wrap with wax paper and chill 10 to 15 minutes, or until the dough feels cool and firm but not hard. Give the dough a fourth and final roll on the floured surface, making the rectangle 7 × 20 inches, again folding it into a book. Wrap tightly with wax paper and chill for 2 hours or up to 3 days. (This dough may be frozen for up to 4 months. Wrap the dough securely in wax paper, then rewrap in aluminum foil.)

"[People] come to me with their heads held high and announce that they do not eat sugar anymore, as though they have tackled one of life's deadly sins. My response is to ask them how long they have had this problem and if they have considered seeing a psychiatrist." —EMILY LUCHETTI

Rolling and Shaping Puff Pastry

- Use a thin, tapered rolling pin. The tapered ends make it easy to angle, which helps to keep the edges of the dough even.
- Always start rolling from the center. Roll away from you, and then toward you, as if you were rowing a boat.
- Flip the dough over once or twice during rolling. This ensures even thickness and will prevent sticking.
- After each turn, when you start to roll, keep the open seam to your right.
- When you fold the dough, be sure to stretch the corners where the two ends meet in the center to keep the seams aligned.
- When rolling the dough, establish the width before the length. Once the dough is rolled lengthwise, if it isn't wide enough, the width is difficult to obtain without making the dough too thin.
- Brush the dough often with a pastry brush to prevent any accumulation of flour.
- Do not allow the pastry to become too cold between "turns" or the butter will harden and not blend smoothly into the dough. If it does become too firm, let the dough stand at room temperature until it softens sufficiently.

kurabia

Middle Eastern pastries are a specialty of my friend Ann Koroghlian, from Hillsdale, New Jersey. Upon hearing about my book, she was anxious for me to try her favorite, Kurabia, a traditional wedding and holiday cookie, sometimes formed in a wooden mold and filled with fruit and nuts. When filling, remember a little goes a long way. While *very* fragile after baking, upon standing, the cookies become firm. With their melting, delicate crumb, they are indeed wonderful.

AT A GLANCE

PAN: Cookie sheets

PAN PREP: Ungreased

OVEN TEMP: 300°

BAKING TIME: 18–20 minutes

DIFFICULTY: ○○

1 cup (2 sticks) unsalted butter, clarified (see page 387)
1½ cups strained confectioners' sugar, divided, spooned in and leveled
1⅔ cups all-purpose flour, spooned in and leveled

Cookie Characteristics

Versatile

Long shelf life

Fragile

1. Position the shelves in the upper and lower thirds of the oven. Heat the oven to 300°.

2. In the bowl of an electric mixer fitted with the paddle attachment, beat the clarified butter on medium speed for 10 minutes. Add ¾ cup of the confectioners' sugar 1 tablespoon at a time, taking 2 to 3 minutes, then continue to mix for 12 to 13 minutes longer, until very light in color. Using a wooden spoon, work in the flour in three additions, mixing *just* until incorporated after each addition. Do not overmix.

3. Divide the dough into 36 1¼-inch balls. Roll into 2-inch logs, tapering the ends, then form into crescents and place about 1 inch apart on the cookie sheets. Bake for 18 to 20 minutes. Toward the end of baking time, rotate the pans top to bottom and front to back to ensure even baking. The Kurabia are done when the bottoms of the cookies *barely* show signs of browning.

4. Remove cookies from the oven and let rest on the sheets for 1 to 2 minutes. Carefully transfer the cookies to wire racks, but *do not touch them,* as they are very fragile when hot. Cool completely and then air-dry for at least 2 hours.

5. Place the remaining confectioners' sugar in a shallow bowl. Using a fork, carefully roll each cookie in the sugar, coating heavily. Air-dry on the wire racks for at least 1 hour.

STORAGE: Store in an airtight container, layered between strips of wax paper, for up to 3 weeks. These cookies may be frozen.

filled kurabia cookies

PAN: Cookie sheets

PAN PREP: Ungreased

OVEN TEMP: 300°

BAKING TIME: 25–27 minutes

DIFFICULTY: ○○○

1 recipe Kurabia cookie dough (page 277), plus remaining confectioners' sugar for garnish

1 recipe filling (below)

pistachio filling

½ cup (4 ounces) finely chopped pistachios, preferably unsalted

2 tablespoons sugar

2 tablespoons unsalted butter, melted

Combine all the ingredients in a small bowl. Chill before using.

walnut filling

½ cup (4 ounces) finely chopped walnuts

2 tablespoons sugar

½ teaspoon ground cinnamon

2 tablespoons unsalted butter, melted

Combine all the ingredients in a small bowl. Chill before using.

date filling

1 cup (6 ounces) coarsely chopped dates

½ cup orange juice

½ cup water

1 teaspoon freshly squeezed lemon juice

¼ teaspoon ground cinnamon

pinch of ground cloves

¼ cup finely chopped walnuts

1. Place the dates, orange juice and water in a small, heavy-bottomed saucepan, cover, and bring to a boil over medium-low heat. Reduce the heat to low and let simmer, covered, for about 15 minutes, or until the dates are completely softened. Check the mixture occasionally to be sure all of the liquid has not evaporated. If it has, add 2 or 3 more tablespoons of water.

2. When the dates are tender, remove from the heat and mix with a fork until you have a thick puree. Stir in the lemon juice, cinnamon, salt, and cloves, then fold in the walnuts. Chill the date filling before using.

TO FILL THE COOKIES USING A KURABIA MOLD

1. Break off a golf ball–size piece of dough and roll into a ball. Brush the Kurabia mold well with flour. Press the dough into the mold, then using your thumb, make a large depression in the center of the dough.

2. Press about 1 teaspoon of the desired filling into the cavity. Using your thumb, ease the edge of the dough from the mold, then enclose the filling with the dough, pinching gently to seal. Cup your hand over the mold to smooth the top. Tap the far edge of the mold firmly on the cookie sheet to release the Kurabia. Repeat with the remaining dough.

TO FILL THE COOKIES BY HAND

1. Break off a golf ball–size piece of dough and roll into an oval. Remove one-fourth of the dough from the oval and set it aside. Place the larger piece of dough in the cupped palm of your hand, and using your opposite thumb, shape the dough into a shallow, oval bowl.

2. Place about 1 teaspoon of the desired filling in the center of the bowl, then bring your fingers inward to reshape the oval form. Set the filled dough on a flat surface. Then take the smaller piece of dough and shape it into an oval large enough to cover the exposed filling. Place it on top of the filling, and press the two pieces of dough together to seal. Gently roll the oval between your hands to smooth the seam and reform the shape.

BAKE THE KURABIA

3. Place about 1 inch apart on the cookie sheets. Bake for 25 to 27 minutes. Toward the end of the baking time, rotate the sheets top to bottom and front to back to ensure even baking. The Kurabia are done when they *barely* show signs of browning on the bottom.

4. Remove from the oven and let rest on the sheets for 1 to 2 minutes before removing with a thin metal spatula. Carefully transfer the cookies to wire racks to cool. Do not touch the cookies. They are very fragile and must cool completely and then air-dry for at least 2 hours before they can be handled.

5. Place the remaining confectioners' sugar in a shallow bowl. Carefully roll the cookies, one at a time, in the sugar, coating them heavily on all sides. Place them back on the wire racks and let air-dry for at least 1 hour longer.

STORAGE: Store in an airtight container, layered between strips of wax paper, for up to 3 weeks. These cookies may be frozen.

petite lavender madeleines

These charming little French tea cakes make a wonderful accompaniment to ice creams, sherbets, and fruit desserts. The batter is made with clarified butter and minced fresh lavender, an herb that is related to the mint family. The herb really perks up the flavor. If you wish to make these without the lavender, omit it, but you will be missing something very special.

While Madeleines should be served fresh out of the oven, the batter can be made up to 3 days ahead and refrigerated. Also, I spoon it into the pans early on the day I plan to bake them, then I refrigerate the pans until ready to bake. I love to serve the Madeleines in a basket hot from the oven, nestled in a linen napkin. Wow! Will your guests be impressed!

AT A GLANCE

PAN: Mini-madeleine pans
PAN PREP: Well-buttered and dusted with strained flour
OVEN TEMP: 375°
BAKING TIME: 6–7 minutes
DIFFICULTY: ○○

⅓ cup (⅔ stick) unsalted butter
3 tablespoons minced fresh lavender
2 tablespoons honey
⅔ cup all-purpose flour, spooned in and leveled
½ teaspoon baking powder
⅛ teaspoon salt
2 large eggs
⅓ cup granulated sugar
1 teaspoon pure vanilla extract
¾ teaspoon freshly grated navel orange zest
¾ teaspoon freshly grated lemon zest
Strained confectioners' sugar, for dusting

1. Position the shelf in the center of the oven. Heat the oven to 375°. Using softened butter and a pastry brush, butter the pans well, being sure to reach into the grooves. Dust well with flour, invert over a sink, and tap two or three times to shake out the excess. To prevent sticking, the interiors of the molds should be completely coated with no metal visible. Chill the pans until ready to use.

2. In a *heavy* small saucepan, melt the butter slowly. As the white foam comes to the surface, skim it with a large spoon periodically until all of the foam is removed and the butter turns a deep golden brown color. Pour the butter through a very fine strainer to remove the dark sediment from the bottom of the pot. While the butter is still warm, stir in the lavender and the honey. Cool until tepid.

3. Strain together the flour, baking powder, and salt three times. Set aside.

4. In an electric mixer fitted with the whip attachment, beat the eggs on medium speed for 2 minutes. Add the sugar 1 tablespoon at a time, beating until light in color and thickened, about 2 minutes longer. Blend in the vanilla and zests.

5. On low speed, add the flour alternately with the tepid butter mixture, three parts flour to two parts butter, starting and ending with flour. Increase the speed to medium and beat for about 10 seconds longer. (The batter may be prepared up to a day ahead and spooned into the pans. It is not necessary to bring the batter to room temperature before baking.)

6. Drop scant ½ teaspoons of batter from the tip of a teaspoon into one of the pans. Be careful not to overfill the molds—they should be two-thirds full. Do not smooth the tops as the cakes should dome during baking. Bake for 6 to 7 minutes or just until golden brown. If baking two pans at once, bake them on the same shelf. (If using nonstick pans, reduce the baking time to 5 to 6 minutes.) *Do not overbake.* Remove from the oven and let cool for 1 minute. Invert the pan and, tipping the pan toward you, give a firm tap on the counter. The Madeleines should pop out. Use a small knife to release any that stick. Dust the Madeleines with confectioners' sugar and serve at once.

STORAGE: Store in an airtight container, layered between strips of wax paper, for up to 3 days. Before serving, freshen the Madeleines in a 300° oven, loosely covered with aluminum foil, for 4 to 5 minutes. Serve at once. While Madeleines may be made ahead or frozen, they are best eaten freshly made.

ginger madeleines

To the strained, clarified butter, add 2 tablespoons minced crystallized ginger along with the honey. Omit the lavender.

Cookie
Characteristics

Festive

Short shelf life

Travel well

athena's baklava

Every Christmas, Athena Sophos, my seamstress, treats her customers to her homemade Baklava. She is an outstanding baker, specializing, of course, in Greek goodies! Her Baklava is the best I have ever tasted.

AT A GLANCE **PAN:** 10½ × 15½ × 1-inch jelly roll pan

PAN PREP: Lightly buttered

OVEN TEMP: 350°

BAKING TIME: 40–45 minutes

DIFFICULTY: ❍❍❍

SYRUP
2 cups water
3 cups sugar
1 tablespoon honey
2 teaspoons fresh lemon juice
1 (3-inch) piece of lemon peel
1 cinnamon stick
5 whole cloves

BAKLAVA
1 package phyllo dough, preferably fresh
2½ cups walnuts
6 tablespoons sugar
½ teaspoon ground cinnamon
1½ cups whole unblanched almonds
1 cup clarified unsalted butter, melted
   (see page 387)

MAKE THE SYRUP

1. Place the water, sugar, honey, lemon juice and peel, cinnamon stick, and cloves in a heavy 2-quart saucepan. Bring to a slow boil, stirring occasionally to dissolve all the sugar. Simmer 2 to 3 minutes, strain, and set aside. (Can be made up to 3 days ahead and refrigerated.)

ASSEMBLE THE BAKLAVA

2. Position the shelf in the middle of the oven. Heat the oven to 350°. Lightly butter the jelly roll pan.

3. Lay a sheet of wax paper on your work surface. Open the phyllo package and unroll onto the wax paper. Lay a second sheet of wax paper on top of the phyllo sheets. Dampen a dish towel or a double thickness of paper towels and lay it over the wax paper to prevent the dough from drying out.

4. Place half of the walnuts in the work bowl of a food processor fitted with the steel blade. Process until coarsely chopped, then empty into a bowl. Process the remaining walnuts with the sugar and cinnamon, and add to the first batch of nuts. Coarsely chop the almonds and combine them with the walnut mixture.

5. On a flat surface, using two phyllo sheets at a time, brush the top with the clarified butter. Repeat until you have six sheets of phyllo. Sprinkle 1 heaping cup of the nut mixture over the top of the phyllo. Spread the mixture with your hand until the nuts are about 1 inch from the edge of the pastry on all sides except for the one closest to you.

6. Brush the exposed left and right edges of the pastry with clarified butter and fold them in. Roll the phyllo, starting with the edge closest to you. This may seem awkward at first, but just continue on. *Do not make the roll too tight.* Place the roll seam down on the prepared pan. Repeat, making three more rolls. Brush the rolls with melted butter and, using a sharp knife, slash the tops at 1-inch intervals.

7. Bake the Baklava for 40 to 45 minutes, or until golden brown. Remove from the oven and immediately pour the room-temperature syrup over the top. (Note: This may seem like too much syrup, but the Baklava will absorb it over time. This will take at least 24 hours, sometimes up to 2 or 3 days. If you wish to eat the Baklava after the first 24 hours, however, it's okay.) When the Baklava is ready, use a serrated knife to cut it into 1-inch slices.

STORAGE: Store at room temperature in a cool place, lightly covered with aluminum foil. The Baklava will keep for about 5 days.

Cookie Characteristics

Versatile

Moderate shelf life

Travel well

florentines

MAKES 80 1 X 1³/₄-INCH COOKIES

Festive Florentines have a thin nut crust topped with chewy, honey-flavored caramel. The golden caramel is covered with sliced unblanched almonds, which are traditional here, and colorful glacé fruits. The jewellike filling sparkles through a web of chocolate zigzagged across the top.

AT A GLANCE

PAN: 10½ × 15½ × 1-inch jelly roll pan

PAN PREP: Buttered heavy-duty aluminum foil

OVEN TEMP: 350°

BAKING TIME: 15– 16 minutes, crust; 13–15 minutes, topping

DIFFICULTY: ◐◐

CRUST
⅔ cup (1⅓ sticks) unsalted butter
1⅓ cups all-purpose flour, spooned in and leveled
⅓ cup confectioners' sugar
¼ teaspoon salt
½ cup sliced blanched almonds

TOPPING
⅔ cup superfine sugar
⅓ cup (⅔ stick) unsalted butter, cut into ½-inch slices
⅓ cup heavy cream
¼ cup honey
⅛ teaspoon salt
¼ cup coarsely chopped glacé cherries
¼ cup coarsely chopped candied orange peel
¼ cup coarsely chopped candied lemon peel
1 teaspoon freshly grated orange zest
1 teaspoon freshly grated lemon zest
1 cup sliced unblanched almonds
2 ounces fine-quality bittersweet or semisweet chocolate, such as Lindt Bittersweet, coarsely chopped
½ teaspoon vegetable or canola oil

1. Position the shelf in the center of the oven. Heat the oven to 350°. Tear a 15 × 18-inch sheet of heavy-duty aluminum foil. Invert the pan and center the foil over the pan, pressing it across the bottom and down the sides. Remove the foil, turn the pan right side up, and place the foil shell into the pan, shaping it smoothly across the bottom and snugly against the sides. Using a pastry brush, grease the bottom and sides with softened butter, taking care not to tear the foil.

MAKE THE CRUST

2. Melt the butter in a medium saucepan. Cool to tepid.

3. Place the flour, confectioners' sugar, salt, and almonds in the work bowl of a food processor fitted with a steel blade. Pulse eight to ten times, then process for 60 seconds, until fine and cakey. Using a fork, stir the mixture into the tepid melted butter and mix thoroughly. Divide into eight portions and place in the pan, pressing it as evenly as you can. Insert a dough scraper, small spatula, or the flat side of a plastic pastry corne between the dough and the sides of the pan to clean and even the edges. Bake the crust for 15 to 16 minutes, or until lightly browned and set on top. Let stand for 8 to 10 minutes to firm.

MAKE THE TOPPING

4. Place the sugar, butter, cream, honey, and salt in a heavy 2-quart saucepan. Bring to a boil, stirring gently but constantly. Brush the sides of the pot with water to be sure the sugar has dissolved, then simmer for 1 minute longer.

5. Mix in the candied fruits, zests, and nuts, blending well. Cook the mixture over low heat for 6 to 8 minutes, or until it begins to thicken and the caramel starts to darken. The thickness of the pot will determine the cooking time. Watch the sides of the pot to see the first signs of thickening.

6. Immediately pour the filling onto the warm crust and spread evenly with a large *buttered* offset spatula, distributing the topping as best you can. Bake for 13 to 15 minutes, until bubbly on top and the surface has begun to brown. Do not overbake. Cool on a wire rack.

TOP WITH THE CHOCOLATE

7. Melt the chocolate in a water bath (see page 393). When the chocolate is almost melted, stir in the vegetable oil. Do not let the chocolate mixure get too hot. Keep the chocolate warm while you unmold the cookies, gently stirring occasionally.

8. Lift the bar from the pan, using the foil as an aid, and place on a cutting board or flat surface. Before you web the bar with chocolate, cut the bar in half and slide each half off the foil.

9. Pour the warm chocolate into a plastic squeeze bottle or an 8-inch pastry bag fitted with a #2 standard writing tip. Starting at an upper corner of one of the cookie bars, make very fine lines at an angle, moving the pastry bag back and forth to the opposite corner until the entire surface is covered; if you wish, reverse the pattern, going in the opposite direction. (See "Webbing," page 399.) Repeat with the remaining cookie bar. Let stand until the chocolate is set, then cut into eighty 1 × 1¾-inch bars.

STORAGE: Store in an airtight container, layered between strips of wax paper, for up to 5 days. These cookies may be frozen.

Cookie
Characteristics

Festive

Moderate
shelf life

Travel well

priama's sicilian wine cookies

MAKES ABOUT 3 DOZEN 2½-INCH CRESCENTS

This recipe was shared by Michael Salvatore, a skilled chef and my teaching partner at Kings Cooking Studio in Short Hills, New Jersey. In addition to being an ebullient addition to the classroom, Michael is a never-ending source of culinary expertise. One day Michael walked in to class and said, "You are including a recipe for Sicilian Wine Cookies in your book, aren't you?" My response was, "Well, Michael, do you have one you would like to share?" And indeed he did. The following week, not only did he bring me his family's favorite recipe, but he also brought me the Chianti with which to make it! He told me that this recipe came from his grandmother's close friend, Priama.

Make it I did, and I loved the cookie. It has an intriguing anise flavor, enhanced with bits of chocolate and citrus zest, all brought together with the mellow flavor of the Chianti.

AT A GLANCE

PAN: Cookie sheets

PAN PREP: Baking parchment

OVEN TEMP: 350°

BAKING TIME: 18–20 minutes

DIFFICULTY: ○

2½ cups all-purpose flour, spooned in and leveled

¾ teaspoon baking powder

½ teaspoon ground cinnamon

1 large egg

¾ cup granulated sugar, plus 2 to 3 tablespoons for rolling

2 teaspoons freshly grated navel orange zest

1 teaspoon freshly grated lemon zest

½ cup canola oil

1½ teaspoons pure anise extract

¼ cup Chianti (or Marsala)

⅔ cup (4 ounces) semisweet chocolate mini-morsels

1. Position the shelves in the upper and lower thirds of the oven. Heat the oven to 350°. Dab the corners of the cookie sheets lightly with butter, then line with baking parchment.

2. Strain the flour, baking powder, and cinnamon together and set aside.

3. Using the whip attachment, beat the egg on medium speed for 1 minute. Add the sugar gradually, taking about 1 minute. Scrape down the side of the bowl. Add the zests and beat for 1 minute longer. Pour in the canola oil and anise extract, beating well, then add the wine in a steady stream and beat again.

4. Remove the bowl from the machine and, using a large rubber spatula, stir in one-half of the dry ingredients. Fold in the mini-morsels, then add the remaining dry ingredients in two additions. The mixture will be very stiff.

5. Shape the dough into 1¼-inch balls and roll in granulated sugar. Form each ball into a 3-inch log and shape the log into a crescent. Roll the crescents in the sugar again, then place on the cookie sheets.

6. Bake the cookies for 18 to 20 minutes, or until they are lightly browned. To ensure even browning, toward the end of baking time rotate the pans top to bottom and front to back. Let cool on the cookie sheets for 3 to 4 minutes before removing to wire cooling racks.

STORAGE: Store in an airtight container, layered between strips of wax paper, for up to 2 weeks. These cookies may be frozen.

Cookie
Characteristics

Versatile

Long shelf life

Travel well

chinese almond cookies

MAKES 32 2½-INCH COOKIES

Chinese almond cookies, once a familiar treat, seem to be disappearing, which is unfortunate because they were always a welcome ending to the meal. Although Almond Cookies are traditionally made with lard, for this recipe I have replaced it with vegetable shortening, which enhances its crispy texture—the perfect complement to a cup of hot Chinese tea.

PAN: Cookie sheets

PAN PREP: Baking parchment

OVEN TEMP: 375°

BAKING TIME: 10–11 minutes

DIFFICULTY: ○

2¼ cups all-purpose flour, spooned in and leveled

1 teaspoon baking soda

¼ teaspoon salt

¾ cup vegetable shortening

¾ cup plus 2 tablespoons granulated sugar, spooned in and leveled, divided

2 large eggs

1½ teaspoons pure almond extract, or to taste

1 egg white, lightly beaten with 1 teaspoon of water

32 (about ⅓ cup) whole blanched almonds

1. Position the shelves in the upper and lower thirds of the oven. Heat the oven to 375°. Dab the corners of the cookie sheets lightly with butter and line with baking parchment.

2. Strain the flour, baking soda, and salt together three times. Set aside.

3. In the bowl of an electric mixer fitted with the paddle attachment, beat the vegetable shortening with ¾ cup of the sugar on medium speed, taking about 1½ to 2 minutes. Scrape down the side of the bowl as needed. Add the eggs one at a time, and beat for another minute. Mix in the almond extract.

4. Reduce the mixer speed to low and mix in the dry ingredients in two additions, mixing until almost incorporated after each addition.

5. Using heaping teaspoonfuls of dough, form walnut-size balls measuring about 1¼ inches in diameter. Place on the sheets, and gently press, using the heel of your hand, into 1½-inch disks. Brush each disk lightly with the egg wash, then place an almond in the center of each cookie. Sprinkle lightly with the remaining 2 tablespoons sugar before placing in the oven.

6. Bake the cookies for 10 to 11 minutes or until lightly browned. To ensure even browning, toward the end of baking time rotate the pans top to bottom and front to back. Remove from the oven and let rest for 2 to 3 minutes. Transfer to wire racks and let cool.

STORAGE: Store in an airtight container, layered between strips of wax paper, for up to 2 weeks. These cookies may be frozen.

Cookie
Characteristics

Homestyle

Long shelf life

Travel well

"All a parent can give a child is roots and wings."

—CHINESE PROVERB

scotch shortbread

MAKES 25 1¾-INCH SQUARES

Scotch shortbread, a thick butter cookie famous for its velvety texture, is a memorable treat. Traditionally made by hand, it has but three ingredients: butter, sugar, and flour. Although it may seem like a "Plain Jane," the freshness of the ingredients and how they are put together make the difference between an ordinary cookie and one that is extraordinary.

Start with the freshest butter and mix it with superfine sugar, which dissolves more readily than ordinary granulated sugar. The velvety texture comes from a combination of wheat flour blended with rice flour, which can be purchased in health food stores or Oriental markets. Because the dough is so rich with butter, it should never be overworked, lest the butter begin to melt and impair the beautiful, fine layers of delicate crumbs.

Scots who take their shortbread very seriously bake their cookies in round wooden patterned molds, which today have become prized among collectors of antique bakeware.

AT A GLANCE

PAN: 9-inch square baking pan and cookie sheet
PAN PREP: Heavy-duty aluminum foil
OVEN TEMP: 300°
BAKING TIME: 1 hour, 10 minutes, baking; 10 minutes, crisping
DIFFICULTY: ○

1¾ cups all-purpose flour, spooned in and leveled
½ cup rice flour, spooned in and leveled
¼ teaspoon salt
1 cup (2 sticks) unsalted butter, slightly softened
½ cup superfine sugar
1 tablespoon sparkling white sugar (available in The Baker's Catalogue; page 403)

1. Position the shelf in the center of the oven. Heat the oven to 300°. Cut a 15-inch square of heavy-duty aluminum foil. Invert the pan and center the foil over the pan, pressing it across the bottom and down the sides. Remove the foil, turn the pan right side up, and place the foil shell in the pan, shaping it smoothly across the bottom and snugly against the sides.

2. Strain the flour, rice flour, and salt together three times and set aside.

3. Place the butter in the bowl of an electric mixer fitted with the paddle attachment. Mix on medium-low speed until smooth and creamy, about 1 minute. Add the sugar gradually, taking about 1 minute, then mix for 1 minute longer,

scraping the side of the bowl as needed.

4. Remove the bowl from the machine and transfer the mixture to a large, wide bowl for ease of mixing. Using a wooden spoon, cut half of the dry ingredients into the butter mixture until it is almost incorporated. Work in the remaining flour by hand, adding it in five or six additions. Gently knead the mixture just until a smooth dough is formed. Be careful not to overwork the dough, as this will result in a tough cookie.

5. Press the dough evenly into the pan using a bâtarde or flat-bottomed glass wrapped in plastic. Be sure the dough is pushed into the corners of the pan. Test for evenness by inserting a toothpick or the point of a knife randomly into the dough. Clean the edges of the pan by inserting the flat side of a plastic pastry corne, a dough scraper, or a small spatula in between the dough and the side of the pan.

6. Bake the shortbread for 55 to 60 minutes, or until the top feels set. Remove from the oven and let stand for 5 minutes. Using a pastry scraper, cut straight down through the dough at 1¾-inch intervals, making five strips. Give the pan a quarter turn and repeat, cutting 25 squares. Sprinkle with sparkling white sugar, return to the oven, and bake for another 10 minutes or until lightly brown.

7. Remove from the oven and let rest for 10 minutes. Have a cookie sheet without sides ready. Using the foil as an aid, lift the shortbread from the pan and place it on the cookie sheet. Gently pull the aluminum foil so it releases from the sides of the shortbread, wrapping longer sides of the foil under the pan and smoothing the foil as best you can to prevent it from sliding. Cut through the shortbread again, and using a thin metal spatula, spread the cookies slightly apart. Return to the oven for 10 more minutes to dry and crisp the cookies. Remove from the oven and let cool for 5 to 10 minutes before transferring to a cooling rack.

STORAGE: Store in an airtight container, layered between strips of wax paper, for up to 3 weeks. These cookies may be frozen.

Cookie Characteristics

Versatile

Long shelf life

Travel well

"Shortbread has beneficial effects on the soul. The warm glow it gives is better than alcohol . . ."

—LUCY ELLMAN

chocolate shortbread nuggets

MAKES 32 1 X 2-INCH COOKIES

Here is a shortbread recipe for the chocolate lovers in the house! The rich, chocolaty cookie is cut into bite-sized nuggets, then dipped in melted chocolate. Whenever I serve these, they are the first to go, and they meet with rave reviews.

PAN: 9-inch square baking pan and cookie sheet

PAN PREP: Heavy-duty aluminum foil

OVEN TEMP: 300°

BAKING TIME: 50–55 minutes, baking; 10 minutes, crisping

DIFFICULTY: ◐◐

1¼ cups all-purpose flour, spooned in and leveled

½ cup rice flour, spooned in and leveled

½ cup strained Dutch-processed cocoa powder, spooned in and leveled

¼ teaspoon salt

1 cup (2 sticks) unsalted butter, slightly softened

⅔ cup superfine sugar

1 teaspoon pure vanilla extract

1 tablespoon sparkling white sugar (available in The Baker's Catalogue; see page 403)

GARNISH   4 ounces fine-quality bittersweet or semisweet chocolate, such as Lindt Bittersweet, melted (see page 392)

1 teaspoon vegetable or canola oil

1. Position the shelf in the center of the oven. Heat the oven to 300°. Cut a 15-inch square of heavy-duty aluminum foil. Invert the pan and center the foil over the pan, pressing it across the bottom and down the sides. Remove the foil, turn the pan right side up, and place the foil shell in the pan, shaping it smoothly across the bottom and snugly against the sides.

2. Strain the flour, rice flour, cocoa, and salt together three times. Set aside.

3. Place the butter in the bowl of an electric mixer fitted with the paddle attachment and mix on medium-low speed until smooth and creamy, about 1 minute. Add the sugar gradually, taking about 1 minute, then mix for 1 minute longer, scraping the side of the bowl as needed. Add the vanilla and mix to combine.

4. Remove the bowl from the machine and transfer the mixture to a large, wide bowl for ease of mixing. Using a wooden spoon, cut half of the dry ingredients into the butter mixture until it is almost incorporated. Work in the remaining dry ingredients by hand, adding in five or six additions. All of the flour does not have to be incorporated after each addition. Gently knead the mixture just until a smooth dough is formed. Be careful not to overwork the dough, as this will result in a tough cookie.

5. Press the dough evenly into the pan, using a bâtarde or flat-bottomed glass wrapped in plastic. Be sure the dough is pushed into the corners. Test for evenness by inserting a toothpick or the point of a knife randomly into the dough. Clean the sides of the pan by inserting the flat side of a dough scraper, small metal spatula, or plastic pastry corne in between the dough and the sides of the pan.

6. Bake for 50 to 55 minutes, or until set on top. Take out and let rest for 5 minutes. Using a dough scraper, cut straight down through the dough at about 1-inch intervals, making eight strips. Give the pan a quarter-turn and cut four more strips at 2-inch intervals. Sprinkle with the sparkling white sugar. Return to the oven and bake for another 10 minutes.

7. Remove from the oven and let rest for 10 minutes. Have a cookie sheet without sides ready. Using the foil as an aid, lift the shortbread from the pan and place it on the cookie sheet. Pull the aluminum foil so it releases from the sides of the shortbread, wrapping the larger sides of the foil under the pan to prevent it from sliding. Wrap loose edges of the foil around the sides of the cookie sheet, smoothing the foil as best you can. Cut through the shortbread again, and using a spatula, spread them slightly apart. Return to the oven for 10 more minutes to crisp and dry the cookies. Remove from the oven and let cool for 5 to 10 minutes before transferring to a cooling rack.

GARNISH THE SHORTBREAD

8. Stir together the melted chocolate and vegetable oil. While the cookies are still tepid, dip each cookie into the chocolate mixture to a depth of ¾ inch. Place on a cooling rack and allow to stand until the chocolate sets.

STORAGE: Store in an airtight container, layered between strips of wax paper, for up to 3 weeks. These cookies may be frozen.

Cookie Characteristics

Versatile

Long shelf life

Temperature sensitive

lemon poppy seed shortbread

MAKES 25 1¾-INCH SQUARES

This pretty shortbread cookie is flecked with poppy seeds and generously flavored with grated lemon zest, along with the addition of lemon oil. The top has a filigree of white chocolate, giving the cookie a more elegant finish.

AT A GLANCE **PAN:** 9-inch square baking pan and cookie sheet

PAN PREP: Heavy-duty aluminum foil

OVEN TEMP: 300°

BAKING TIME: 50–55 minutes, baking; 10 minutes, crisping

DIFFICULTY: ◐◐

1¾ cups all-purpose flour, spooned in and leveled

½ cup rice flour, spooned in and leveled

¼ teaspoon salt

3 tablespoons poppy seeds

1 cup (2 sticks) unsalted butter, slightly softened

2 tablespoons freshly grated lemon zest

½ teaspoon lemon oil (see page 376)

½ cup superfine sugar

GARNISH 2 ounces fine-quality white chocolate, such as Lindt Classic Swiss White, melted (see page 393)

1. Position the shelf in the center of the oven. Heat the oven to 300°. Cut a 15-inch square of heavy-duty aluminum foil. Invert the pan and center the foil over the pan, pressing it across the bottom and down the sides. Remove the foil, turn the pan right side up, and place the foil shell in the pan, shaping it smoothly across the bottom and snugly against the sides.

2. Strain the flour, rice flour, and salt together three times. Stir in the poppy seeds and set aside.

3. Place the butter in the bowl of an electric mixer fitted with the paddle attachment. Mix on medium-low speed until smooth and creamy. Add the lemon zest and lemon oil and mix for 1 minute. Add the sugar gradually, then mix for 1 minute longer, scraping the bowl as needed.

4. Remove the bowl from the machine, and transfer the mixture to a large, wide bowl. Using a wooden spoon, cut half of the dry ingredients into the butter mixture until almost incorporated. Work in the remaining flour by hand, adding it in 5 or 6 additions. Gently knead the mixture just until a smooth dough is formed. Be careful not to overwork the dough, as this will result in a tough cookie.

5. Press the dough evenly into the pan, using a bâtarde or flat-bottomed glass wrapped in plastic to spread it. Be sure the dough is pushed into the corners. Test for evenness by inserting a toothpick or the point of a knife randomly into the dough. Clean the edges of the pan by inserting a dough scraper, a small spatula, or a plastic pastry corne in between the dough and the sides of the pan.

cookie closest to you, and using the paper toweling as an aid, tightly roll the cookie around the chopstick, pressing the edge to seal. Repeat with the remaining three cookies. You must work quickly because, as the cookies cool, they become hard to roll. If so, return them to the oven for a few seconds to soften. Place the rolled cookies on a cooling rack. They will crisp as they cool.

5. Repeat with the remaining batter. It is not necessary to rebutter the pan each time. If desired, the batter may be refrigerated for up to 5 days and the cookies baked as needed.

STORAGE: Store in an airtight container, layered between strips of wax paper, for up to 3 weeks. These cookies may be frozen.

Cookie
Characteristics

Festive

Long shelf life

Fragile

sand tarts

MAKES ABOUT 12 DOZEN 2-INCH COOKIES

Sand Tarts are crisp, not-too-rich Danish butter cookies that are glazed with egg white, sprinkled with finely chopped almonds, and then dusted with sparkling white sugar. The hallmark of the cookies is that they are made from a somewhat dry dough that is rolled wafer-thin.

Thanks to my friend Marcia Germanow for this recipe, which came, she said, from Paula Marshall of Boxford, Massachusetts.

AT A GLANCE

PAN: Cookie sheets

PAN PREP: Ungreased

EQUIPMENT: 2-inch scalloped cookie cutter

OVEN TEMP: 400°

CHILLING TIME: 1 hour

BAKING TIME: 8 minutes

DIFFICULTY: ○

3 cups all-purpose flour, spooned in and leveled

1 teaspoon salt

¾ cup (1½ sticks) unsalted butter, slightly firm, cut into 1-inch pieces

1¼ cups superfine sugar

1 large egg

1 large egg yolk

1 teaspoon pure vanilla extract

1 large egg white, lightly beaten with 2 teaspoons water

½ cup finely chopped toasted sliced almonds

Sparkling white sugar, for sprinkling (available in The Baker's Catalogue; see page 403)

MAKE THE DOUGH

1. Whisk together the flour and the salt. Set aside.

2. In the bowl of an electric mixer fitted with the paddle attachment, beat the butter on medium speed until smooth and creamy. Gradually add the sugar, taking about 2 minutes, beating until well blended. Add the egg and the egg yolk, and beat for 1 minute longer, then blend in the vanilla extract.

3. Reduce the mixer speed to low and add the dry ingredients in three addi-

with a few of the finely chopped nuts and sparkling white sugar.

6. Bake the cookies for about 8 minutes, or until the edges are very lightly browned. Watch carefully—the cookies brown quickly! To ensure even browning, toward the end of baking time rotate the pans top to bottom and front to back. Remove from the oven and let rest on the cookie sheet for 1 minute before loosening with a thin metal spatula. Transfer to cooling racks.

STORAGE: Store in an airtight container, layered between strips of wax paper, for up to 3 weeks. These cookies may be frozen.

tions, mixing until the flour is blended in and all of the crumbly pieces on the bottom of the bowl are incorporated. Remove the dough from the bowl and divide into three equal portions. Form into disks, cover each securely with plastic, and refrigerate for at least 1 hour or up to 3 days. (The dough may be frozen for up to 1 month.)

BAKE THE COOKIES

4. Position the shelves in the upper and lower thirds of the oven. Heat the oven to 400°.

5. Cover a flat surface or cutting board with a pastry cloth. Flour the cloth. Cover a rolling pin with a pastry sleeve and flour it also. Working with one portion of the cookie dough at a time, roll thinly, slightly less than ⅛ inch thick, and cut with a 2-inch scalloped cookie cutter or other desired shapes. (Note: To re-roll scraps of dough, gather the scraps together on a piece of plastic wrap. Lift the ends up and over the dough, twist them together, and form a ball of dough, then re-roll.) Brush the tops lightly with the egg wash and sprinkle the centers

Cookie
Characteristics

Versatile

Long shelf life

Travel well

"A good cook is like a sorceress who dispenses happiness."

—ELSA SCHIAPARELLI

krumkake

MAKES 2 DOZEN 5 ½-INCH CONES

Krumkake are wafer-thin cone-shaped cookies that are traditional Christmas fare in Norway. These Old World cookies are made in a special krumkake iron, similar to a waffle or pizzelle iron. The iron has decorative grids that leave an impression on the cookies when they are cooked. When the cookie is released from the iron, it is immediately rolled into a cone. They can be served plain, or if you choose to fill them, unlike sturdy sugar cones, which can handle the weight of ice cream, these feathery cookies are best filled with whipped cream when ready to serve.

Jeanne Greco, one of my testing team, shared her family recipe with me, along with her krumkake iron. Jeanne told me that when you pour the batter into the iron, directing it toward the back instead of the center of the grid will prevent it from spreading outside the iron. And indeed it worked!

It takes patience and a certain knack to make these special cookies. But I promise that when you do, whether for family or friends, they will queue up in anticipation of this special treat.

AT A GLANCE

PAN: Krumkake iron
PAN PREP: Lightly buttered
RESTING TIME: 1 hour
BAKING TIME: 2 minutes
DIFFICULTY: ❍❍❍

BATTER

1 cup all-purpose flour, spooned in and leveled
6 tablespoons cornstarch
1½ teaspoons ground cardamom, preferably freshly ground
1 cup eggs (about 4 or 5 large)
1 cup sugar
1 cup (2 sticks) unsalted butter, melted and cooled
1 teaspoon pure vanilla extract

3 tablespoons cold water, or more as needed
Clarified butter for greasing the iron (see page 387)

FILLING

Whipped cream (see page 356)
Candied violets (available from Maison Glass; see page 403)

MAKE THE BATTER

1. Strain together the flour, cornstarch, and cardamom. Set aside.

2. In the bowl of an electric mixer fitted with the whip attachment, beat the eggs on medium speed until frothy, then add the sugar in a steady stream and beat for 1 minute. Pour in the butter and vanilla, beating well to combine. Remove the bowl from the machine and stir in the flour mixture. Let the batter rest for 1 hour. (Note: This batter can be made up to 3 days ahead and refrigerated until ready to use.)

COOK THE KRUMKAKE

3. Prepare the Krumkake iron by heating it over medium-low heat until hot. Test the iron by sprinkling a few drops of water on it. The water should sizzle. Have ready 24 individual paper towels. Brush the iron very lightly with clarified butter, taking care to thoroughly butter the crevices of the design.

4. When ready to bake the Krumkake, stir in the 3 tablespoons of water. Using a 1-ounce (2-tablespoon) ladle, pour the batter onto the back portion of the iron, just above the center. (Alternatively, use measuring spoons to spoon 2 tablespoons of batter onto the iron.) Hold the iron closed for 10 seconds, then release the handles. *Take care not to squeeze the handles too tightly,* or the batter will ooze out of the iron.

5. Cook for 1 minute and 15 seconds on the first side. Flip the iron over and cook 45 seconds more. Flip the iron again and bake for another 10 seconds. Open the iron and, using a thin metal spatula, carefully remove the Krumkake onto a paper towel and let rest for 5 seconds. (The first one or two cookies will not come out well, but as the iron seasons, this will improve. After baking three or four cookies, it will no longer be necessary to butter the iron. If too much butter accumulates on the iron, wipe off excess with a paper towel.)

6. Without inverting the Krumkake, roll

it into a cone using a wooden cone-shaped dowel. Alternatively, use a single layer of paper towel to help roll the hot cookie into a cone shape. To do this, lift one corner of the paper towel and roll it toward the opposite corner. This will help to guide the rolling of the cookie. Note: The rolled cookies are very fragile. Handle them carefully.

FILL THE KRUMKAKE

7. Using an 18-inch pastry bag fitted with a #847 large star tube, pipe whipped cream into the cones and garnish each with a candied violet. Serve at once. (Note: One recipe of whipped cream should fill five to six cones, depending on how tightly they are curled.)

STORAGE: Store unfilled Krumkake in an airtight container for at least 1 week. These cookies may be frozen for up to 3 months.

Cookie Characteristics

Festive

Long shelf life

Fragile

janhagels

MAKES 4 DOZEN 4 X 1-INCH COOKIES

Janhagels, crisp Dutch cookies, are made with almond-scented dough that is spread thinly in a jelly-roll pan. The top of this delicate cookie is sprinkled generously with sliced blanched almonds, then showered with cinnamon and sugar.

This recipe was inspired by one shared with me by Leslie Sporn of Short Hills, New Jersey. Leslie's busy schedule does not allow her much time to play in the kitchen, but when she does, her time is put to good use. Since baking is her forte, I welcomed the addition of one of her recipes. While Leslie cuts her cookies into diamonds, they will taste just as good cut into rectangles or squares.

AT A GLANCE   **PAN:** 10½ × 15½ × 1-inch jelly roll pan
PAN PREP: Buttered
OVEN TEMP: 350°
BAKING TIME: 25 minutes
DIFFICULTY: ⚙

1 cup (2 sticks) unsalted butter, slightly firm
½ cup plus 2 tablespoons granulated sugar, divided
½ cup lightly packed light brown sugar
1 large egg, separated
1 teaspoon pure vanilla extract
½ teaspoon pure almond extract
2 cups all-purpose flour, spooned in and leveled
1 cup sliced blanched almonds
½ teaspoon ground cinnamon

1. Position the shelf in the center of the oven. Heat the oven to 350°. Generously butter the jelly roll pan.
2. In the large bowl of an electric mixer fitted with the paddle attachment, mix the butter on medium-low speed until it is creamy and lightened in color. Add ½ cup of the granulated sugar along with the light brown sugar, and mix for 1 minute, then mix in the egg yolk and the extracts.
3. Remove the bowl from the mixer. Using a wooden spoon or oversized rubber spatula, work 1 cup of flour at a time into the dough, being careful not to overmix. Divide the dough into eight portions and place in the pan, pressing it as evenly as you can. Insert a dough scraper, small spatula, or the flat side of a plastic pastry corne between the dough and the sides of the pan to clean the edges.
4. In a small bowl, mix the egg white with a fork until frothy, then spread evenly over the dough. Sprinkle with the sliced almonds. Combine the remaining sugar with the cinnamon and sprinkle over the almonds. Bake for 25 minutes or until golden brown.

5. Remove from the oven and place on a cooling rack. Let stand for 10 minutes. While still warm, slice the cookies into eight lengthwise strips. Turn the pan (a quarter turn) and cut 12 strips on the diagonal to create diamond shapes. Remove the cookies from the pan using a thin metal spatula.

STORAGE: Store in an airtight container, layered between strips of wax paper, for up to 3 weeks. These cookies may be frozen.

Cookie
Characteristics

Versatile

Long shelf life

Travel well

10 Biscotti and Such

toasted pecan mandelbrot

MAKES ABOUT 4 DOZEN 4-INCH MANDELBROT

My students often ask me what cookie is my husband, Gene's, favorite. Without hesitation, I always reply, "Toasted Pecan Mandelbrot!" This recipe, which originated with Rita Hirsch, from Greensboro, North Carolina, has been in my repertoire for years. Because my husband liked them so much, his mother asked for the recipe.

Whenever we visited her, she always made the Mandelbrot. The only problem for me was that hers were better than mine! I repeatedly asked her, "Mom, what did you do differently with the recipe?" And she repeatedly said, "Nothing!" Years later, after she had passed away, I saw her recipe lying on the counter in my sister-in-law's kitchen. As my eyes glanced at it, the mystery was solved. Instead of the 1 teaspoon of baking powder that I used, Mom used 1 tablespoon! And what a difference that made! The cookie was lighter and crispier than the original. This was one mistake that we all benefited from!

AT A GLANCE

PAN: Jelly roll pans
PAN PREP: Buttered
OVEN TEMP: 350°, 325°
CHILLING TIME: 1 hour
BAKING TIME: 20 minutes, baking; 15–18 minutes, toasting
DIFFICULTY: ○

2½ cups *less* 2 tablespoons all-purpose flour, spooned in and leveled
1 tablespoon baking powder
3 large eggs
1 cup plus 2 teaspoons sugar, divided
2 teaspoons pure vanilla extract
½ cup canola or safflower oil
1 cup broken pecans, lightly toasted
½ teaspoon ground cinnamon

MAKE THE DOUGH

1. Strain together the flour and baking powder three times. Set aside.
2. In the large bowl of an electric mixer fitted with the whip attachment, beat the eggs on medium speed until lightened in color, about 2 minutes. Gradually add 1 cup of the sugar, taking about 2 minutes, then beat in the vanilla. Pour the oil down the side of the bowl and beat 30 seconds longer.
3. Reduce the mixer speed to low and add the dry ingredients in two additions, mixing only to combine. Using an oversize rubber spatula, fold in the pecans. Cover with plastic and refrigerate for 1 hour or longer.

BAKE THE DOUGH

4. Position the shelves in the upper and lower thirds of the oven. Heat the oven to 350°. Butter the jelly roll pans.

5. Spoon the chilled batter onto the prepared pans, forming three 16-inch logs. Using your hands, even the sides of the logs as best you can. If the mixture is too sticky, moisten your hands with a little water.

6. Combine the remaining 2 teaspoons sugar and the cinnamon and sprinkle *lightly* over the surface of the logs. (A sugar shaker is best for this; see page 398.) Bake for 20 minutes or until set on top and just beginning to brown. To ensure even browning, toward the end of baking time, rotate the pans top to bottom and front to back. Cool in the pans for 5 minutes.

TOAST THE SLICES

7. Reduce the oven temperature to 325°. Using a serrated knife, cut the logs on the diagonal into ½-inch-thick slices. Turn the pieces on their sides. Sprinkle the cut side *lightly* with cinnamon and sugar and toast for 8 to 10 minutes. Turn the Mandelbrot over and sprinkle the second side *lightly* with cinnamon and sugar and toast for 6 to 8 minutes

longer or until very crisp and the edges show signs of browning. To ensure even browning, rotate the pans top to bottom and front to back. Let cool in the pans.

STORAGE: Store in an airtight container, layered between strips of wax paper, for up to 3 weeks. These cookies may be frozen.

Cookie Characteristics

Versatile

Long shelf life

Travel well

chocolate chocolate chocolate biscotti

MAKES 6 DOZEN 3½-INCH BISCOTTI

Here is a recipe for Chocolate Biscotti from my former assistant, Judie Levenberg. Judie, an excellent baker, was the owner of Bake My Day, and much to her clients' delight, one of her specialties was biscotti. Her father recently told me that his favorite cookie of Judie's was Chocolate Chocolate Chocolate Biscotti. I asked him if he would give me the recipe, and when he did, there was a certain familiarity to it. Eventually, I came to discover that Judie adapted it from a recipe by Nick Malgieri, who in turn had adapted it from my recipe for Toasted Pecan Mandelbrot (page 308)! The old adage, "What goes around, comes around," certainly did come true!

Nibbling on these rich, chocolaty bars brought back many happy memories of the hours Judie and I spent baking together. Once you try them, I know they will create wonderful memories for you, also.

AT A GLANCE

PAN: Jelly roll pans
PAN PREP: Baking parchment
OVEN TEMP: 350°, 325°
BAKING TIME: 20–25 minutes, baking; 20 minutes, toasting
DIFFICULTY: ✪

2 cups all-purpose flour, spooned in and leveled
⅓ cup strained Dutch-processed cocoa powder, spooned in and leveled
1 tablespoon baking powder
3 large eggs
Pinch of salt
1 cup sugar
1 teaspoon pure vanilla extract
½ cup (1 stick) unsalted butter, melted and cooled to tepid
1 cup coarsely chopped walnuts
1 (12-ounce) bag semisweet chocolate chips

CHOCOLATE GLAZE
⅓ cup water
⅓ cup light corn syrup
1 cup sugar
8 ounces fine-quality bittersweet or semisweet chocolate, such as Lindt Bittersweet, chopped

1. Position the shelves in the upper and lower thirds of the oven. Heat the oven to 350°. Lightly dab the corners of the jelly roll pans with butter and line them with baking parchment. Set aside.

2. Whisk together the flour, cocoa, and baking powder. Set aside.

3. In the bowl of an electric mixer fitted

slices. Place the slices on their sides in the pan and return to the oven for 12 minutes. Turn the slices over and bake for another 12 minutes, or until lightly browned. Remove from the oven and let cool on the pan.

STORAGE: Store in an airtight container, layered between strips of wax paper, for up to 3 weeks. These cookies may be frozen.

Secrets to Making Biscotti and Such

- If the dough sticks to your hands when shaping the loaves, you can either wet the palms of your hands with cold water, flour your palms, or rub them lightly with bland salad oil.
- When shaping biscotti loaves, it's okay if the sides are somewhat irregular.
- Before baking the biscotti loaves, the tops can be finished with sugar, nuts, or both.
- Sugar will adhere to biscotti dough, but an egg wash must be used to attach the nuts.
- Baking biscotti on buttered pans encourages browning when toasting.
- While necessary at times, pans lined with baking parchment are more awkward to use because the paper slides. Anchoring it with dabs of butter to hold it in place is helpful.
- Jelly roll pans or pans with rimmed sides are the easiest to use for toasting because the biscotti slices are less likely to fall off.
- Since biscotti and mandelbrot are twice-baked, do not overbake the logs during the first baking. They should show signs of light browning on the bottom and the top should be firm to the touch.
- If you like softer biscotti, you can either toast them on one side or reduce the toasting time. Or, instead of laying the pieces flat, keep the loaves intact with the slices slightly separated when re-baking.
- To give the cookies extra crunch, when the oven cools down to warm, return the biscotti and mandelbrot to the oven to crisp further.
- Biscotti should rest at least 10 minutes before slicing. Biscotti containing chunky pieces of nuts and/or fruit should rest longer.
- A serrated bread knife usually works best for smooth or less textured biscotti. Avoid moving the knife back and forth. Just cut down while drawing the knife toward you.
- Cut straight down with a dough scraper to slice coarse-textured, fruity biscotti that a knife would tear (for example, Jeweled Almond Biscotti or Shaved Chocolate and Pistachio Biscotti).
- Cutting biscotti on the diagonal will give larger slices; cutting straight across the loaves makes them smaller.
- Biscotti made without fat are usually hard, and therefore are best sliced in thin pieces, about ¼ inch.
- Biscotti made with fat will be more delicate and are best sliced in thicker pieces, about ⅜ to ½ inch.

tuscan almond anise biscotti

MAKES ABOUT 8 DOZEN 3½-INCH BISCOTTI

Distinctive Italian flavors—anise and almonds—combine with orange and lemon zests in this biscotti. Classic Italian biscotti do not have butter, making them especially crisp and perfect for dunking in an espresso or cappuccino.

AT A GLANCE

PAN: Jelly roll pans
PAN PREP: Moderately buttered
OVEN TEMP: 350°, 300°
BAKING TIME: 18–20 minutes, baking; 20 minutes, toasting
DIFFICULTY: ○

2½ cups all-purpose flour, spooned in and leveled
1 teaspoon baking powder
½ teaspoon salt
4 large eggs
2 teaspoons freshly grated orange zest
1 teaspoon freshly grated lemon zest
1 cup sugar
¾ teaspoon anise extract
¾ teaspoon almond extract
2 cups toasted sliced almonds

1. Position the shelves in the upper and lower thirds of the oven. Heat the oven to 350°. Butter the jelly roll pans.
2. Strain together the flour, baking powder, and salt. Set aside.
3. In the bowl of an electric mixer fitted with the whip attachment, beat the eggs and the zests on medium speed for 2 minutes. Slowly add the sugar and beat until thickened. Blend in the extracts.
4. Reduce the mixer speed to low and add the dry ingredients in two additions, mixing just until incorporated. Using an oversized rubber spatula, gently fold in the almonds.
5. Spoon the batter into the pans, making four logs measuring 12 inches long. With slightly moistened hands, smooth the logs as best you can. (The batter will be somewhat sticky.)
6. Bake for 18 to 20 minutes, or until set on top and lightly browned. To ensure even browning, toward the end of baking time rotate the sheets from top to bottom and front to back.
7. Remove from the oven and let rest on the pan for 10 to 15 minutes. Reduce the oven temperature to 300°. Using a serrated knife, cut each log into ⅜-inch-thick slices and lay them flat side down on the pan. Toast the biscotti for 10 minutes on each side, or until lightly golden.

STORAGE: Store in an airtight container, layered between strips of wax paper, for up to 3 weeks. These cookies may be frozen.

peppery almond anise biscotti

Add 1 to 1½ teaspoons freshly ground black pepper, medium-fine grind, to the flour in the Master Recipe.

Cookie Characteristics

Homestyle

Long shelf life

Travel well

chocolate marble biscotti

MAKES ABOUT 5 DOZEN 3-INCH BISCOTTI

The flavor combination of a vanilla dough temptingly swirled with chocolate has always had a big audience, and these biscotti provided the perfect vehicle for incorporating this popular duo into my book. To achieve the classic marbled effect, the chocolate must be added carefully so it does not blend through the dough. When you form the logs, it's all right to see some "wet" patches of chocolate!

AT A GLANCE

PAN: Cookie sheets
PAN PREP: Buttered baking parchment
OVEN TEMP: 350°, 300°
BAKING TIME: 20 minutes, baking;
18–20 minutes, toasting
DIFFICULTY: ○

2¾ cups all-purpose flour, spooned in and leveled
1 teaspoon baking powder
½ teaspoon salt
¾ cup (1½ sticks) unsalted butter, slightly firm
1 teaspoon freshly grated lemon zest
1 cup sugar
3 large eggs
1½ teaspoons pure vanilla extract
1 cup toasted walnuts, coarsely chopped
3 ounces fine-quality bittersweet or semisweet chocolate, such as Lindt Bittersweet, melted (see page 392)

1. Position the shelves in the upper and lower thirds of the oven. Heat the oven to 350°. Dab the corners of the cookie sheets lightly with butter. Line the cookie sheets with baking parchment and lightly butter the baking parchment.

2. Strain together the flour, baking powder, and salt. Set aside.

3. In the bowl of an electric mixer fitted with the paddle attachment, mix the butter with the lemon zest on medium speed until smooth and lightened in color, about 1 minute.

4. Add the sugar in a steady stream, then beat for 2 minutes longer. Beat in the eggs one at a time, scraping down the side of the bowl as needed. Add the vanilla and beat again.

5. Reduce the mixer speed to low and mix in the flour in two additions, mixing only to combine. Remove the bowl from the machine, and using an oversize rubber spatula, stir in the walnuts.

6. Divide the dough into 2 large mixing bowls. Working one bowl at a time, drizzle spoonfuls of one-half of the slightly warm chocolate over the top, then cut through the dough with a spatula. *Do not stir in the chocolate or overwork the dough.* Scoop the dough onto the first cookie sheet, forming two logs about 12 inches long and 2 inches wide. It's okay if streaks of melted chocolate are visible in the batter. It will dry after bak-

ing. Repeat with the remaining dough and melted chocolate, forming a total of four logs.

7. Bake for 20 minutes, or until the bottom of each loaf is lightly browned. To ensure even browning, toward the end of baking time rotate the sheets top to bottom and front to back.

8. Remove from the oven and reduce the oven temperature to 300°. Let the loaves rest on the cookie sheets for at least 15 minutes, then cut into ½-inch-thick slices with a serrated knife. Lay the slices flat side down on the cookie sheets and return to the oven for 10 minutes, then turn the slices over and bake for another 8 minutes or until the edges are lightly browned. Transfer to cooling racks.

STORAGE: Store in an airtight container, layered between strips of wax paper, for up to 3 weeks. These cookies may be frozen.

Cookie Characteristics

Versatile

Long shelf life

Travel well

Chocolate Marble Biscotti

Glazed Lemon–Pine Nut Biscotti

Cinnamon Toasts

Tuscan Almond Anise Biscotti

shaved chocolate and pistachio biscotti

MAKES 5 DOZEN 4-INCH BISCOTTI

Pistachio and chocolate is a flavor combination that was a favorite of my mother's, and I fell for its charm, too. These special biscotti are made with lots of toasted green pistachios and streaks of shaved chocolate. The dough is highlighted with the tang of orange and lemon zests. These are habit forming!

AT A GLANCE **PAN:** Jelly roll pans

PAN PREP: Buttered

OVEN TEMP: 350°, 300°

CHILLING TIME: 1 hour

BAKING TIME: 25 minutes, baking; 22–25 minutes, toasting

DIFFICULTY: ○

2½ cups all-purpose flour, spooned in and leveled

1 teaspoon baking powder

¼ teaspoon baking soda

½ teaspoon salt

¾ cup (1½ sticks) unsalted butter, slightly firm

2 teaspoons freshly grated navel orange zest

2 teaspoons freshly grated lemon zest

1 cup plus 1 tablespoon sugar, divided

2 large eggs

1 teaspoon pure vanilla extract

1 cup plus 2 tablespoons (about 5 ounces) coarsely chopped unsalted, unskinned, toasted pistachios, divided

1 (3.5-ounce) bar Lindt Bittersweet chocolate, shaved (about ¾ cup) (see "Shaving and Slivering Chocolate," page 393)

1 large egg, beaten with 2 teaspoons water

MAKE THE DOUGH

1. Strain the flour, baking powder, baking soda, and salt together three times. Set aside.

2. In the bowl of an electric mixer fitted with the paddle attachment, mix the butter with the zests on medium-high speed until smooth, about 1 minute. Slowly add 1 cup of sugar and beat for 1 minute longer.

3. Add the eggs one at a time, then beat again for 1 minute more, scraping down the bowl as needed. Beat in the vanilla. Reduce the mixer speed to low and add the dry ingredients in three additions, mixing *just* until combined.

4. Remove the bowl from the machine and, using a large rubber spatula, fold in 1 cup of the pistachios and the shaved chocolate. Cover the bowl with plastic wrap and chill for 1 hour.

BAKE THE COOKIES

5. Position the shelves in the upper and lower thirds of the oven. Heat the oven to 350°. Butter the jelly roll pans and set aside.

6. Divide the dough into thirds, and on a lightly floured surface, roll each piece into a 14-inch log and place on the pans.

Brush each log with the egg wash, then
sprinkle the tops with the remaining
pistachios and the tablespoon of sugar.
7. Bake the logs for 25 minutes or until
just lightly browned. To ensure even
browning, toward the end of baking time
rotate the pans from top to bottom and
front to back. Remove from the oven
and let rest on the pan for 5 minutes.
8. Reduce the oven temperature to 300°.
Using a dough scraper, cut the logs into
½-inch-thick slices. Lay the slices on

their sides and return to the oven for
15 minutes, or until they just start to
brown. Remove from the oven, turn the
slices over, and bake for another 7 to 10
minutes. Let rest on the pan for 5 minutes before transferring to cooling racks.

STORAGE: Store in an airtight container,
layered between strips of wax paper, for
up to 3 weeks. These cookies may be
frozen.

cinnamon toasts

MAKES ABOUT 40 3-INCH TOASTS

Here is a recipe for a simple yet very satisfying treat. These little, cinnamon-scented biscotti are the perfect complement to your morning cup of coffee, late-afternoon cup of tea, or after-dinner espresso. As my daughter-in-law, Marla, munched on these, she said, "They are real comfort food."

Instead of baking the loaves free-form, I use disposable foil loaf pans, available in the bakeware section of most supermarkets. The pans give the cookies a uniform look, replicating the shape of a loaf of bread. A sugar shaker is the perfect tool to distribute the cinnamon sugar evenly over the cookies.

AT A GLANCE

PAN: Two 4½ × 8½-inch disposable aluminum foil loaf pans, baking; cookie sheet, toasting

PAN PREP: Buttered

OVEN TEMP: 350°, 300°

BAKING TIME: 22–25 minutes, baking; 28–30 minutes, toasting

DIFFICULTY: ✪

½ cup (1 stick) unsalted butter
1½ cups all-purpose flour, spooned in and leveled
½ teaspoon baking powder
¼ teaspoon baking soda
¼ teaspoon salt
4 teaspoons ground cinnamon, divided
2 large eggs
½ cup plus 2 tablespoons sugar, divided
1 teaspoon pure vanilla extract

1. Position the shelf in the middle of the oven. Heat the oven to 350°. Butter the loaf pans and the cookie sheet and set aside.

2. Place the butter in a small, heavy-bottomed saucepan over low heat. Using a large spoon, skim the white foam that rises to the surface and discard. Continue to cook the butter, skimming any additional foam that rises, until the butter begins to deepen in color and turns a rich, golden color. This can take up to 15 to 20 minutes. Let stand 5 minutes. Pass through a fine-mesh strainer, discarding any sediment that forms on the bottom of the saucepan. You should have about 6 tablespoons of butter.

3. Strain together the flour, baking powder, baking soda, salt, and 2 teaspoons of the cinnamon. Set aside.

4. In the bowl of an electric mixer fitted with the whip attachment, beat the eggs for 1 minute on medium speed until lightened in color. Add ½ cup of the sugar in a steady stream, beating until thickened, about 1 minute. Scrape down the side of the bowl. Drizzle in the *tepid* nut butter, beat for about 1 minute, then beat in the vanilla.

5. Reduce the mixer speed to low and add the dry ingredients all at once, mixing only to combine.

6. Divide the batter into the loaf pans and smooth the tops. Stir together the remaining 2 teaspoons of cinnamon and 2 tablespoons of sugar and sprinkle evenly over the loaves. A sugar shaker is best to use. Bake the loaves for 22 to 25 minutes, or until lightly browned and firm to the touch. Remove from the oven and let cool for at least 15 minutes.

7. Reduce the oven temperature to 300°. Remove the loaves from the pans and, working one loaf at a time, cut ¼-inch slices with a serrated knife. Lay the slices flat side down on the cookie sheet. Sprinkle lightly with half of the cinnamon–sugar mixture and toast in the oven for 15 minutes. Turn the slices over, sprinkle again with the cinnamon sugar, and bake for another 13 to 15 minutes, or until the edges are just beginning to brown. Remove from the oven and let cool.

STORAGE: Store in an airtight container, layered between strips of wax paper, for up to 3 weeks. These cookies may be frozen.

Cookie Characteristics

Homestyle

Long shelf life

Travel well

"In the childhood memories of every good cook, there's a large kitchen, a warm stove, a simmering pot and a mom." —BARBARA COSTIKYAN

cardamom cornmeal biscotti

MAKES 10 DOZEN 3½-INCH BISCOTTI

My assistant, Kathie Finn Redden, and I share a passion for find-ing new restaurants. One day, she arrived and proudly produced a small, napkin-wrapped package. "Wait until you taste these!" she said. Unwrapping the parcel, I found two golden biscotti, flecked with jewel-like pieces of raisin. I took one small bite, followed by another, then another. "Where did you get these?!" I exclaimed. Kathie told me that her husband, Michael, had discovered a new restaurant in Manhattan's theatre district (called, appropriately, District). Having dined there the previous evening, Kathie dili-gently pilfered her husband's biscotti and brought them for me to sample.

I telephoned the chef, Sam DeMarco, and he graciously shared the recipe with me. These crispy, not-too-sweet biscotti flavored with cardamom are the perfect accompaniment to gelato or sorbets, or fresh fruit. My applause to District—these are showstoppers!

AT A GLANCE

PAN: Jelly roll pans
PAN PREP: Baking parchment
OVEN TEMP: 350°, 250°
CHILLING TIME: 2 hours
BAKING TIME: 15–20 minutes, baking; 10–12 minutes, toasting
DIFFICULTY: ◐

1½ cups all-purpose flour, spooned in and leveled
½ cup stone-ground cornmeal, spooned in and leveled
1 tablespoon ground cardamom, preferably freshly ground
2 teaspoons baking powder
½ cup golden raisins
½ cup (1 stick) unsalted butter, slightly firm
¾ cup sugar

2 large eggs
1 cup finely ground toasted slivered almonds

MAKE THE DOUGH

1. Stir together the flour, cornmeal, car-damom, and baking powder. Set aside.

2. Place the raisins on a cutting board. Using a chef's knife dipped in very hot water and then dried, cut into ¼-inch dice. Set aside.

3. In the bowl of an electric mixer fitted with the paddle attachment, beat the butter and sugar on medium speed until smooth and lightened, about 2 minutes. Add the eggs one at a time, then beat for 1 minute more.

4. Reduce the mixer speed to low and blend in the flour mixture, then the

BAKE THE BISCOTTI

5. Position the shelf in the middle of the oven. Heat the oven to 350°. Butter the jelly roll pan.

6. Divide the dough in half. Place one piece on a lightly floured surface and shape into a log that is 16 inches long and 2 inches wide. Place the log off center on the pan and repeat with the remaining dough. Bake the logs for 22 to 25 minutes, or until lightly browned on the bottom and firm to the touch. Remove from the oven and let rest for 5 to 10 minutes.

7. Reduce the oven to 300°. Using a dough scraper, slice each log on the diagonal into ½-inch-thick slices. Turn the slices on their sides and bake for 10 minutes, then turn the slices over and bake for another 7 minutes or until lightly browned on the edges. Remove from the oven and let cool on the pan.

STORAGE: Store in an airtight container, layered between strips of wax paper, for up to 3 weeks. These cookies may be frozen.

Cookie Characteristics

Homestyle

Long shelf life

Travel well

"As for Rosemary, I let it run all over my garden walls . . . because it is the herb sacred to remembrance and to friendship."

—SIR THOMAS MORE

11 Meringues and Macaroons

meringue kisses

MAKES 3 DOZEN 1½-INCH COOKIES

While developing recipes for a Christmas cookie class that I was teaching, I thought that a low-fat cookie would be especially welcome during the holidays. These meringue cookies are made with toasted pecans and fine-flaked unsweetened coconut. Some of the snowy cookies I garnish with colorful red glacé cherries, and others I give a dusting of cocoa powder.

Do make these with desiccated coconut, which can be found in specialty food stores and health food stores. This unsweetened coconut is the perfect foil for the sweetness of the meringue. These Meringue Kisses continue to be a favorite among my students, family, and friends.

AT A GLANCE

PAN: Cookie sheets

PAN PREP: Heavy-duty aluminum foil

OVEN TEMP: 250°

BAKING TIME: 50–60 minutes

DRYING TIME: 15 minutes

DIFFICULTY: ◗

THE COOKIES

1 cup broken pecans, lightly toasted

3 tablespoons unsweetened, flaked coconut

⅓ cup plus 2 tablespoons superfine sugar, divided

2 large egg whites, at room temperature

Pinch of salt

¼ teaspoon fresh lemon juice

½ teaspoon pure vanilla extract

THE GARNISH

About 9 glacé cherries, halved (optional)

½ teaspoon unsweetened cocoa powder, for dusting

1. Position the shelves in the upper and lower thirds of the oven. Heat the oven to 250°. Line the cookie sheets with heavy-duty aluminum foil.

2. Combine the pecans, coconut, and 2 tablespoons of the sugar. Set aside.

3. In the bowl on an electric mixer fitted with the whisk attachment, beat the egg whites on medium speed until frothy. Add the salt and the lemon juice. Increase the speed to medium-high and beat until firm peaks form. Add the remaining ⅓ cup of sugar, 1 teaspoon at a time, taking about 2 minutes, then add the vanilla.

4. Remove the bowl from the mixer and gently fold the pecan–coconut mixture into the meringue. Drop the batter from the tip of a teaspoon onto the cookie sheets. Press a candied cherry half into the tops of *half* of the meringues.

5. Bake the meringues for 50 to 60 minutes, or until they can be lifted off the foil without sticking. To ensure even baking, rotate the sheets from top to bottom and front to back toward the end of baking time. (Note: The longer the meringues bake, the better.) Let the meringues stand in the turned-off oven to dry for 15 minutes. Transfer to cooling racks.

6. When the meringues are completely cool, lightly dust the tops of the plain meringues with cocoa, sifting it through a very fine strainer.

STORAGE: Store the meringues in a container with a loose-fitting lid for up to 2 weeks, layered between strips of wax paper.

Cookie
Characteristics

Versatile

Long shelf life

Travel well

Secrets for Making Meringues and Macaroons

- To ensure that meringue cookies will have a good shape after baking, do not start beating the whites on high speed. Start on medium speed and gradually increase the speed. When egg whites and sugar are heated over a water bath before beating, it's okay to start beating the mixture on a higher speed.

- To form a strong, shiny meringue, add the sugar to the beaten egg whites when the whites have formed straight, firm peaks.

- Be sure to use a fine-grained sugar and sugar that is free of lumps.

- Most meringue batters can be piped through a pastry bag fitted with a 1/2-inch tip unless they contain ingredients that are coarsely chopped.

- An alternative to shaping meringue cookies with a pastry bag is to pinch the tops with your fingertips.

- Meringue batters perform best if they are baked soon after they are prepared.

- In most instances, meringue cookies are at their best when baked in a low oven.

- If meringue cookies are finished baking, they will release from the cookie sheets. If they show resistance, they are not ready.

- In damp or humid weather, meringues frequently need to bake longer than the specified time.

- When making macaroons with almond paste, for the best results the paste should always be soft.

- Overmixing macaroon batters will cause the cookies to deflate during baking.

- If piping macaroon batter with a pastry bag, don't overfill the bag because macaroon batters are dense and somewhat difficult to pipe.

- Air-drying macaroons before baking will often improve their shape.

walnut orange meringue mounds

MAKES ABOUT 5 DOZEN 1¾-INCH COOKIES

Knowing my passion for nuts, you can imagine my delight when my cousin Nancy Schwartz asked for my advice with her walnut meringue cookie recipe. While Nancy liked her recipe, she felt that it needed a bit more pizzazz, and when I saw the amount of walnuts in the recipe, I was more than happy to oblige! A bit less sugar, some grated orange zest, and violà! An ordinary little meringue is transformed into a walnut-filled Cinderella of a cookie!

PAN: Cookie sheets

PAN PREP: Baking parchment

OVEN TEMP: 225°

BAKING TIME: 30 minutes

DRYING TIME: 20 minutes

DIFFICULTY: ◔

4 large egg whites, at room temperature

2½ cups strained confectioners' sugar, spooned in and leveled

1½ teaspoons pure vanilla extract

4 teaspoons white vinegar

1½ teaspoons freshly grated navel orange zest

3½ cups (about 11 ounces) broken walnuts

Cookie
Characteristics

Versatile

Long shelf life

Fragile

1. Position the shelves in the lower and upper thirds of the oven. Heat the oven to 225°. Dab the corners of the cookie sheets lightly with butter and line them with baking parchment.

2. Place the egg whites and sugar in the bowl of an electric mixer and stir by hand with a whisk. Place the bowl over a saucepan filled with about 1 inch of simmering water. Whisk lightly for about 2 minutes, or until the mixture reaches a temperature of 115 to 120 degrees. Note: The sugar will form lumps at first, but it will smooth out as the mixture warms.

3. Remove the bowl from the saucepan and dry the bottom. Using the whip attachment, beat the egg mixture on medium-high speed for 4 to 5 minutes, or until it cools and a thick meringue is formed. Reduce the speed to medium, then add the vanilla, vinegar, and orange zest and mix for 1 minute longer.

4. Remove the bowl from the machine and, using a large rubber spatula, fold in the walnut pieces.

5. Drop heaping teaspoons of the meringue onto the cookie sheets, spacing them about 1½ inches apart. (As the last of the batter is used, the nuts may become sparse; if so, you may want to mix in a few additional walnuts.)

6. Bake the meringues for 30 minutes, or until they feel set to the touch. To ensure even baking, rotate the sheets from top to bottom and front to back toward the end of baking time. They should *not* show signs of browning. Turn the oven off and leave the meringues in the oven for another 20 minutes to dry.

7. Remove from the oven and let cool on the cookie sheets.

STORAGE: Store in a container with a loose-fitting lid, layered between strips of wax paper, for up to 3 weeks. These cookies may be frozen.

"Love and eggs are best when they are fresh." —RUSSIAN PROVERB

chocolate meringue gondolas

MAKES 40 2½-INCH OVAL COOKIES

During one of the photography sessions for this book, I had assembled a group of these cookies on a platter. While they were waiting to have their picture taken, one of my assistants looked at them and exclaimed, "Look at those meringues! They look like a little armada!" Upon reflection, I realized that they did, indeed, resemble little oval boats and decided to incorporate that characteristic in their name. After much pondering, I turned to my husband, Gene, who came up with the perfect name.

The simple technique for shaping these oval chocolate-flecked meringues is similar to the one used for shaping quenelles, the classic French dumplings. The finished cookie is glazed with a Dark Chocolate Honey Glaze and garnished with chopped pistachios—a fitting addition to any captain's galley! Try to use unsalted pistachios, which are available in specialty food and health food stores. The lime-green color of these nuts is far more intense than that of the salted variety.

AT A GLANCE
PAN: Cookie sheets
PAN PREP: Baking parchment
OVEN TEMP: 275°
BAKING TIME: 50 minutes,
DRYING TIME: 15 minutes
DIFFICULTY: ◉

MERINGUES
2 ounces unsweetened chocolate, broken into pieces
4 large egg whites, at room temperature
⅛ teaspoon salt
1 cup superfine sugar, divided
½ teaspoon pure vanilla extract

DARK CHOCOLATE HONEY GLAZE
4 ounces fine-quality bittersweet or semisweet chocolate, such as Lindt Bittersweet, coarsely chopped
2 tablespoons half-and-half

1 tablespoon honey
2 teaspoons hot water
¾ teaspoon pure vanilla extract
¼ cup medium-chopped unsalted pistachios

MAKE THE MERINGUES

1. Position the shelves in the upper and lower thirds of the oven. Heat the oven to 275°. Lightly dab the corners of the cookie sheets with butter, then line with baking parchment.

2. Finely chop the chocolate in the work bowl of a food processor fitted with the steel blade.

3. Place the egg whites in the bowl of an electric mixer fitted with the whip attachment and beat on medium speed until frothy. Add the salt, increase the speed to medium-high, and beat to firm peaks. Add ⅔ cup of the sugar, 1 tablespoon at a time, taking about 1 minute. Add the vanilla and beat 1 minute longer to stiff peaks.

4. Remove the bowl from the mixer, and using a large rubber spatula, fold in the remaining ⅓ cup sugar in four additions, then fold in the chocolate.

5. Fill 1 tablespoon with meringue. Place a second tablespoon on top at a 90-degree angle and ease it down over the edge of the first tablespoon. Repeat the procedure on the second side. Then push the oval of meringue from the side of the spoon onto the cookie sheet. You should have an egg-shaped mound of meringue. Repeat with remaining meringue, spacing the cookies about 2 inches apart.

6. Bake about 50 minutes, or until firm and crisp. To ensure even baking, toward the end of baking time rotate the sheets top to bottom and front to back. Turn the oven off and let the meringues dry for 15 minutes. Remove from the oven and let stand 5 minutes. Using a thin metal spatula, carefully release the meringues from the parchment.

MAKE THE GLAZE

7. Place the chocolate and the half-and-half in a small, heavy-bottomed saucepan. Stir constantly over low heat until the chocolate is melted and blended with the half-and-half. Off the heat, stir in the honey and hot water to achieve a spreading consistency. Add the vanilla.

8. Apply the glaze to the meringues using the bottom of a tablespoon, spreading it on the raised areas of the cookies. Sprinkle each meringue with a scant ½ teaspoon of the pistachios. Let rest for at least 2 hours or until the glaze is set.

STORAGE: Store in a container with a loose-fitting lid, layered between strips of wax paper, for up to 3 weeks. These cookies may be frozen.

Cookie Characteristics

Versatile

Long shelf life

Fragile

Black Bottom Coconut Macaroons; Italian Macaroons; Golden Almond Amaretti

golden almond amaretti

In order for the finished cookie to have a chewy texture, it is important that the almonds be very finely ground (see Chopping Nuts in the Food Processor, page 390) and the cookies not be overbaked.

AT A GLANCE

PAN: Jelly roll pan

PAN PREP: Buttered baking parchment

OVEN TEMP: 375°

BAKING TIME: 10–11 minutes

DIFFICULTY: ○

COOKIES

2 cups sliced unblanched almonds
¾ cup sugar, divided
1½ teaspoons ground cinnamon
4 large egg yolks
½ teaspoon pure vanilla extract
½ teaspoon almond extract

GLAZE

2 large eggs
3 tablespoons Amaretto liqueur
1 cup sliced unblanched toasted
   almonds, crunched into small pieces
   with your hand
½ cup sugar

Cookie
Characteristics

Versatile

Long shelf life

Travel well

1. Position the shelves in the upper and lower thirds of the oven. Heat the oven to 375°. Dab the corners of the jelly roll pans lightly with butter and line with baking parchment. Lightly butter the parchment.

2. Place the almonds, ¼ cup of the sugar, and the cinnamon in the work bowl of a food processor fitted with the steel blade. Process until the mixture begins to clump together, 45 to 60 seconds.

3. In the bowl of an electric mixer fitted with the paddle attachment, beat the yolks on medium speed, then increase the speed to medium-high. Beat until thickened and lightened in color, 1½ to 2 minutes. Add the remaining ½ cup sugar, taking about 1 minute, then mix for another 30 seconds. Beat in the extracts.

4. Reduce the mixer speed to low and add the almond mixture in two additions.

5. For the glaze: place the eggs and the Amaretto in a low, flat dish, such as a pie plate, and whisk to blend. In another low, flat dish combine the crushed almonds and the sugar.

6. Shape the dough into 1-inch balls. Roll each ball in the egg mixture, then in the almond-sugar mixture. Repeat the dipping procedure before placing the balls on the pans.

7. Bake the cookies for 10 to 11 minutes, or *just* until the bottoms are lightly browned. To ensure even browning, toward the end of baking time, rotate the sheets from top to bottom and front to back. *Do not overbake.* Let rest on the pan for 4 to 5 minutes, then remove to cooling racks.

STORAGE: Store in an airtight container, layered between strips of wax paper, for up to 3 weeks. These cookies may be frozen.

midnight macaroons

Lots of coconut, blended with cocoa powder and espresso, are the flavors of this deep chocolate, chewy macaroon. A whole toasted almond sets off the center along with a webbing of melted chocolate.

AT A GLANCE   **PAN:** Cookie sheets

PAN PREP: Buttered baking parchment

OVEN TEMP: 300°

BAKING TIME: 18–20 minutes

DIFFICULTY: ○

1 cup blanched slivered almonds

⅔ cup plus 2 teaspoons superfine sugar, divided

3 cups sweetened, flaked coconut

¼ cup strained, Dutch-processed cocoa powder, spooned in and leveled

2 tablespoons cornstarch

4 large egg whites, at room temperature

¼ teaspoon salt

2 cups strained confectioners' sugar, spooned in and leveled

2 teaspoons instant espresso powder, dissolved in 1 teaspoon boiling water

2 teaspoons pure vanilla extract

4 ounces unsweetened chocolate, melted and cooled to tepid (see page 392)

48 toasted whole blanched almonds

GARNISH   2 ounces fine-quality bittersweet or semisweet chocolate, such as Lindt Bittersweet Chocolate, broken into pieces

½ teaspoon vegetable oil

1. Position the shelves in the upper and lower thirds of the oven. Heat the oven to 300°. Dab the corners of the cookie sheets with butter and line with baking parchment. Butter the baking parchment. Set aside.

2. Place the almonds and 2 teaspoons of the superfine sugar in the work bowl of a food processor fitted with the steel blade. Pulse 5 to 6 times, then process until fine crumbs form, about 15 seconds. Empty into a bowl. Then place the remaining superfine sugar, coconut, cocoa powder, and cornstarch in the processor bowl, pulse three times to blend, then process 12 to 15 seconds, or until the coconut is finely chopped but still retains some texture. Empty into a second bowl.

3. In the bowl of an electric mixer fitted with the whip attachment, beat the egg whites on medium speed until frothy. Add the salt and beat until soft peaks *barely* begin to form. Add the confectioners' sugar, then scrape the sides of the bowl with a rubber spatula. Stir together the espresso liquid and the vanilla and add to the egg white mixture, then beat for 1 minute longer.

4. Reduce the mixer speed to low and mix in the *tepid* chocolate. Remove the bowl from the machine, and using a large spatula, fold in the ground almonds. Then fold in the coconut mixture in two additions, folding *just* until blended.

5. Drop the batter by teaspoonfuls onto the cookie sheets, making 1½-inch mounds and spacing them about 2 inches apart. Alternatively, working with half of the batter at a time, spoon it onto a piece of plastic wrap. (See Techniques, Using a Pastry Bag, page 398.) Wrap the batter in the plastic and insert it into a large (18-inch) pastry bag. You do not need a pastry tube. Pipe 1½-inch mounds onto the cookie sheets, spacing them about 2 inches apart.

6. Press a whole almond in the center of each macaroon. Bake for 18 to 20 minutes, or until the cookies are just set. Do not overbake. To ensure even baking, rotate the sheets from top to bottom and front to back toward the end of baking time.

MAKE THE GARNISH

7. Place the chocolate in a small bowl and set it over simmering water. When the chocolate has melted, stir in the vegetable oil.

8. While the cookies are still warm, dip a fork in the chocolate and wave the tines back and forth over the cookies to create stripes. When the cookies are cool, transfer to cooling racks.

STORAGE: Store in an airtight container, layered between strips of wax paper, for up to 5 days. These cookies may be frozen.

Cookie Characteristics

Versatile

Moderate shelf life

Temperature sensitive

"The greatest tragedies were written by the Greeks and by Shakespeare. Neither knew chocolate. (The Swiss are known for nonviolence. They are also known for superb chocolate.)" —SANDRA BOYNTON, *CHOCOLATE: THE CONSUMING PASSION*

black bottom coconut macaroons

MAKES ABOUT 40 1¾-INCH CONE-SHAPED COOKIES

There is no doubt that this macaroon will bring back memories of a favorite chocolate-covered coconut candy bar. It is made with almond paste and coconut, two ingredients that are packed with flavor. To give the cookie its eye-catching cone shape, pipe the batter through a star-tipped pastry bag. After baking, the bottoms of the cookies are dipped into melted chocolate, creating a combination of flavors that I, for one, find impossible to resist!

AT A GLANCE

PAN: Cookie sheets

PAN PREP: Buttered baking parchment

OVEN TEMP: 325°

BAKING TIME: 20 minutes

DIFFICULTY: ☉

2 cups sweetened, flaked coconut

16 ounces almond paste, at room temperature

¾ cup granulated sugar

¾ cup strained confectioners' sugar, spooned in and leveled

¼ cup strained cake flour, spooned in and leveled

4 large egg whites, at room temperature

¼ teaspoon salt

½ teaspoon coconut extract

DIPPING CHOCOLATE

4 ounces fine-quality bittersweet or semisweet chocolate, such as Lindt Bittersweet Chocolate, broken into pieces

1 teaspoon vegetable oil

1. Position the shelf in the middle of the oven. Heat the oven to 325°. Dab the corners of the cookie sheets lightly with butter and line with baking parchment. Lightly butter the parchment.

2. Place the coconut in the work bowl of a food processor fitted with the steel blade. Process for 10 to 15 seconds, or until finely chopped. Set aside.

3. Break the almond paste into pieces and place in the bowl of an electric mixer fitted with the paddle attachment. Add the granulated and confectioners' sugars and mix on medium-low speed for 5 minutes, or until the almond paste is broken into tiny, meal-size pieces. Then mix in the flour.

4. Combine the egg whites and salt in a separate bowl and whisk lightly to break up the whites. With the machine on low speed, pour the whites into the almond paste mixture and mix just until blended, about 15 seconds.

5. Remove the bowl from the machine, and using a large rubber spatula, fold in the coconut and the extract. Let the batter stand for about 10 minutes. (The batter will firm up slightly.)

6. Place the batter in an 18-inch pastry bag fitted with a large #828 star tip, filling it one-third full. Twist the top of the bag to close, then, holding the bag almost straight up, pipe 1½-inch stars onto the cookie sheets, placing them about 1½ inches apart. Alternatively, with moistened hands, shape heaping teaspoonfuls of the batter into 1½-inch balls, then taper the balls into cones, Place them about 1½ inches apart on the cookie sheets.

7. Bake the macaroons one sheet at a time for 20 minutes, or *just* until the tops of the cones are golden and the bottoms of the cookies are lightly browned. Remove from the oven and let rest on the pan for 10 minutes.

MAKE THE DIPPING CHOCOLATE

8. Place the chocolate in a small bowl and set it over simmering water. When the chocolate has melted, stir the vegetable oil into the chocolate. While the cookies are still warm, dip the bottom of each into the chocolate to a depth of ¼ inch. Place the dipped cookies back on the cookie sheets and let dry for several hours. When the chocolate is set, the macaroons will release from the parchment.

STORAGE: Store in an airtight container, layered between strips of wax paper, for up to 3 days. These cookies may be frozen.

Cookie Characteristics

Versatile

Short shelf life

Temperature sensitive

"Probably one of the most private things in the world is an egg until it is broken."

—M. F. K. FISHER

chocolate-dipped pignoli crescents

MAKES 4 DOZEN 2¼-INCH COOKIES

Imagine indulging in a cookie packed with a gold mine of ingredients—that's what these Pignoli Crescents are all about! They are loaded with chewy almond paste, generously sprinkled with pine nuts, and finished with a dip in chocolate ganache. A platter of these on a dessert buffet does make quite a stunning statement. This is a cookie that—I am not embarrassed to say—I could indulge in every day. (Although, I must hasten to add, I do indulge in *small* portions . . . most of the time.)

AT A GLANCE

PAN: Cookie sheets
PAN PREP: Buttered baking parchment
OVEN TEMP: 300°
CHILLING TIME: 1 hour
BAKING TIME: 28–30 minutes
DIFFICULTY: ○○

16 ounces almond paste, at room temperature
¾ cup sifted confectioners' sugar, spooned in and leveled
¾ cup granulated sugar
¼ teaspoon salt
4 large egg whites, at room temperature
3 cups pine nuts
Granulated sugar, for sprinkling
1 recipe Ganache Glaze (page 360)

Cookie Characteristics

Versatile

Moderate shelf life

Temperature sensitive

MAKE THE DOUGH

1. In the bowl of an electric mixer fitted with the paddle attachment, combine the almond paste and sugars and mix on low speed for 6 to 8 minutes, or until the mixture forms meal-size crumbs.

2. Add the salt to the egg whites and whisk to blend. Add the egg whites to the almond paste mixture in four additions. Continue to mix until it starts to liquefy and stick to the bottom of the bowl. This will take about 15 to 20 seconds. Cover lightly with plastic wrap and chill for 1 hour.

BAKE THE COOKIES

3. Position the shelves in the upper and lower thirds of the oven. Heat the oven to 300°. Dab the corners of the cookie sheets lightly with butter and line with baking parchment. Butter the parchment.

4. Place the pine nuts in a shallow dish, such as a pie plate. Have ready a bowl of ice water. Remove the dough from the refrigerator and roll into 1¼-inch balls, moistening your palms with the ice water to keep the dough from sticking. Roll the balls in the pine nuts, pressing gently to adhere, then shape into crescents. Place about 2 inches apart on the cookie sheets. Sprinkle the crescents with additional granulated sugar.

5. Bake the cookies for about 28 minutes, or until lightly brown on the bottom. To ensure even baking, toward the end of baking time rotate the sheets from top to bottom and front to back.

Do not overbake; the centers should remain chewy. Remove from the oven and let rest for 10 minutes, then transfer to cooling racks.

6. When the cookies are cool enough to handle, dip the ends into the ganache and place on a cooling rack set over a sheet of wax paper. Let stand at least 1 hour or until the ganache sets.

STORAGE: Store in an airtight container, layered between strips of wax paper, for up to 5 days. These cookies may be frozen.

"Give me the luxuries of life and I will willingly do without the necessities."

—FRANK LLOYD WRIGHT

french chocolate
almond macaroons

MAKES ABOUT 30 1½-INCH SANDWICH COOKIES

When you are looking for that special recipe to remind you of those wonderful macaroons you savored all over France, look no further! This popular French cookie bears little resemblance to the classic macaroon that we are familiar with. It is crisp on the outside with a soft, chewy center. They are often made in a variety of flavors and sandwiched while still warm, the soft bottoms adhering to each other.

My chocolate macaroons are sandwiched with ganache. Whether you choose White Chocolate–Orange Ganache or Chocolate Ganache, these delectable little sandwiches will dazzle your guests. Do pay attention to the baking time—these cookies must not be overdone.

AT A GLANCE
PAN: Jelly roll pans
PAN PREP: Buttered baking parchment
AIR-DRYING: 20 to 30 minutes
OVEN TEMP: 325°
BAKING TIME: 10 minutes
DIFFICULTY: ❍❍❍

1 scant cup slivered, blanched almonds
    (about 4½ ounces)
2 cups strained confectioners' sugar,
    divided, spooned in and leveled
3 tablespoons strained Dutch-processed
    cocoa powder
3 large egg whites, at room temperature
⅛ teaspoon salt
½ recipe White Chocolate–Orange
    Ganache Filling (page 357), or
    ½ recipe Ganache Glaze (page 360)

1. Position the shelf in the middle of the oven. Heat the oven to 325°. Dab the cor-

ners of the jelly roll pans lightly with butter and line with baking parchment. Butter the parchment.

2. Place the almonds, 1 cup of the confectioners' sugar, and the cocoa in the work bowl of a food processor fitted with the steel blade. Pulse the mixture five or six times to combine, then process for 1 minute or until very powdery. Set aside.

3. In the bowl of an electric mixer fitted with the whip attachment, beat the egg whites on medium speed until frothy. Add the salt and beat until firm peaks form. Add the remaining 1 cup sugar, 1 tablespoon at a time, taking about 2 minutes, scraping down the bowl as needed, then beat 1 minute longer until stiff and shiny.

4. Remove the bowl from the machine. Place the nut mixture in a large-gauge strainer and sprinkle over the meringue in five or six additions, folding in with a large rubber spatula. Discard any remaining large pieces of nuts.

5. Empty the meringue into an 18-inch pastry bag fitted with a #805 or ½-inch piping tube. (For ease of filling, you can stabilize the bag by standing it in a tall jar or glass.) Fold the bag down over the jar, making a 4-inch cuff, and spoon the meringue into the bag. Twist the top of the bag to close, then pipe 1-inch dots onto the prepared cookie sheets. (Keep the mixer bowl handy in case the batter drips from the tip of the bag.

6. After the meringues are piped, smooth the tops with barely moistened fingertips, then air-dry for 20 to 30 minutes. Bake the cookies, one sheet at a time, for 10 minutes or *just until set*. Do not overbake or the cookies will crack. The tops of the cookies should be smooth.

7. Remove from the oven and let the cookies rest for 1 or 2 minutes, then gently lift up two corners of the parchment on each end of the pan. The cookies will release easily once the air flows under the parchment. Let cool.

8. Fit a 12-inch pastry bag with a #802 large round pastry tube. Empty the ganache into the pastry bag. Pipe a ½-inch dot, centered, onto the flat side of one of the cookies. Top with another cookie (choosing one of equal size) and press together, making a sandwich. Alternatively, spread a scant ½ teaspoon of ganache on the bottom half of each sandwich cookie.

STORAGE: Store in an airtight container, layered between strips of wax paper, for up to 5 days. These cookies may be frozen.

Cookie Characteristics

Festive

Moderate shelf life

Temperature sensitive

italian macaroons

MAKES 3 DOZEN 2-INCH COOKIES

Here is a recipe for the classic Italian macaroon. Rich almond paste provides the cookie with a luxurious texture and flavor, while the combination of confectioners' sugar and granulated sugar gives the cookie a wonderfully crisp-chewy texture. Be sure the almond paste is very fresh. It does make a difference.

AT A GLANCE

PAN: Cookie sheets

PAN PREP: Buttered baking parchment

OVEN TEMP: 350°

BAKING TIME: 16–18 minutes

DIFFICULTY: ○

16 ounces almond paste, at room temperature

¾ cup strained confectioners' sugar, spooned in and leveled

¾ cup granulated sugar

¼ teaspoon salt

4 large egg whites, at room temperature

2 tablespoons granulated sugar, for sprinkling

Cookie Characteristics

Versatile

Moderate shelf life

Travel well

1. Position the shelves in the upper and lower thirds of the oven. Heat the oven to 350°. Dab the corners of the cookie sheets lightly with butter and line them with baking parchment. Butter the parchment.

2. In the bowl of an electric mixer fitted with the paddle attachment, mix the almond paste with the sugars on low speed until the mixture is the consistency of meal-size crumbs, 6 to 8 minutes.

3. Add the salt to the egg whites and whisk to blend. Add the egg whites to the almond paste mixture in four additions. Continue to mix until it starts to liquefy and stick to the bottom of the bowl. This will take 15 to 20 seconds. Let stand 10 minutes to thicken slightly.

4. Drop slightly full teaspoons of the batter, forming 1½-inch mounds, from the tip of a teaspoon onto the prepared cookie sheets, spacing them about 2 inches apart. If the mounds are uneven, they may be smoothed with moistened fingertips. Sprinkle with granulated sugar.

5. Bake for 16 to 18 minutes, or until just lightly browned around the edges. To ensure even baking, rotate the sheets from top to bottom and front to back toward the end of baking time. Let rest on the cookie sheet for 5 minutes before transferring to cooling racks.

STORAGE: Store in an airtight container, layered between strips of wax paper, for up to 5 days. As the macaroons age they develop flavor and become softer. These cookies may be frozen.

nick malgieri's coffee pecan eclairs

MAKES 2 DOZEN 3-INCH SANDWICH COOKIES

This recipe comes from my good friend, master baker Nick Malgieri. I have no doubt that you will become addicted to this sinfully rich combination of cinnamon-scented pecan meringues filled with decadent coffee buttercream as quickly as I (and my assistants) did! Upon standing, the buttercream softens the meringue, melding a marvelous mouthful of flavors. I like to serve my Eclairs in petit-four cups for an especially elegant presentation.

AT A GLANCE

PAN: Cookie sheets
PAN PREP: Baking parchment
OVEN TEMP: 300°
BAKING TIME: 25–30 minutes
DIFFICULTY: ❍❍❍

ECLAIRS

¾ cup pecans (about 3 ounces)
1 cup sugar, divided
2 tablespoons cornstarch
¼ teaspoon ground cinnamon
4 large egg whites, at room temperature
⅛ teaspoon salt

COFFEE
BUTTERCREAM

1 tablespoon instant coffee powder
⅓ cup very strong hot coffee
4 large egg whites
1 cup sugar
Pinch of salt
1½ cups (3 sticks) unsalted butter, cut into 1-inch pieces, at room temperature
2 tablespoons dark rum

GARNISH

2 tablespoons finely chopped, toasted pecans
1 teaspoon cocoa powder, for dusting

MAKE THE ECLAIRS

1. Position the shelves in the upper and lower thirds of the oven. Heat the oven to 300°. Dab the corners of the cookie sheets lightly with butter and line with baking parchment.

2. Grind the pecans: Place the pecans in the work bowl of a food processor fitted with the steel blade. Process for about 45 to 50 seconds, stopping the machine at five-second intervals. Watch carefully to be sure the pecans do not form a paste.

3. In a small bowl, whisk together ½ cup of the sugar, the ground pecans, cornstarch, and cinnamon. Set aside.

4. Place the egg whites in the bowl of an electric mixer fitted with the whip attachment and beat on medium speed until frothy. Add the salt, increase the speed to medium-high, and beat to firm peaks. Add the remaining ½ cup of sugar 1 tablespoon at a time, taking about 1 minute.

5. Remove the bowl from the machine, and using a large rubber spatula, fold in the dry ingredients.

6. Place the meringue in an 18-inch pastry bag fitted with a ½-inch plain (#806) pastry tip. Pipe 3-inch "fingers"

Cookie
Characteristics

Festive

Short shelf life

Temperature
sensitive

onto the cookie sheets, piping the fingers 1½-inches apart at an angle on the
parchment so you can fit more. Bake for
25 minutes, or until golden and fairly
dry. To ensure even baking, rotate the
sheets from top to bottom and front to
back toward the end of baking time.
(Watch carefully; the meringues overbake easily.) Remove from the oven, let
rest for 5 minutes, then use a thin metal
spatula to carefully loosen the
meringues. Let cool.

MAKE THE BUTTERCREAM

7. Dissolve the instant coffee in the very
strong hot coffee. (Alternatively, 3 tablespoons instant coffee can be dissolved in
⅓ cup boiling water.) Cool before using.
8. Place the egg whites, sugar, and salt
in the bowl of an electric mixer over a
pan of simmering water. The bowl
should not touch the water. Whisk gently and constantly until the egg whites
are hot (about 140°) and the sugar is
dissolved.
9. Remove the bowl from the heat, and
using the whip attachment, beat the
mixture on medium-high speed until it
is thick and cooled, about 5 minutes.
Change to the paddle attachment and on
medium-low speed add the butter, one
or two pieces at a time, mixing until the
butter is thoroughly incorporated before
adding the next pieces. Reduce the
mixer speed to low and blend in the
coffee and rum.

ASSEMBLE THE ECLAIRS

10. Line up half of the meringues, flat
side up, on a clean piece of baking
parchment. Transfer the buttercream to
a pastry bag fitted with a star tip and
pipe a line of buttercream on each
meringue. Top the buttercream with the
remaining meringues, flat side down,
then turn the fingers sideways and pipe
a rosette of buttercream on each cookie.
Sprinkle each rosette with chopped
pecans and refrigerate for up to 3 days.
11. To serve, put the cocoa powder in a
fine strainer and tap *gently* over the
eclairs. Place in petit-four papers with
the rosettes facing up.

STORAGE: Store in a shallow pan in the
refrigerator covered with aluminum foil
for up to 3 days. These cookies may be
frozen.

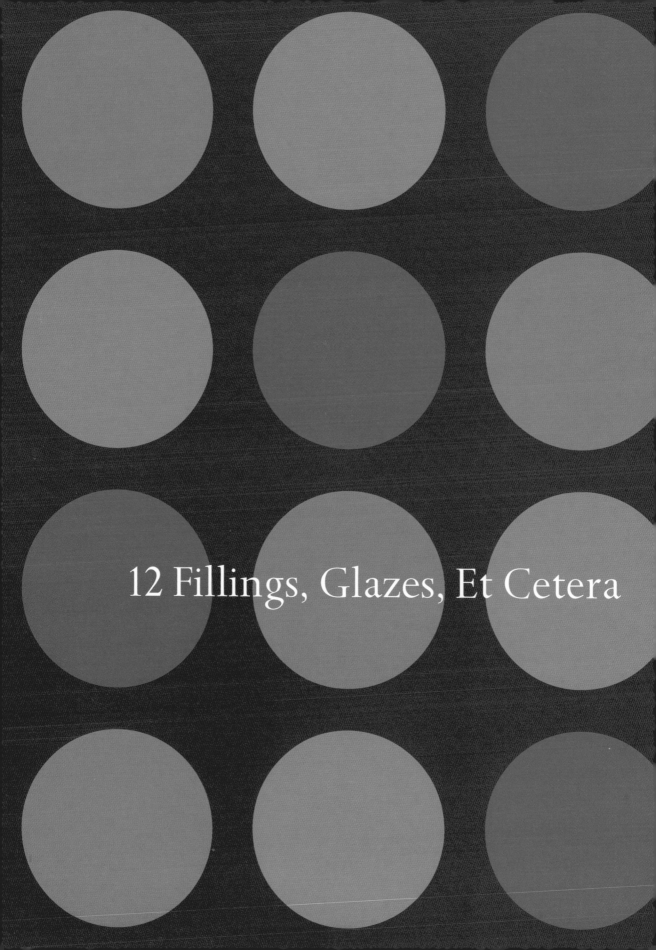

12 Fillings, Glazes, Et Cetera

Fillings for Sandwich Cookies

powdered sugar buttercream

MAKES ABOUT 2 CUPS; ENOUGH FOR 4 DOZEN 2-INCH SANDWICH COOKIES
(ABOUT 2 TEASPOONS PER SANDWICH)

This buttercream is the kind that children lick off their cookie when they separate it in two. Its creamy texture is perfect for sandwich cookies.

½ cup (1 stick) unsalted butter, at room temperature
¼ teaspoon salt
3 cups strained confectioners' sugar, spooned in and leveled
3 to 4 tablespoons milk
1 teaspoon pure vanilla extract

1. In the large bowl of an electric mixer fitted with the paddle attachment, mix the butter with the salt on low speed until smooth.

2. Add the confectioners' sugar alternately with the milk, beginning and ending with the sugar. Mix until smooth, but *do not overmix*. Blend in the vanilla extract.

STORAGE: Place in an airtight container and refrigerate. For easy spreading, remove from the refrigerator at least 1 hour before using. This frosting may be frozen for up to 3 months. Thaw in the refrigerator for 24 hours, then let stand at room temperature until spreadable, about 1 hour.

VARIATIONS: coffee buttercream
1 teaspoon instant espresso powder
½ teaspoon boiling water

Stir the espresso powder and boiling water together. Add to the milk and proceed with the recipe as written.

chocolate buttercream
½ cup unsweetened cocoa powder, spooned in and leveled
3 tablespoons corn syrup

Strain the confectioners' sugar and salt from the Master Recipe with the cocoa. Add to the creamed butter in the Master Recipe alternately with the milk and corn syrup, beginning and ending with the sugar. Then blend in the vanilla extract.

peanut butter buttercream
¼ cup peanut butter (smooth or crunchy)
¼ cup (½ stick) unsalted butter, at room temperature
⅓ cup medium-chopped peanuts

In the large bowl of an electric mixer fitted with the paddle attachment, cream the peanut butter and the butter on low speed. Proceed with the Master Recipe, then fold in the peanuts.

walnut orange buttercream

2 tablespoons freshly grated navel
  orange zest
½ cup medium-chopped, toasted
  walnuts

In the large bowl of an electric mixer
fitted with the paddle attachment, cream
the butter and the orange zest on low
speed. Proceed with the Master Recipe,
folding in the walnuts with the vanilla
extract.

Secrets for Fillings, Glazes, et Cetera

- Always check the consistency of the filling before applying. It should be as spreadable as smooth peanut butter.

- Arrange the cookies on a flat surface, matching the tops to the bottoms, before the filling is applied.

- Apply fillings to the center of the cookie.

- Piping the filling through a pastry bag gives a more professional finish to the cookie.

- When the filling is applied, gently press the bottom and top together, applying pressure in the center first, then *lightly* pressing around the edge.

- Be sure to use hot liquid for making a glaze.

- The amount of liquid needed for a glaze can vary according to climate conditions or slight variables in measuring equipment.

- All glazes are best made immediately before using because they thicken as they stand.

- If a glaze becomes too thick, thin with a *few* drops of hot water. Remember, a little goes a long way.

- If glazes are made ahead they should be carefully warmed in a water bath or on the defrost cycle in the microwave to achieve the proper consistency. Watch carefully; they soften in seconds.

- Glazes can be applied by dipping a 4-prong fork into the glaze and swiggling it back and forth (see "Decorating and Garnishing," page 398).

- Apply the glaze with the back of a large soup spoon.

whipped cream

When you purchase heavy cream for whipping, do not buy the freshest cream on the shelf. Heavy cream that is more aged will whip better. Resist the temptation to use a higher mixer speed for beating the cream. Cream that is beaten more slowly will retain its shape.

	MAKES 2 CUPS	MAKES 3 CUPS
Heavy cream, well chilled	1 cup	1½ cups
Strained confectioners' sugar	2 tablespoons	3 tablespoons
Pure vanilla extract	1 teaspoon	1½ teaspoons

1. Put the cream in the chilled bowl of an electric mixer. Using a chilled whip attachment or beaters, beat the cream on medium-low speed until it begins to thicken, then add the sugar and vanilla, or any other flavoring of your choice.
2. Continue to beat until the sugar and vanilla are blended and the cream falls in soft mounds when the whip or beaters are lifted. Remove from the mixer. With a hand-held balloon whisk, whip until the cream is thick, smooth, and holds its shape. Do not overbeat or the cream will become grainy.
3. Refrigerate the whipped cream for two to three hours, loosely covered with plastic.

caramel mascarpone cream

MAKES ABOUT 1½ CUPS

Mellow caramel and smooth mascarpone blended together are the perfect complement to chocolate.

4 ounces caramels, such as Hershey's Classic Caramels, unwrapped (20–22 pieces)
2 teaspoons heavy cream
1½ cups (12 ounces) mascarpone cheese, at room temperature
¼ teaspoon pure vanilla extract
⅛ teaspoon salt

1. Place the caramels and cream in a small microwave-safe bowl. Cook on high for 30 seconds, stir, and continue to cook for an additional 25 seconds to melt the caramels. Stir briefly until all of the caramel pieces are melted. Transfer to a 2-quart bowl and cool to tepid; it will only take a few minutes to cool.
2. Using a rubber spatula, fold ¼ cup mascarpone into the caramel, folding gently until completely blended. Gently fold the caramel mixture into the remaining mascarpone. Blend in the vanilla and salt. Be careful to avoid overmixing or the mascarpone will break and separate. Refrigerate until ready to use.

STORAGE: Store in an airtight container for up to 3 days. This cream may be frozen for up to 1 month.

gingery mascarpone cream

MAKES 2⅔ CUPS

Tangy mascarpone cream and snappy ginger are the ideal complement to sugary lace cookies. Mascarpone is a very delicate cheese. Be gentle when mixing!

⅓ cup strained confectioners' sugar, spooned in and leveled
2 teaspoons ground ginger
⅛ teaspoon salt
8 ounces mascarpone cheese, at room temperature
¼ cup minced crystallized ginger
1½ teaspoons freshly grated lemon zest
1 cup heavy cream, divided
1½ teaspoons pure vanilla extract
1 to 2 tablespoons Grand Marnier liqueur or light rum

1. Strain together the confectioners' sugar, ground ginger, and salt. Set aside.

2. Place the mascarpone in a medium bowl. Using a spatula, gently fold in the crystallized ginger and lemon zest, then gently fold in ⅓ cup of the heavy cream.

3. In a chilled bowl with chilled beaters, on medium-low speed whip the remaining ⅔ cup of cream to soft peaks, then add the confectioners' sugar mixture, the vanilla extract, and Grand Marnier. Whip just until firm peaks form. Gently fold one-third of the whipped cream into the mascarpone mixture. It is essential not to overwork the mascarpone so that it does not separate and appear grainy. Then fold in the remaining whipped cream.

STORAGE: Store in an airtight container for up to 3 days. Freezing is not recommended.

white chocolate–orange ganache filling

MAKES ABOUT 1 CUP; ENOUGH FOR FILLING 30 2-INCH SANDWICH COOKIES

This ganache turns any cookie into a decadent luxury.

½ cup heavy cream
2 teaspoons freshly grated orange zest
6 ounces fine-quality white chocolate, such as Lindt Classic Swiss White, melted (see page 393)

Heat the cream in a small saucepan until just simmering. Off the heat, add the orange zest, then let stand until barely warm. Stir into the melted chocolate and whisk gently just until smooth and creamy. Chill for 3 to 5 minutes, or until it just starts to set.

STORAGE: Ganache may be held at room temperature for several hours, but should be refrigerated in an airtight container for up to 2 weeks or frozen for up to 9 months. To thaw frozen ganache, warm *slowly* in a double boiler or place entire container in a pan of hot water.

Cookie Glazes

vanilla glaze

MAKES ABOUT ⅔ CUP; ENOUGH FOR 4 DOZEN 2-INCH COOKIES

Making this glaze with milk gives a thicker covering while water makes a more translucent finish. Use less liquid when piping.

2 cups strained confectioners' sugar, spooned in and leveled
2–3 tablespoons hot milk or water, plus additional as needed
1 tablespoon light corn syrup
½ teaspoon pure vanilla extract
Pinch of salt

Place the confectioners' sugar in a large bowl and add the remaining ingredients. Stir with a small whisk or spoon until very smooth. The glaze should pour from a spoon in a steady stream. Use additional liquid sparingly. A little bit goes a long way.

STORAGE: Store the glaze tightly covered in the refrigerator for up to 3 days.

lemon or lime glaze

Substitute hot, fresh lemon or lime juice for the milk. Omit the vanilla extract.

orange glaze

Substitute hot, fresh orange juice for the milk and add ¼ teaspoon orange oil. Omit the vanilla extract.

vanilla sugar

MAKES 2 CUPS

Vanilla sugar is a European favorite that is used for coating the surface of buttery cookies. The traditional method for making it is to store a vanilla bean in a jar with sugar for at least a week. The bean perfumes the sugar, leaving a lovely vanilla flavor. While this method works, I tried toasting the bean first and then pulverizing it with sugar in a food processor. What a wonderful result I had! The sugar had a more pronounced vanilla flavor with minuscule bits of bean throughout.

1 6- to 7-inch vanilla bean
2 cups superfine sugar, spooned in and leveled

1. Position the shelf in the center of the oven. Heat the oven to 325°. Place the vanilla bean on a small cookie sheet and toast for 8 to 10 minutes. Remove from the oven and let cool.

2. Break the vanilla bean into 1-inch pieces and place it and the sugar in the work bowl of a food processor fitted with the steel blade. Pulse five or six times, then process for 2 minutes; pulse 3 or 4 times, and then process again for 1 minute or until the bean is pulverized. Pass through a fine strainer and discard any small particles of bean.

STORAGE: Store in a tightly sealed jar for up to 1 year.

quick chocolate glaze

This recipe has been a favorite of mine for years. It has a lovely gloss that holds well under refrigeration or freezing.

Melt the chocolates and butter in a shallow bowl set over simmering water, stirring until smooth. Remove from the heat and add the sugar alternately with the water. Stir in the corn syrup and vanilla. Beat well with a wooden spoon until very smooth.

STORAGE: The glaze may be held at room temperature for several hours, refrigerated for up to 2 weeks, or frozen for up to 9 months. To thaw, warm slowly in a double boiler or place the entire container in a pan of hot water. Adjust the consistency with a few drops of hot water as needed. Leftover glaze can be refrozen and used again as needed.

	SMALL	LARGE
Unsweetened chocolate, coarsely chopped	1 ounce	1½ ounces
Semisweet chocolate, coarsely chopped	1 ounce	1½ ounces
Unsalted butter	2 teaspoons	1 tablespoon
Strained confectioners' sugar, spooned in and leveled	⅔ cup	1 cup
Boiling water, plus additional as needed	2 tablespoons	3 tablespoons
Light corn syrup	2 teaspoons	1 tablespoon
Pure vanilla extract	½ teaspoon	¾ teaspoon

chocolate candy glaze

Nothing can be faster than melting a candy bar for a glaze.

8 ounces high-quality bittersweet or semisweet chocolate, such as Lindt Bittersweet or Classic Swiss White
1 tablespoon vegetable oil

Slowly melt the chocolate and vegetable oil together over hot water. (See Techniques: Melting Chocolate, page 392.) When the mixture is smooth, remove from the water. Cool briefly.

ganache glaze

The versatility of ganache is a gift to a sweet kitchen. It makes a mirrorlike glaze when pourable. When chilled, it thickens to a consistency suitable for filling cookies or it can be piped into rosettes, lines, or other beautiful ornamentations.

6 ounces fine-quality semisweet or
    bittersweet chocolate, such as Lindt
    Bittersweet, cut into 1-inch chunks
¾ cup heavy cream
1 tablespoon light corn syrup
¾ teaspoon vanilla extract
½ to 1 teaspoon hot water, if needed

1. Place the chocolate in the work bowl of a food processor fitted with the steel blade and process until finely chopped.
2. In a small saucepan, over low heat, heat the heavy cream and corn syrup together until it comes to a simmer. *Immediately* pour the hot cream over the chocolate in the processor bowl. Let stand for 1 minute so that the chocolate begins to melt. Pulse three or four times, then let rest 1 additional minute. Add the vanilla and pulse three or four more times.
3. Empty into a container. If the ganache's surface appears oily, add the hot water, a few drops at a time, stirring well after each addition. The ganache will thicken as it stands, but should remain pourable. If the sauce fails to thicken, refrigerate it for 4 to 5 minutes.

STORAGE: Ganache may be left at room temperature for several hours, but should be reheated over low heat if being used as a glaze. When ganache is used as a filling for a drop or sandwich cookie, it is best chilled to spreading consistency. It may also be made ahead and stored in the refrigerator in an air-tight container for up to 2 weeks or frozen for up to 9 months. To thaw frozen ganache, heat slowly in a water bath or a double boiler or place entire container in a pan of hot water.

Et Cetera

cashew brittle

**ENOUGH FOR A 9 X 13 X 2-INCH
PAN OF BAR COOKIES**

This brittle makes an addictive topping to use as a garnish for bar or other cookies. Nuts such as blanched almonds or hazelnuts are also good choices for brittle.

5 ounces (1 level cup, packed) cashews, salted or unsalted
⅔ cup superfine sugar, spooned in and leveled
½ teaspoon lemon juice

1. Heat the oven to 325°. Place the cashews on a sheet pan and toast for 8 to 10 minutes, or until fragrant. Set aside. Have ready a buttered wooden spoon, a buttered heat-resistant square spatula (approximately 3 inches), and a jelly roll pan lined with buttered baking parchment or a Silpat nonstick baking mat.

2. Place the sugar and the lemon juice in a heavy-bottomed 10-inch skillet. Stir gently to combine. The mixture will look like coarse sand. Melt the sugar over medium-low heat, swirling the pan occasionally, taking care not to burn the sugar. Brush the sides of the pan with water to remove any sugar crystals.

3. When the sugar is completely melted and reaches a rich amber color, it is caramelized and should be removed from the heat. Using the buttered wooden spoon, stir in the nuts and separate the clusters. Return to low heat and use the buttered spatula to press the cashews into the caramel. Lifting from underneath, turn the nuts over into the caramel. Cook until the mixture barely starts to bubble. Remove from the heat immediately. *Take care when working with the syrup at this point, as it is dangerously hot.*

4. Turn the mixture out onto the jelly roll pan, spreading it as evenly as you can. As it cools, it will harden into a brittle. Break the brittle into pieces for storage.

5. When ready to use, place the brittle on a cutting board and, using a chef's knife, chop into small pieces. Never use plastic wrap to cover cookies trimmed with brittle. The condensation will cause the brittle to melt.

STORAGE: Store in an airtight container in a cool, dry place completely free of humidity. Do not refrigerate.

II The Teacher's Secrets
for Sensational Cookies

About Ingredients

Flours and Leavenings

Flours are one of the prime building blocks of most baked goods.

Wheat flour—the flour most commonly used for cookie baking—is harvested from the tiny kernels, or berries, on wheat stalks. Every berry contains three parts: the outer shell, or bran; the starchy center, or endosperm; and the heart, or germ. All-purpose white flour is milled from the endosperm, while the entire kernel is ground for whole wheat flour. Some flours are chemically bleached with hydrogen gas and benzoyl peroxide or other substances; generally, bleached and unbleached flours can be used interchangeably in cookies.

Protein is present in all flours. The greater the protein content of the flour, the more liquid it will absorb. Unbleached flour has a slightly higher protein value than bleached flour, and because of this doughs made with unbleached may require a little more liquid. The protein content of a flour is indicated in the nutritional label on the side of the package.

If you are buying a new or unfamiliar brand, it's a good idea to check the protein count on the package. Be aware that there can be differences in flour protein levels and moisture content in different lots of the same brand because of varying climate and soil conditions in the fields.

STORAGE
Ideally, flour should be used within a few weeks. For longer storage, refrigerate for about three months or freeze for up to a year.

Whole wheat flour can taste old and turn rancid rather quickly; therefore, it is best to keep whole wheat and other specialty flours in the freezer. Bring flour to room temperature before using.

I have listed here the commonly available flours. These do not include premium flours produced by small specialty companies because their protein contents are variable.

WHEAT FLOURS
Bleached All-Purpose Flour (3 grams protein per ¼ cup flour): This is an enriched, pure white flour that has been bleached to whiten and even out its liquid absorption. Bleached all-purpose flour is used interchangeably with unbleached all-purpose flour. Unless otherwise specified, I used Gold Medal All-Purpose Bleached Flour in the development and testing of the recipes in *Great Cookies*.

Unbleached All-Purpose Flour (3 grams protein per ¼ cup flour): Unbleached flour has a slight cream color, which indicates that it has not been chemically bleached. It has a slightly higher protein value than bleached and, because of this, may require increased liquid.

Whole Wheat Flour (varies, 3 to 5 grams per ¼ cup flour): Whole wheat flour is flour that is milled from the entire wheat kernel. It is composed of three parts: the bran or the outer shell, the endosperm or white starchy center, and the germ or heart. Whole wheat flour is more nutritious than white flour because it is higher in fiber. It is

rich in protein with a content that can range from 12 grams to 20 grams per cup depending on the manufacturer. Graham flour, named for its developer, Dr. Sylvester Graham, is less refined than regular whole wheat flour but can be used interchangeably with regular whole wheat flour. Stone-ground whole wheat flour is ground between two giant stones that are propelled by water. This process keeps the flour cool during milling, retaining more of the natural vitamins and nutrients. It is more flavorful than commercially processed whole wheat flour. Highly perishable, this flour should be stored in the refrigerator or freezer.

Cake flour (2 grams protein per ¼ cup): Cake flour is milled especially for cakes and delicate pastries. It is an enriched white flour produced from high-quality soft wheat. Cake flour is usually packaged in 2-pound boxes rather than bags. If you cannot locate it in the flour section of your supermarket, you may find it shelved with the cake mixes. Be sure to purchase *plain* cake flour, not self-rising, which has leavening and salt added to it.

NON-WHEAT FLOURS AND MEALS
Cornmeal: Cornmeal is made from either white or yellow corn kernels. It is sometimes combined with wheat flour in baking to achieve added flavor and texture. Although yellow cornmeal is more nutritious than white, their baking properties are the same. You will see "stone-ground" on some packages of corn-

meal; this means that the whole kernels are ground into meal between two huge, water-powered stones. Because the water keeps the grain cool during milling, more natural vitamins and nutrients are retained. In electric-milled commercial cornmeal, the hull and germ are removed and the meal is finer textured. Stone-ground cornmeal is coarser and more flavorful. You can store "regular" cornmeal at room temperature. Stone-ground cornmeal goes rancid more quickly and is better stored in the refrigerator for up to three months or in the freezer for one year.

Cornstarch: Cornstach is the endosperm or starchy center of the corn kernel. For baking cookies, replacing some of the wheat flour with cornstarch reduces the strength of the protein, resulting in a more tender finished product. Cornstarch is also an excellent medium for coating or dusting rolling surfaces or doughs. It provides ease of rolling and gives a flaky finish to the baked cookie.

Nut Flours: Nut flours are an example of non-wheat products that have been refined to a powdery texture and are used instead of, or in combination with, wheat flour in baking. Almond, chestnut, and hazelnut flours are familiar examples used in cookies, cakes, and ethnic pastries (see Specialty Sources, page 403). The process used to produce flours from nuts cannot be duplicated in the home kitchen with the best results. Yes, the nuts can be pulverized in your food processor or blender, but the oils that are released create a moist, oily texture. While adding a little flour or sugar to absorb the oil helps, optimum results are achieved with commercially refined nut flours. These flours are highly perishable and

should be either refrigerated or stored in the freezer.

Rice Flour: Rice flour, made from white rice, is a very soft, powdery flour. It contains protein but does not form gluten. For those who cannot tolerate gluten, rice flour can be a suitable substitute. Use ⅞ cup of rice flour for 1 cup of wheat flour in baked goods. Do not confuse regular rice flour with sweet rice flour, which is used in Oriental cooking. In cookie baking, rice flour combined with wheat flour produces a fine crumb and unique, velvety texture.

Rolled Oats (Oatmeal): Oats are a healthful grain high in protein and unsaturated fats. Using oatmeal in baking adds flavor, nutrition, and interesting texture to the final product. Old-fashioned oats are coarser textured than quick-cooking oats and produce a rustic, chewier cookie, while quick-cooking oats are cut finer and impart a more refined quality. In many recipes, an equal amount of ground oatmeal can be substituted for flour. Be sure to grind it before measuring. Steel-cut oats imported from Ireland or Scotland make a hearty breakfast cereal but are not suitable for baking because of the lengthy cooking time required and their very chewy, coarse texture.

LEAVENINGS

Baking Soda: Also known as sodium bicarbonate, baking soda is a component of baking powder. It has four times the leavening power of baking powder and is used as a neutralizing agent in batters and doughs containing acidic ingredients such as buttermilk, yogurt, and sour cream, as well as honey, molasses, fruits, and chocolate. A pinch of baking soda (⅛ teaspoon) added to a batter or dough deepens its color.

Cream of Tartar: A component of baking powder, it is sometimes used in combination with baking soda (sodium bicarbonate) as a leavening agent for baking cookies. Cream of tartar is an acid made from the residue formed inside wine vats during fermentation. It is frequently used to stabilize beaten egg whites; additionally, it helps prevent the crystallization of sugar during caramelization.

Double-acting Baking Powder: A leavening that releases gas in two stages: when it initially comes into contact with the liquid in a recipe, and in the heat of the oven during baking. Batters and doughs containing double-acting baking powder are able to stand without losing their leavening power, which is helpful when baking cookies in batches. Cookies made with baking powder spread less and bake faster.

Single-acting Baking Powder: Single-acting baking powder releases all its gas when it comes into contact with liquid. Batters and doughs made with single-acting baking powder lose rising power as they stand; therefore, the cookies should be baked as soon as possible.

Yeast: Primarily made of the cells of a minute fungus, yeast is widely used as a leavening agent for baking breads, sweet doughs, and sometimes cookies.

Sugars and Other Sweeteners

All sweeteners are carbohydrates that come from the leaves, stems, or roots of plants. Sugar is the most commonly used sweetener, and it comes from either sugarcane or sugar beets.

Beet sugar is a root crop grown in more places than sugar cane. Since it requires only one refining process, it is cheaper to bring to market. Cane sugar, which grows above ground, is produced only in four states, and it requires two processes at two different facilities. If your package does not say "cane sugar," there is a high possibility that it is beet sugar.

BROWN SUGAR

Brown sugar, a combination of refined white sugar and molasses, comes in both light and dark varieties. Light brown sugar contains less molasses than dark brown sugar. It has a more delicate flavor and imparts a lighter color to the finished product. Dark brown sugar has a more robust taste and gives deeper color and flavor. While light and dark brown sugars may be used interchangeably in most cookie recipes, when used in abundance, the flavor of the finished product will differ.

Brown sugar will harden quickly when exposed to air; therefore, reseal a package tightly after it is opened. Squeeze all the air out, fold the top over, and secure with a rubber band or adhesive, and return it to the box for storage. I find that storing the entire box, with the sealed inner bag in a large zipper plastic bag, in the refrigerator helps to keep the brown sugar soft. An alternative is a small terracotta "sugar bear," available through The Baker's Catalogue (see Specialty Sources, page 403). The bear is moistened with water and stored in the bag with the sugar.

Granulated brown sugar is available and may be used in equal amounts for the nongranulated type. It pours for easy measuring; however, it is quite costly and the benefit does not seem to justify the expense.

CONFECTIONERS' SUGAR

This powdery blend of granulated sugar and 3 percent cornstarch is processed to a fineness ten times that of granulated sugar. Thus, it may be referred to as "10X sugar" or "powdered sugar." It is less sweet than granulated sugar and is not interchangeable in recipes. Because of its powdery texture, it does not hold air as well as either granulated or brown sugars, and it produces a very tight, velvety crumb when used in baking. Confectioners' sugar tends to lump, even in a new box, and should be strained before measuring.

CORN SYRUP

Corn syrup, made from cornstarch, comes in two varieties: light and dark. Light corn syrup has been clarified and is clear and sweet but flavorless. Dark corn syrup is flavored with caramel and adds flavor and color. Corn syrup has a long shelf life and should be stored at room temperature.

GOLDEN SYRUP

Golden syrup, an English import, is a syrupy, liquid sweetener that can be used instead of corn syrup. Its golden color is similar to honey, but the toasty intensity of the flavor is unique. Called "light treacle" in Britain and sold under the Lyle's label, it can be purchased in the United States in some supermarkets and specialty food stores.

GRANULATED SUGAR

Granulated sugar is the all-purpose sweetener of choice in the American home. In addition to sweetness, sugar contributes tenderness, moistness, color, and texture to cookies. Try to purchase cane sugar with a fine crystal that will dissolve readily and will incorporate air when creamed with butter or beaten with eggs. If you find your sugar has large crystals, you can grind the sugar, preferably in a blender; however a food processor can be used. I like to grind a whole 5-pound bag and save it just for my baking. It will keep indefinitely in an airtight container.

HONEY

The most common types of honey found at the grocer's today come from the nectars of orange blossom, clover, or lavender flowers. Usually, the darker the honey, the stronger the flavor. Although honey can be used in place of sugar in equal amounts, the flavor, texture, and consistency will be different from a cookie made with granulated or brown sugar. Those made with honey will have a softer, more chewy consistency. Honey stored at room temperature may develop sugar crystals, which can be liquefied by putting the container in hot water that does not exceed 160 degrees—hotter temperatures alter the flavor of the honey. Alternatively, honey may be stored in the refrigerator, but must be warmed briefly in hot water to restore the proper consistency.

MAPLE SYRUP

Pure maple syrup is distilled from the sap of mature maple trees. It comes in grades that are identified by color. Grade A is the most commonly available. The lightest and most delicate is light amber. Medium and dark amber are more intense in flavor. Maple-flavored syrups found in the supermarkets are a combination of corn syrup, artificial flavoring, and a small amount or no maple syrup. Keep real maple syrup in the refrigerator after opening to prevent mold from forming. Gentle heating liquefies any crystallization that may occur.

SUPERFINE SUGAR

This finely grained, premium cane sugar is also referred to as "bar sugar" or "dessert sugar" because it dissolves readily. It can be used interchangeably with regular sugar and has many of the same benefits of baker's sugar. Superfine sugar, manufactured by Domino Sugar, is sold in 1-pound boxes and is usually stocked with the brown and confectioners' sugars. It will form lumps if not kept in an airtight container.

Fats

The importance of fat in cookie baking is unparalleled to any other ingredient with the exception of flour. It not only contributes fantastic flavor, it also maintains freshness and provides moisture.

Fat greatly affects the texture of cookies depending upon the type used. It can give them a remarkable melting tenderness or an extraordinary crispiness. Because it is such a major player, the significance of learning about this ingredient cannot be minimized.

BUTTER

Butter contains about 80 percent animal fat and from 10 to 16 percent water along with curd and minerals. The new, premium, ultra-creamy butters, such as Land O' Lakes and Plugrá, a European-style butter, are about 83 percent fat. If substituting these high-fat butters for regular butters, you will find the consistency of cookie doughs can be affected.

Butter is available in salted and unsalted forms. While both may be used in baking, unsalted butter is far superior. Unsalted butter has less moisture and a fresher, sweeter, clearer flavor than salted.

Reduce the added salt in the recipe if salted butter is used. Never substitute a whipped or "lite" butter in a recipe because it is aerated or has a higher water content.

Butter must be refrigerated to prevent it from becoming rancid. It should be kept covered because it picks up refrigerator odors and flavors. Pay attention to the expiration date on the package. For longer storage, butter may be frozen up to six months to prolong its rather limited shelf life.

HYDROGENATED VEGETABLE SHORTENING

This product, processed with heat and hydrogen, is 100 percent fat and made from soybean, corn, cottonseed, palm, or peanut oil. Classic shortening is pure white and neutral flavored. A recent addition to the product line is the yellow-colored, butter-flavored vegetable shortening. My preference is for unflavored vegetable shortening because it does not contain artificial flavoring. If you substitute vegetable shortening for butter, your cookies may not spread as much. This is because vegetable shortening does not contain water. Although shortening can be stored at room temperature, I prefer to keep it in the refrigerator to maintain the white color and freshness. When baking cookies, bring it to room temperature before combining it with other ingredients.

MARGARINE

Margarine is made from a blend of vegetable oils and hydrogenated hardened fats mixed with skim milk or water. It is softer than butter, but has the same fat calories. Some margarines are either "lower cholesterol" or "cholesterol free." Other margarines are low in fat by virtue of a very high moisture con-

tent. Whipped and "lite" margarines are not recommended for baking.

Stick margarine can be substituted for butter in most recipes. However, where the butter flavor is essential to the recipe, butter by far gives the best results.

VEGETABLE AND OTHER OILS

Peanut, canola/rapeseed, safflower, corn, soybean, and pure or extra-virgin olive oil can all be used in baking. When using oil, consider the taste or flavor of the oil. Generally the more neutral the flavor, the better; however, for recipes that use olive oil, the fruitier-flavored extra-virgin oil is recommended. Do not substitute oil for solid fats because the consistency of the dough is greatly affected.

Dairy Products

Everyone knows that milk and cookies go together. Milk is good, not only with cookies but also *in* cookies: it provides color, tenderizes the crumb, and gives flavor. Other dairy products, too, lend their various properties to moist, tender cookies.

MILK

Cow's milk is the most commonly consumed milk in the United States. Whole milk has about 3½ percent milkfat. Low-fat versions are 2 percent, 1 percent, and skim, which has less than ½ percent milkfat. Unless specified, whole milk and low-fat milks are interchangeable in most recipes. It is the lactose, or milk sugar, that caramelizes to contribute crisp texture and brown color to cookies. Evaporated whole or skim milk may be substituted for bottled milk if it is reconstituted with 50 percent water. Sweetened, condensed milk is not a suitable substitute because it contains sugar and should be used only if specified.

CREAM

Most *heavy* cream is ultra-pasteurized to lengthen shelf life. This cream contains small amounts of mono and diglycerides, carrageenan, polysorbate, cellulose gum, and guar gum. Pure cream is 100 percent heavy cream and is more difficult to find. This type of cream is better for whipping properties and has a fresher flavor. *Light* cream most commonly contains 20% milkfat. *Half-and-half* is exactly that—half cream and half milk. It is important to use the type of cream specified in the recipe because the fat content of the finished product has been calibrated to be in proportion with the other ingredients.

CHEESE

Soft cheeses can be used for a variety of rich, tender cookies and for making flaky doughs as well as for flavorful fillings.
Cream Cheese: This cheese is made from cow's milk and must contain at least 33 percent milkfat and no greater than 55 percent moisture. Its firm texture comes from the addition of gum arabic. Whipped cream cheese is lighter in calories by virtue of the addition of air. It is not a suitable substitute for regular cream cheese in baking.
Mascarpone: Mascarpone is a rich double- or triple-cream Italian cream cheese, made from cow's milk and added cream. The result is smooth and "buttery" and versatile enough to stand on its own with fruit or be used in combination with other ingredients.
Ricotta: A fresh cheese of Italian origin, ricotta is commonly manu-factured in the United States. It is made from the whey or by-product of mozzarella or provolone cheese production and whole or skim milk. Whole-milk ricotta is similar to a smoother-textured cottage cheese and has a sweetness to it. As fat is reduced, the texture gets grainier and the sweetness is lost. Nonfat ricotta bears little resemblance to the whole-milk variety.

Eggs

Eggs are as essential to cookies as they are to most baked goods. They are 75 percent water. Eggs have two basic parts, the yolk and the white. The yolk is high in fat and adds richness, tenderness, and color to cookies. The high-protein white provides strength, stability, and moisture. Eggs are graded for quality and size. Most consumers buy AA eggs, although there are also A and B eggs. Unless otherwise specified, most recipes call for large eggs. On average, a large, unshelled egg weighs 2 ounces. The shell accounts for about 25 percent or ½ ounce and the interior liquid is about 1½ ounces. That equates to about 3 tablespoons, with the yolk being about 1 tablespoon and the white measuring about 2 tablespoons. Whether the eggs are white or brown depends upon the breed of chicken and does not influence the nutritional value or flavor of the egg.

Eggs must be stored and handled properly to avoid salmonella poisoning. Refrigerate eggs in their original cartons with the pointed tip facing down. Avoid open containers or refrigerator egg bins because eggshells are porous and can absorb bacteria and odors. Do not use eggs that have cracked shells and resist the temptation to taste dough or batter containing raw eggs before it is baked. Wash your hands before and after handling eggs and keep your measuring and stirring utensils clean to avoid cross-contamination.

Unshelled, whole eggs can be stored in the refrigerator, tightly covered, for up to three days. Unbroken egg yolks can be covered with a little water to prevent a skin from forming and stored in the refrigerator for two or three days. If the yolk is broken, omit the water and tightly cover with plastic wrap. Yolks may be frozen if a small amount of sugar is added. However, they become grainy when thawed, which limits their use. Egg whites can be tightly covered and stored in the refrigerator for four days or frozen for several months. Egg whites pick up a little moisture when frozen and so they may not be ideal for meringue cookies or meringue-style toppings.

EGG SUBSTITUTES

Egg substitutes are made almost entirely from egg whites with added stabilizers and color. Egg substitutes may be used for some or all of the whole eggs in many recipes. I recommend using 3 tablespoons per egg instead of the ¼ cup per egg directed on the container. Three tablespoons approximates the volume of a large egg without the shell.

MERINGUE POWDER

Meringue powder is made from egg whites with modified food starch, sugar, cream of tartar, and other additives. It is the preferred solution for safely making icings that depend upon egg whites that are not heated, like royal icing, for decorating cookies. Because the whites are processed, the risk of salmonella is eliminated.

Meringue powder can be found in most supermarkets, cake decorating departments of craft or party stores, and by mail order.

Liquids

Liquids, or moisteners, are the "binders" or ingredients that pull the batter together. Sometimes the moistener is as mundane as tap water; other times it is as rich as heavy cream.

CITRUS JUICES AND OTHERS

Lemon, lime, and orange, along with apple, are some of the common juices used to bind and flavor cookie doughs and batters.

Citrus fruits frequently play a dual role in cookie baking. Their juice adds moisture while their zests add intense flavor. Look for fruit that yields slightly to pressure and feels weighty for its size. Thin-skinned Florida oranges are primarily used for juice. For juice and zest, look for thick-skinned, brightly colored oranges, like California navel and Valencia or Florida Honeybell. Lemons and limes should also feel heavy and have brightly colored skins.

All varieties of citrus fruits can be kept at room temperature for a few days, and up to 2 weeks in the refrigerator. The juice may be frozen for later use.

WATER

Tap water at room temperature (unless you are directed to heat the water) is just fine. If there are excessive amounts of chlorine or minerals in the tap water, opt for bottled water.

Chocolate

The world of chocolate has risen to unbelievable heights in recent years. Today's baker may choose from a wealth of chocolate resources, both domestic and imported. Whether the chocolate is melted, chunked, or chipped in a dough or batter, or used as a finishing touch, I can't imagine a cookie book without a healthy helping of this seductive ingredient.

HOW TO STORE CHOCOLATE

Because of the cocoa butter, chocolate readily absorbs flavors from nearby ingredients. Therefore, always wrap chocolate securely in aluminum foil, then rewrap in plastic. Store it in a cool, dry place with low humidity and *away from light;* 65 degrees is the optimum storage temperature.

Frequently, a "bloom" will appear on chocolate, meaning that its color has changed during storage. There are two types of bloom that can form on the surface: fat bloom and sugar bloom. Fat bloom will form if chocolate becomes too warm, causing the stable cocoa butter crystals to melt and become unstable. If the chocolate solidifies again, the surface becomes mottled and streaked. Sugar bloom results when chocolate is exposed to excessive moisture. This causes the surface of the chocolate to become grainy. Chocolate that forms fat bloom can be remelted and used for baking and, if tempered, can be used for candy making. Chocolate that forms sugar bloom can be melted and used for most purposes other than candy making.

The shelf life of chocolate is determined by the amount of cocoa butter it contains. The longest-lived chocolates are unsweetened, bittersweet, and semisweet. Well wrapped and stored in a cool dry

place, they will keep for years. Far more perishable are milk and white chocolate. Milk chocolate should be used within 1 year and white chocolate within 8 months of purchase.

Ideally, chocolate should not be refrigerated. This may be unavoidable, however, if you live in a warm, humid environment. Milk and white chocolate may be frozen by breaking the chocolate into usable size pieces, then wrapping it well for the freezer. Do not unwrap the chocolate before thawing to prevent condensation from forming on the surface.

BITTERSWEET AND SEMISWEET CHOCOLATES

These authentic (or "real") chocolates must, by federal regulation, contain no less than 27 percent cocoa butter and at least 35 percent chocolate liquor. According to United States Standards of Identity, they are not "real" chocolates if they do not have the liquor.

Each manufacturer's distinct formula produces varying degrees of sweetness, intensity, and smoothness. Both semisweet and bittersweet chocolates contain sugar, chocolate liquor, cocoa butter, lecithin (a natural soybean product), and vanilla. Because they are sold under a variety of names (including semisweet, bittersweet, extra bittersweet, bitter, special dark, Eagle Sweet, dark sweet, and German's sweet), purchasing these chocolates is sometimes confusing since the labels do not indicate the amount of sugar added to a particular brand. It is entirely possible that a semisweet chocolate may be less sweet than a bittersweet. The only way to tell is by tasting.

Well-known domestic brands include Nestlé Semisweet Chocolate, Baker's Semisweet Chocolate,

Baker's German's Sweet, which is sweeter than the basic semisweet, and Ghirardelli Semisweet. Premium domestic chocolates include Mercken's, Peter's Burgundy, Scharffen Berger, and Guittard.

These are some of the more widely known, luxurious imported chocolates on the market: Lindt Bittersweet or Surfin, Tobler Tradition, and Godiva, all from Switzerland; Callebaut Semisweet or Bittersweet from Belgium; Valrhona and Cacao Barry from France; Perugina from Italy; El Rey from Venezuela; and Maillard Eagle Sweet Chocolate from England. See The Baker's Catalogue (Specialty Sources, page 403).

Many of the recipes in this book call for "best quality" bittersweet or semisweet chocolate. Because the quantity of sugar varies in many chocolates, it is not always wise to make substitutions. Should you have difficulty in locating premium chocolate in your supermarket baking aisle, be sure to check the candy section.

MILK CHOCOLATE

Also termed a "real" chocolate, milk chocolate is recognizable by its light color. It must be made from at least 10 percent chocolate liquor and 12 percent milk solids. Sugar and vanilla are also added. Although not commonly used melted in batters, milk chocolate, cut into bits, can be added to cookie doughs.

UNSWEETENED CHOCOLATE (BITTER OR BAKING)

This chocolate contains between 53 percent and 55 percent cocoa butter and 45 percent to 47 percent chocolate liquor. Because it does not contain sugar do not substitute bittersweet or semisweet chocolate for unsweetened chocolate. Popu-

lar brands are Nestle's, Baker's, Hershey's, and Ghirardelli. Premium chocolates like Scharffen Berger, Guittard, and Callebaut are worth seeking out (see Specialty Sources, page 403).

WHITE CHOCOLATE

Because it does not contain chocolate liquor, white chocolate is not classified as "real" chocolate. It is made of cocoa butter, butterfat, sugar, milk solids, lecithin, and vanilla and is extremely sweet. It contains about 30 percent milk and is rich in fat. White chocolate is extremely perishable, so buy it in small quantities unless you use it frequently. Some premium brands found in the candy aisles of many supermarkets are Lindt Swiss White; Perugina White; Lindt Blancor; Tobler Narcisse, and Valrhona Ivoire.

CHOCOLATE CHIPS

Chocolate chips bring us to the distinction between real chocolate and compound chocolate. Real chocolate must contain some chocolate liquor. Compound chocolate is chocolate-flavored candy. It is used to make novelty candies and decorations. When you purchase chocolate chips, buy *real* chocolate. It matters because real chocolate and compound chocolate behave and taste differently when baked.

Chocolate chips are available in sizes and shapes that are different from the familiar dollop. Mini-chips or morsels give you more chocolate pieces per measure. You can also find jumbo chocolate chips and chocolate chunks.

Semisweet Chocolate Chips: Made from "real" chocolate, these contain less cocoa butter than regular semisweet chocolate. This is why the chips hold their shape when baked. When melted semisweet

chocolate is used in a recipe, substituting chocolate chips for semisweet bar chocolate is not a good idea because chocolate chips do not melt as readily and the consistency is not as smooth.

Milk Chocolate Chips: These are "real" chocolate made from at least 10 percent chocolate liquor, 12 percent milk solids, sugar, and vanilla (or vanillin). Substituting milk chocolate chips for semisweet in chip-style cookies is certainly fine.

White Chocolate Chips: These contain cocoa butter but no chocolate liquor. The absence of chocolate liquor allows for the white color, but these chips are not considered "real" chocolate. White chocolate chips do not keep well because of their high fat content, so buy just what you need. While they are okay to use in a chocolate chip cookie, they should not be substituted for "real" chocolate because they have entirely different properties when melted and combined with other ingredients.

Flavored Chips: These are chips that wander beyond the traditional chocolate chip. They include peanut butter, cinnamon, cappuccino, cherry, or lemon. You may have trouble finding the more exotic flavors in the baking section, but they are available in The Baker's Catalogue (see Specialty Sources, page 403).

UNSWEETENED COCOA POWDER

Two types of cocoa powder are available for bakers: nonalkaline and Dutch-processed, or alkaline. When chocolate liquor is placed under hydraulic pressure, it is possible to remove at least 75 percent of the cocoa butter. The remaining cocoa solids, called a presscake, are ground into a powder. Even

(continued on page 372)

Not All Chocolate Chips Are Created Equal

Because of the popularity of chocolate chips, I did an experiment with the many kinds of chocolate chips and premium chocolate bags on the market. I wanted to test their melting properties, texture after melting, and most important, their taste. My assistants and I awakened our taste buds and conducted the following test:

A small amount of chips and pieces of chocolate bars, were baked in small, ovenproof glass containers in a 350° oven. Chocolate chips, chunks, and bite-size pieces of chocolate bars were baked for 5 minutes, while milk and white chocolates were baked for 3 minutes. The chocolates were then tasted after 5 minutes and 3 minutes, respectively. While it is true that these ingredients are enrobed in doughs and batters or used as toppings, our findings are still of significance. There were a few surprises, especially with the performance of some premium bars of chocolate. Here are our conclusions.

MILK CHOCOLATES

Perugina Milk Chocolate Bar	Visual:	Glossy
	Flavor:	Rich milk chocolate flavor
	Texture:	Smooth, silky
Lindt Swiss Milk Chocolate Bar	Visual:	Glossy
	Flavor:	Milky taste
	Texture:	Creamy
Ghirardelli Milk Chocolate Bar	Visual:	Glossy
	Flavor:	Smoky, medicinal taste
	Texture:	Smooth
Nestle's Milk Chocolate Chips	Visual:	Did not melt
	Flavor:	Acceptable milk chocolate taste
	Texture:	Fairly smooth, waxy

WHITE CHOCOLATE BARS AND CHIPS

Lindt Swiss Classic White Chocolate Bar	Visual:	Glossy
	Flavor:	Rich, full-bodied
	Texture:	Velvety and silky
Perugina White Chocolate Bar	Visual:	Glossy
	Flavor:	Rich, full-bodied
	Texture:	Velvety and silky
Ghirardelli Classic White Chips	Visual:	Glossy
	Flavor:	Basic white chocolate flavor
	Texture:	Moderately smooth

SEMISWEET CHOCOLATE CHIPS AND CHUNKS

Ghirardelli Double Chocolate Chips

Visual:	Glossy
Flavor:	Full-bodied chocolate flavor
Texture:	Smooth, velvety

Ghirardelli Semisweet Chocolate Chips

Visual:	Glossy
Flavor:	Good chocolate flavor
Texture:	Less velvety than Double Chips

Saco Chocolate Chunks

Visual:	Glossy
Flavor:	Fruity, mellow
Texture:	Smooth

Nestle's Semisweet Morsels

Visual:	Not as glossy
Flavor:	Good depth of flavor
Texture:	Somewhat grainy

Hershey's Semisweet Chocolate Chips

Visual:	Glossy
Flavor:	Very sweet, no depth of flavor
Texture:	Somewhat grainy, very soft

Baker's Semisweet Chocolate Chunks

Visual:	Not as glossy
Flavor:	Harsh
Texture:	Somewhat waxy, grainy

DARK, BITTERSWEET, SEMISWEET CHOCOLATES

Lindt Swiss Bittersweet Bar

Visual:	Glossy
Flavor:	Rich, melly chocolate flavor
Texture:	Smooth, velvety

Perugina Dark Chocolate Bar

Visual:	Glossy, rich chocolate color
Flavor:	Fruity chocolate flavor
Texture:	Creamy, somewhat waxy

Scharffen Berger Semisweet Bar

Visual:	Glossy
Flavor:	Intense chocolate flavor
Texture:	Smooth, velvety

Baker's German's Sweet Chocolate Bar

Visual:	Porous
Flavor:	Poor
Texture:	Grainy

though most of the cocoa butter has been removed, the resulting cocoa powder still contains 8 to 24 percent fat.

The most popular cocoa sold in the United States is nonalkaline cocoa, manufactured by Hershey's, Baker's, or Ghirardelli. This acidic cocoa has a strong, full-bodied flavor. Since nonalkaline cocoa does not have the acid removed, baked goods that contain leavening generally use baking soda in order to neutralize the acid.

In Dutch-processed cocoa, the acid is neutralized with alkali. This dark powder is favored by baking professionals for its rich, delicate flavor. Here, baking powder may be used for leavening. Popular Dutch-processed cocoas are Dröste, Poulain, Feodora, and Van Houten, along with Hershey's, who introduced its own Dutch-processed cocoa powder, boxed in a silver tin.

Dried Fruits and Preserves

Raisins, currants, prunes, dates, figs, and apricots are the familiar dried fruits. In recent years, the selection has increased vastly, largely owing to the emphasis on healthier eating. Dried fruits like apples, cherries, cranberries, bananas, pears, peaches, and mangoes are but a few of the many varieties available. A new addition to the market is baking raisins, a super-moist version of the standard variety.

I cannot stress enough how important high-quality dried fruits are to baked goods. Seek out soft, moist fruits and be sure to read the labels thoroughly before you buy. Try to purchase only those fruits that are grown in places where pes-

ticides and herbicides are monitored, and that have a minimum of chemical additives. I make an exception with fruits treated with sulphur dioxide, which is added to preserve color, freshness, and flavor. Oddly, I have found that fruits treated with sulphur dioxide cook into a softer purée than dried fruits without this additive. Avoid precut, smaller pieces of dried fruits because they can quickly lose their flavor. If you are purchasing fruit from bulk containers, taste a piece to be sure the flavor and moisture content indicate quality and freshness. If your supermarket does not stock the variety you are looking for, check out The Baker's Catalogue and order by mail (Specialty Sources, page 403).

After opening dried fruit, reseal the package tightly, expelling as much air as possible, and cover with plastic wrap or place in plastic air-tight bags. Bulk fruit should be stored in a tightly sealed glass jar. If you will not be using the fruit within two or three weeks, put it in the refrigerator, where it will keep for up to three months.

ABOUT GLACÉ AND CRYSTAL-LIZED FRUITS AND FLOWERS

The best selection and freshest glacé fruits can be found from September through December, when holiday baking gets underway. At other times, they can be difficult to find and when you do, the selection is limited and the fruit is often dried out and tasteless. When glacé fruit reaches this state, it is not worth spending the time nor the money to use it for baking. Glacé fruits found in supermarkets cannot be compared to the high-quality fruits that specialty stores stock (see Specialty Sources, page 403). If commercial fruit is the only alternative, focus on buying it at

holiday time when baking season is at its peak.

Glacé fruits are fruits that have been candied. The fruit is boiled with sugar, flavorings, and other ingredients. A coating of transparent, heavy syrup makes it shiny. Not only does its jewellike appearance enhance a plain cookie, the fruit also provides flavor, sweetness, and texture. While glacé red and green cherries are the most popular, other varieties include orange and lemon peel, citron, pineapple, and mixed fruit combinations.

Crystallized fruit is prepared similarly to glacé fruit but instead of a syrup finish, the fruit is rolled in granulated sugar. Other forms of crystallized accent ingredients are candied violets, rosebuds, and rose petals. These are processed in the same manner as other crystallized fruits. These costly ingredients are difficult to obtain, but a little goes a long way and they do make a stunning finish.

PRESERVES, JAMS, AND JELLIES

Preserves, jams, jellies, and marmalades are popular partners in a myriad of cookie recipes. They are essential components for sandwich cookies and all kinds of rolled pastries. When choosing one of these fruity mixtures, select one that complements the cookie's base flavor. Quality also pays off here. Many less expensive brands have higher quantities of water, so seek out those laden with fruit. This will help to prevent the messy runoff of watery products. Preserves and marmalades are the best to use for making cookies. Jams, while delicious, are more difficult to obtain unless homemade. Jellies have no pulp and therefore have less flavor. I find them the least desirable for cookies.

Nuts and Seeds

NUTS

The versatility of nuts is endless. They impart wonderful flavor, immeasurable texture, and visual beauty to cookies. Nuts form the foundation of dough when ground into nut meal, while larger pieces act as "spacers" by changing the density of baked products. Chopping nuts to the correct size can sometimes determine the difference between the success and failure of a recipe. Through years of teaching, I've noted some confusion as to what size is a medium chopped nut, a finely chopped nut, and so forth. See page 129 for examples of different nut sizes. When purchasing nuts, you pay for quality. Be sure to read the ingredient listing on the package and always take note of the country of origin. If you purchase nuts in bulk, be sure to sample the nut to make sure it is fresh. Nuts that are past their prime will have a stale or rancid taste.

Nuts should be stored in a cool, dark place until opened. Store nuts after opening in a well-sealed container in the refrigerator for up to three months or in the freezer for up to one year. Always date your package and rotate your stock. Refresh frozen nuts by heating them in a 325° oven for 8 to 10 minutes.

Almonds: While California almonds are the most familiar to us, almonds are also grown in Australia, the Near East, Spain, and other countries around the Mediterranean. Almonds come blanched and unblanched, whole, sliced, slivered, and chopped. Because they are firm nuts, they are good candidates for grinding into meal, either alone or paired with hazelnuts. Almonds have very little saturated fat.

Almond paste is a dense nut paste made from finely ground blanched almonds, sugar, and water, and sometimes glucose or egg white. It is a primary ingredient in many Italian pastries, especially macaroons, as well as in Scandinavian baking. Look for the Solo brand, which is sold in 8-ounce cans, rather than the plastic-wrapped, imported almond paste. Do not confuse almond paste with marzipan, which has a smoother consistency and sweeter flavor. Leftover almond paste should be well wrapped in plastic and refrigerated for up to six months.

Brazil Nuts: The seeds of giant trees, Brazil nuts are grown in South American countries. The hard, triangular shell is difficult to remove, so they are best purchased already shelled.

Cashews: Native to Brazil, India, and the West Indies, cashews are rich in protein and have a high proportion of unsaturated fatty acid. They lend a rich, buttery taste to cookies and are excellent paired with chocolate. Cashews are almost one-half oil and should be purchased in smaller quantities and stored in cool environments.

Hazelnuts: Also known as filberts, hazelnuts are grown throughout Europe and the United States. They are small and roundish wild nuts, with thin brown skins and hard interiors, that grow in clusters on hazel trees. Because of their firmness, they are especially suited for nut flours and meals. Although the skin can have a strong flavor, at times this can be complementary to certain cookies. Hazelnuts may be purchased already skinned and chopped, which is a real time-saver for the baker.

Macadamia Nuts: Macadamia nuts, were originally grown in Australia, before being exported in the late nineteenth century to Tasmania and Hawaii. Now grown in California as well, the golden brown, marble-size macadamia's buttery rich flavor pairs well with both white and dark chocolates. Usually sold with their extremely hard shells removed, these nuts are very high in fat and should be refrigerated or frozen to prevent them from becoming rancid.

Peanuts: The most widely recognized peanut variety is the Virginia peanut, an oval nut slightly larger than the small red-skinned Spanish peanut. It is a legume, like the pea, but with pods that ripen underground. Shelled peanuts, when purchased in vacuum-packed containers, may be stored for up to one year. Refrigerate open jars for up to three months.

Peanut butter debuted in 1890 and was marketed at the 1904 World's Fair as a health food. It has since become an American diet staple. There are many varieties to choose from: smooth or chunky, salted or unsalted, sweetened or unsweetened. Primarily, this nut butter is a creamy mixture of ground peanuts and vegetable oil. Natural peanut butter, made without preservatives, should be refrigerated after opening.

Pecans: A member of the Hickory family, the pecan has a higher fat content than any other nut. These nuts are grown primarily in the southern part of the United States and are available year-round. They are sold shelled and unshelled, in halves or pieces. These rich nuts are best stored in the refrigerator or frozen to prevent rancidity.

Pine Nuts: The pine nut, also known as the pignoli, pignon, or Indian nut, is actually the seed of the pinecone. It can come from several varieties of pine trees. To gather the nuts, pinecones are heated until they open, then the seeds are removed. Pine nuts are pricey because extracting the seeds from the pinecones is an expensive process. Pine nuts are grown in the Mediterranean (Spain and Italy), China, Mexico, North Africa, and the southwestern United States. There are two varieties of these small, ivory-colored nuts. The Mediterranean (or Italian) pine nut, with its oval shape and delicate flavor, is harvested from the stone pine. The triangular Chinese pine nut, usually available in Asian markets, has a more intense pine flavor and is generally less expensive. Pine nuts are extremely high in fat. They should be refrigerated or frozen, and care should be taken when toasting as they easily burn. In baking and cooking, pine nuts are usually left whole.

Pistachios: Pistachios are grown in the Mediterranean and the Middle East, as well as in California. They are a mainstay of Middle Eastern pastries. Pistachios are sold either in their pale tan shells or with shells that are dyed red. The color of the nuts can range from a brownish green to a beautiful bright green. Pistachios are available in many forms—shelled, unshelled, raw or roasted, salted, unsalted—and are available year-round. The unsalted pistachios have the brightest green color. When buying unshelled pistachios, look for shells that are slightly open. Not only is the nut easier to remove, it also indicates ripeness.

Walnuts: Native to southwestern Europe and Central Asia, walnuts in France are simply called *le noix*. Over time, the prefix *wal* was added, meaning "foreign," hence the name *walnut*. Although there are different varieties, the English walnut is the one most familiar and most frequently used in bak-

ing. Walnuts are in supply year-round and are sold both shelled and unshelled. They should be plump, meaty, and crisp. Dark-colored, shriveled walnuts are past their prime and may have a bitter overtone. Walnuts are rich in oil and protein, and should be stored in a cool place, refrigerated or frozen to keep them from turning rancid.

COCONUT

Although we think of Hawaii as its native land, coconut—the fruit of the palm tree—is believed to have originated in Malaysia. Coconut is also grown in other tropical islands throughout the Pacific, as well as in India and parts of South America.

The most common type of coconut used for making cookies is sweetened packaged or canned coconut, sold either flaked or shredded. Sweetened coconut is treated with propylene glycol to preserve freshness and sodium metabisulfate to retain whiteness.

Unsweetened or desiccated coconut, sold in health food stores, is more nutritious because it is unsulphured. This coconut, when eaten out of hand, is very dry and flavorless, but when mixed through a batter, it becomes more pleasing to the palate.

Both sweetened and unsweetened coconut should be well sealed after opening and stored in the refrigerator or freezer to retain freshness. Coconut is very high in saturated fat, however, it is rich in potassium and vitamins.

SEEDS

Seeds make wonderful accent ingredients for cookies. They are visually attractive, add texture, and contribute flavor. Store your seeds in cool, dark places and be aware

that too much time on the shelf will alter their flavor.

Anise Seeds: Anise is an annual plant and member of the parsley family. It bears a sweet licorice flavor and is particularly notable in Springerle, the traditional German Christmas cookie.

Caraway Seeds: A European seed dating back to 1552 B.C., caraway seeds are prevalent in the baked goods of Germany, Russia, and other Central European countries.

Mustard Seeds: Mustard seeds, available either whole or powdered, come in two major species: white (or yellow) and brown (Asian). The small, brown (Asian) seed is used in pickling and seasoning, as well as in Chinese and European mustards. The larger white (or yellow) variety, mainly used in American-style mustard, is much less pungent.

Pepita Seeds: These edible, dark green pumpkin seeds, with their white shells removed, have a delicate flavor that is enhanced by toasting and salting. Popular in Mexican cooking, pepitas are sold raw, roasted and salted, and with or without hulls. Buy them in health food stores, supermarkets, or Mexican markets.

Poppy Seeds: Well known in Central European, Middle Eastern, and Indian cooking, poppy seeds provide a crunchy texture and nutty flavor to cookies, cakes, coffee cakes, and pastries, as well as toppings for breads. You may purchase these tiny, bluish-gray seeds of the poppy plant in supermarkets. They are also ground for pastry fillings. Poppy seeds are high in fat; therefore, they should be refrigerated or frozen.

Sesame Seeds: This tiny seed is of an herbaceous plant native to Indonesia, India, and Africa. Sesame seeds can be purchased both hulled or unhulled. The black variety is frequently used in southern Indian cuisine. Sesame seeds have a slightly sweet, nutty flavor that encourages a variety of uses, from savory to sweet. Purchase hulled sesame seeds in supermarkets. Unhulled seeds can be found in health food stores. Middle Eastern and Indian markets usually sell sesame seeds in bulk, while Oriental markets often carry black sesame seeds. Because of their high oil content, they should be stored in the refrigerator or freezer.

Spices, Herbs, and Seasonings

SPICES

Dried spices are very intense and should be used sparingly to provide balance and nuance, not distraction, to the finished product. Purchase spices in small amounts so you will use them within a reasonable time. If the pleasant, distinctive aroma of a spice has diminished, discard the package and buy a fresh container. Heat and light hasten the deterioration of spices, so store them in a cool, dark place and make sure the caps are tightened.

Allspice: With a flavor reminiscent of cinnamon, cloves, and nutmeg, allspice is used in both sweet and savory dishes. The dried, pea-sized berry of the pimiento tree (indigenous to South America, the West Indies, and Jamaica) is used either whole or ground into a powder.

Cardamom: Cardamon, a member of the ginger family, has a spicy-sweet flavor and distinct aroma. Because of the intensity of flavor, with cardamom, a little goes a long way! The seeds may be purchased either whole (decorticated) or ground.

Cinnamon: Cinnamon is actually the inner skin of tree bark. Cinnamon sticks, which are frequently used to flavor ciders and coffees, are gathered from the younger branches, while cinnamon that will eventually be ground is harvested by removing large chunks of bark, which are cleaned, sorted, and stored, then cracked into smaller pieces before shipping. Native to Southeast Asia, cassia cinnamon, with its strong, spicy-sweet flavor, is most familiar to us. Ceylon cinnamon, frequently used in English and Mexican cookery, has a slightly citrus, less sweet flavor and is reddish brown in color.

Cloves: The pungent, peppery clove derived its name from the Latin *clavus*, meaning "nail," because of its unique shape. When dried in the sun, the unopened, pink flower bud of the evergreen clove tree turns reddish brown and may be sold either whole or ground. When used sparingly, the flavor of cloves is very complementary.

Coriander: This tiny, yellowish-tan seed of the cilantro plant offers an interesting citrus flavor that combines well with ginger. This spice is frequently found in Scandinavian baked goods, as well as Indian curries. Coriander may be purchased either whole or ground.

Curry: Curry is a combination of spices most associated with Indian cuisine. Authentic curry differs from region to region, dish to dish, and cook to cook. Most American bakers will use curry powder from the spice section in the supermarket, which is a mild, sweeter blend. Before using, curry powder should always be enlivened by toasting in a dry skillet, over low heat, until fragrant.

Ginger: Ginger, often associated with savory Asian and Indian cuisine, is also a mainstay of the baker's kitchen. Ginger's flavor depends on where it is grown and when it is harvested. Preferred by bakers and candy makers, Australian ginger, harvested from a first spring cutting, is tender and delicate. Oriental ginger comes from second and third cuttings and is more fibrous and pungent. When purchasing fresh ginger, look for knobs with smooth skin and a spicy fragrance. While it is not necessary to peel very young "spring" ginger, older ginger's light tan skin must be carefully removed to reveal the flesh. Store the unpeeled root in the refrigerator in plastic wrap for up to three weeks.

Crystallized (or candied) ginger has been peeled, cut, cooked in sugar syrup, and tossed in coarse sugar. Because it is fiber-free, it is especially good to use in baking. Look for Australian ginger (see Specialty Sources, page 403) when purchasing crystallized ginger.

Dried ground ginger appears in various desserts, including fruit compotes, cakes, pies, and cookies (think Gingerbread People), and should not be used in place of fresh ginger.

Nutmeg: Native to East India, nutmeg, the seed from the tropical evergreen tree, is covered with a lacy membrane; when the membrane is split, the nutmeg seed is removed and then dried. (The membrane, also dried and ground, becomes mace.) Nutmeg's familiar spicy-sweet flavor can be found in numerous cookies, pastries, and desserts. It is commonly sold whole, although ground nutmeg is also available. If substituting preground nutmeg for freshly grated, reduce the amount by one-third to one-half because of its finer grain.

HERBS

At times, herbs provide a complementary flavor contrast and savory taste to certain cookies. For this type of baking they should balance flavors, but never overwhelm. Like spices, dried herbs should be purchased in small quantities and used within a reasonable time—about a year—to maintain flavor. They should be stored in a dark, cool place in tightly sealed containers. After measuring, rub dried herbs between your hands to release the flavor oils. Fresh herbs should be refrigerated and used within a few days.

Lavender: A member of the mint family, lavender is noted for its pungency and aromatic scent. It can be used either fresh or dried to impart a delicate flavor to pound cakes and cookies. You will find it with the fresh herbs or in the dried spice section in the supermarket.

Mint: The most familiar mints are peppermint and spearmint. This easy-to-grow herb is cultivated in the United States, Europe, and Asia. When purchasing, look for leaves that are bright green in color, with no signs of blemishing or drooping. Refrigerate stems standing in water, and cover the leaves with a plastic bag. The water should be changed every other day.

Rosemary: A strong pungent herb, rosemary has an almost pine flavor. It is relatively easy to grow in an herb garden or window box and is easily dried. If it is fresh, chop the leaves finely to release the aromatic oils. If dried, crumble between your fingers to release the essence.

Thyme: A member of the mint family, thyme grows tiny, pointy green-gray leaves on clusters of thin stems. Its aromatic flavor is a combination of mint with hints of lemon. It is available fresh in season, but is more likely found dried, either in leaf form or ground, in the spice section.

SEASONINGS

Salt: Sodium chloride, or salt, is used to flavor or enhance the flavor of other ingredients. Often, it just takes a pinch to raise a taste from so-so to memorable and you do not even realize it is there. In baking cookies, use ordinary table salt unless otherwise directed.

Pepper: Used sparingly, pepper, preferably black, can add punch to cookies, especially in combination with chocolate. The recipe will direct you to use freshly ground or pre-ground pepper. The general rule of thumb is that freshly ground pepper will require one-third to one-half more because of its coarser grain.

Flavoring, Spirits, and Coloring

COFFEE AND ESPRESSO

Coffee or espresso, when used in concentrated form, is a wonderful flavor accent for chocolate, spice, or nut cookies. Freeze-dried instant coffee, such as Tasters' Choice, is acceptable, as is instant espresso powder, such as Medaglio d'Oro. I like to make a coffee or espresso "zest": for coffee zest, dissolve three parts instant coffee with one part boiling water; for espresso zest, dissolve two parts espresso powder with one part boiling water. Use coffee and espresso zests like an extract flavoring—that is, judiciously. Be sure to store your opened jars in the refrigerator to retain freshness.

FLAVORED EXTRACTS

Check out the baking aisle or any cook's catalogue and you will find a wide variety of pure flavored extracts along with imitation flavors. Pure almond, lemon, orange, banana, raspberry, hazelnut, spearmint, and peppermint are available, as well as imitation maple and coconut. If you do not see the pure extract, you can substitute an imitation with reasonable success.

FLAVORED OILS

Flavored oils are highly concentrated and should be used in small amounts. The fruit oil is squeezed from the rind with no other oils added, hence the intensity. The Baker's Catalogue (see page 403) sells "dropper caps" which screw onto bottles and can precisely measure a drop or two when a quarter teaspoon is too much. Some of the more popular flavors are orange, lemon, lime, peppermint, and anise. Because these oils are highly concentrated, use them sparingly. A few drops will go a long way. After opening, it is best to store them in the refrigerator.

SESAME OIL

Sesame oil is pressed or extracted from sesame seeds. The flavor is intensified when the seeds are toasted. The lighter sesame oil has a mild, nutty flavor while the dark, Asian sesame oil has a much stronger taste. Some supermarket sesame oils are a blend of sesame oil and canola oil, so read the fine print.

FOOD COLORING

Various dyes are used to tint batter and/or icings. Liquid food coloring is available in almost any supermarket, while the paste form, preferred by professionals, is sold in specialty stores.

LIQUEURS (CORDIALS), BRANDIES, AND RUM

Liqueurs, also referred to as cordials, and brandies can add a fruity nuance to dried fruit fillings used for cookies. Liqueurs are prepared by redistilling various spirits with flavoring materials like herbs, seeds, berries, and roots. An average liqueur can contain up to 35 percent sweetening agent. This accounts for their slightly syrupy consistency. Liqueurs commonly used are Grand Marnier, Cointreau, and triple sec (orange); Kahlùa and Tía Maria (coffee); Amaretto (almond); and Crème de Menthe (mint). B and B (Benedictine and Brandy) is a dry sweetened brandy-based cordial made from a spicy aromatic plant that is combined with cognac. Brandies are a potable spirit aged in wood and are obtained from the distillation of wine or a fermented mash of fruit. Fruit brandies fall into three categories: those made with apples and pears, those made from stone fruits, and those made from berries. Fruit brandies do not contain added sugar and have a lighter consistency. Popular brandies are Kirschwasser (from wild black cherries) and Calvados and applejack (from apples). Rum is an alcoholic spirit distilled from fermented sugarcane, sugarcane syrup, sugarcane molasses, or other sugarcane by-products. White or silver rums, usually from Puerto Rico, are clear, dry, and light. Golden rums have a deeper tone with a flavor to match, while the darker Jamaican rums are the most full-bodied.

VANILLA

Vanilla is produced from the tropical vanilla orchid, the only orchid to produce an edible fruit. The orchid flowers are hand-pollinated and the newly harvested bean must be cured for six months before it can be processed into *pure vanilla extract*. Pure vanilla extract is made from vanilla beans combined with at least 35 percent alcohol, water, and sugar, which acts as a preservative. *Vanilla flavor extract* and *natural vanilla flavor* are natural vanilla products, but are weaker in flavor than the pure extract. Imitation vanilla flavorings or vanillin, a by-product of paper making, do not begin to compare with the natural vanilla flavorings and should not be used in fine baking.

The gold standard of vanilla beans is grown on the islands of Madagascar, Réunion, and the Comoros in the Indian Ocean. Be wary of purchasing Mexican vanilla. While some products are of high quality, others may contain coumarin, a substance banned by the FDA because it may cause liver or kidney damage. Since it is impossible to tell which vanilla contains coumarin, it is best to buy Mexican vanilla *beans* only from a reputable supplier.

Vanilla beans are superior to use for making vanilla sugar, which in turn is used as a coating or finish for baked cookies (see page 358). The used bean can be dried and put in a jar with granulated sugar to produce the aromatic vanilla sugar. As a point of information, a 2-inch piece of vanilla bean equals 1 teaspoon of vanilla extract.

Vanilla, as all extracts, is very concentrated and should be measured carefully and used judiciously to avoid overwhelming your baked goods. Since vanilla contains alcohol, it will evaporate quickly if the cap is not sealed tightly. Premeasured vanilla should always be kept covered until ready for use.

Candies and Decorative Sugars

Many candies and sprinkles are available for cookie embellishment, performing magic on an ordinary cookie.

Nonpareils: These are tiny sugar balls that commonly come in white and also in a rainbow of colors. They are usually color-coded for the season so you can plan on reds and greens or combinations at Christmas; lavender, yellow, pink, and green—anything pastel— make an appearance in spring; and birthday-party blue, orange, neon green and yellow can be found year-round.

Chocolate Nonpareil Candies: These are a cluster of tiny nonpareils, usually white, on chocolate disks. Again, candy-store versions are superior to the mass-produced, tasteless compound-chocolate varieties.

Jimmies: Rod-shaped, chocolate jimmies or sprinkles purchased at the supermarket are nondescript in taste and freshness. Shop around or look in a quality catalogue and you will find chocolate jimmies that actually taste chocolate. It is worth the time and money.

Dragées: Tiny, silver balls, dragées can be used for special effect but are *not edible*. There are other, edible ways to get shine without the dental repair that dragées incur.

Coarse Sugars: Available in brown (Demerara) and sparkling white, these lend an attractive finish and add crunch to your cookie.

Pearl Sugar: With super-white, large, irregular-shaped sugar grains, pearl sugar's main attraction, beyond appearance, is that it does not melt in baking.

Sparkling White Sugar: Clear, large crystal sugar grains, commonly from Scandinavia, slow-melting, used to decorate cookies and pastries.

Snow White Sugar: A confectioners'-type sugar, featured in The Baker's Catalogue (see Specialty Sources, page 403). It does not disappear as confectioners' sugar does when it comes in contact with moisture in frostings or under plastic wrap.

Glazing Sugar: This is another sugar featured in The Baker's Catalogue (see Specialty Sources, page 403). It is a confectioners'-type sugar that sets up fast and glossy and does not melt into your cookie.

Glitter: Not sugar at all, glitter is edible gum arabic and color manufactured to look like airy flakes of shimmer. Sprinkled on frosting, it catches the light for a dramatic presentation.

MARSHMALLOWS

Marshmallows are really in a class by themselves, as they are neither candy nor sugar. Whether in ½-inch miniature or 1½-inch airy puffs, they are very sweet, but can add unusual texture to cookies. Today, marshmallows are made from corn syrup, gelatin, gum Arabic, and flavorings and are readily available in supermarkets in a variety of colors.

About Equipment

At first glance, the equipment for preparing cookies appears daunting. How can so much be needed when all your grandmother used to turn out those heartwarming treats was a bowl, a wooden spoon, and a baking pan?

A closer look reveals that many of the items used for everyday cooking and baking are already in your kitchen. Other items, like the bâtarde (a tool used for pounding meat), can be used in innovative ways to facilitate some cookie preparations.

When you need to make a purchase, remember that quality equipment will pay off in the end.

Dry and Liquid Measures

Dry ingredients should always be measured in graduated and/or dry measures, preferably heavy stainless steel cups with sturdy handles. They are available in sets of ¼-, ⅓-, ½-, and 1-cup capacities, with some sets now including ⅔-, ¾-cup and 2-cup measures.

It is well worth spending a bit extra for stainless steel or good-quality plastic measuring spoons. They come in sets of ¼, ½, 1 teaspoon, and 1 tablespoon. Some newer sets add a ⅛ teaspoon and a 1½ teaspoon (equal to ½ tablespoon) to the standard four.

The most common liquid measures are heat-proof glass or plastic with a spout for spill-proof pouring. They come in 1-, 2-, or 4-cup (1-quart) capacities. Be aware that variations in the manufacturing process of liquid heat-proof glass measuring cups, even among popular brands, can produce inac-curately stamped measuring lines, resulting in too much or too little liquid in the recipe. To double-check the accuracy of your liquid measuring cup, fill a dry measuring cup to the *brim* with water, empty it into the new liquid measure, and see if the volumes are comparable. If not, when measuring, adjust the liquid accordingly.

Kitchen Scales

A good-quality digital scale can be used, but they may be pricey. An alternative is a small spring scale manufactured by Cuisinart. While the total weighing capacity is only 10 ounces, it does an adequate job for such ingredients as chocolate, nuts, dried fruit, and coconut. If the items to be weighed are just beyond the capacity of your scale, you may have to weigh in batches; however, this is not as accurate.

Thermometers

There are two essential thermometers needed for a baker's kitchen, an oven and a candy, each serving its own purpose. Since oven temperatures are frequently incorrect, owning an oven thermometer enables you to make any necessary minor adjustments in the thermostat. Candy thermometers are used for testing the temperature of sugar syrups for making nut brittles. These thermometers register between 100 and 400 degrees and often have clips for attaching them to pots.

Pastry (or Dough) Scraper

A pastry scraper performs many tasks in the preparation of cookie dough. If you have difficulty handling dough, this is the purchase to make. Uses include leveling the cup when measuring dry ingredients, cutting and portioning dough, releasing pastry that sticks to the rolling surface, cleaning the rolling surface, moving pastry, turning the dough and even slicing or cutting cookies. Select one that feels weighty, with a stainless steel blade and a wooden or plastic handle. Avoid those with metal handles as they are slippery and hard to grip.

Pastry Cloth and Rolling Pin Cover

Once you own a pastry cloth, your troubles with rolling dough will be a thing of the past. I highly recommend my custom canvas pastry cloth made by Ateco, paired with a knitted rolling pin cover or "stocking" (see Specialty Sources, page 403). Rubbing flour into the weave of the cloth and stocking creates an almost nonstick surface. This greatly reduces the amount of flour absorbed by the dough. In addition, dough sticking, breaking, or tearing is virtually eliminated. Washing the pastry cloth and rolling pin cover after each use will make them softer over time. After drying, store the cloth and cover rolled flat around a rolling pin. Do not fold the cloth because folding creates creases that will mark future batches of dough.

Rolling Pins and Surfaces

For rolling cookie dough, I recommend a heavy-duty 12-inch ball-bearing rolling pin made by Ateco (see Specialty Sources, page 403) for basic rolling needs and a tapered French rolling pin, 19 to 21 inches long, without handles for rolling thin doughs.

Cookie dough can be rolled on any flat surface; however, the one you choose may help or hinder your efforts. My favorite rolling surface is a large wooden pastry board that I cover with a canvas cloth to prevent the dough from sticking. To keep the board from sliding while working, I anchor it with a 12-inch square of rubber shelf liner. A dampened linen towel or several layers of moist paper towels are good alternatives. If you don't have a pastry board, roll the dough on your kitchen counter, be it granite, Formica, Corian, or wood.

Silpat

A French baking mat, silicone treated, nonstick surface, flexible fiber. Ideal for baking lace and other delicate cookies. Pricey, but worth the investment.

Pastry Docker

A pastry docker is a cylinder approximately 5 inches long with sharp spikes at ½-inch intervals around the entire surface. Older models are made of wood and nails while newer models are plastic. It is for piercing holes in sheets of dough to relax the gluten and reduce elasticity. This prevents the dough from shrinking and rising during baking. If you don't want to make the investment for a docker, a four-pronged table fork serves the same function, but it will take more time.

Graters

The grating called for in this book is primarily zesting citrus fruits and grating whole nutmeg. To do the job properly, the size and shape of the cutting edges are of utmost importance. I prefer a small, flat, stainless steel shredder with an easy-to-grasp handle and tiny scalloped cutting edges. This grater is safe for your knuckles and produces the perfect size zest. A flat hand grater with medium-sized scalloped cutting edges is a good choice to use for shredding ingredients like almond pastes; however, the traditional four-sided box grater is okay to use, too.

The Microplane grater is a kitchen essential. Basically a rasp, this grater is useful for zests and hard cheeses. Numerous variations are now available, including one with a handle (specifically for cheese), as well as a smaller model for nutmeg.

Strainers and Sifters

Strainers are essential for removing lumps and aerating flour. They also incorporate leavenings and salt. For incorporating dry ingredients with leavening, I recommend using an 8-inch strainer, preferably double-mesh, made by Cuisipro or Best. It is wise to have an assortment of sizes and mesh densities on hand to suit varying functions. It is worthwhile to invest in those that are well constructed. The mesh on less expensive equipment is easily bent out of shape.

Most of the sifters manufactured today, both single- and triple-mesh, suffer from poor construction and materials. The handles break easily under the stress of sifting and the mesh layers clog readily. If you do use a triple-mesh sifter, rather than stressing the handle through repeated squeezing, it is better to firmly tap the sifter with the side of your hand to shake the dry ingredients through. Never wash a sifter. Wipe it with damp paper towels.

Food Processors

Food processors have become an almost indispensable piece of equipment in today's modern kitchen. They are marvelous time savers, having the ability to perform tasks that are difficult to do by hand. Like most electric appliances, there are subtle differences that make one operate differently from another. The timing depends on the model and age of your machine. Differences in motors from model to model (and even machine to machine in the same model) will affect the size of the crumbs when making pastry doughs, as well as chopping nuts and chocolate. A dull blade can chop for the amount of time specified in the recipe but not achieve the desired consistency. If necessary, return your dull blade to the manufacturer for sharpening.

Electric Mixers

Electric mixers come in two major categories: the stand mixers and the hand mixers. When it comes to making cookie doughs, their use and convenience cannot be minimized.

The most versatile unit is the KitchenAid stand mixer. For normal home use, I recommend the

5-quart Artisan Tilt Head model with 325 watts of power. It is costly but worth the investment. Other brands of stand and hand mixers lack the power and accessories of the KitchenAid, but are quite suitable for mixing and whipping purposes. They perform well as long as the mixtures being combined are not too dense, which would overheat the motor.

Pots and Pans

The importance of using high-quality cooking equipment cannot be overstated. While only a few key pieces are needed for cookies, the performance of well-constructed, heavy-duty cookware like that manufactured by All-Clad, Calphalon, and KitchenAid will contribute to the success of a recipe. A well-insulated saucepan and frypan ensure an even reduction of liquid. Although a double boiler is recommended for heat-sensitive mixtures, especially melting chocolate, this method of cooking can be improvised. Placing a covered stainless steel or heatproof glass bowl over a pot of simmering water is a good alternative. Teflon and nonstick cookware are not recommended for these recipes.

Baking Pans

Half-Sheet or Jelly Roll Pan: These rimmed, shallow, rectangular aluminum pans are frequently used for bar cookies. Their low sides keep dough contained, while the aluminum bottom assures even baking without warping. Also used for baking and toasting biscotti, the sides of these pans keep the cookies from sliding off. Turned upside down, these pans may easily substitute for cookie sheets.

Square and Rectangular (Brownie) Pans: These deeper baking pans are also used for bar cookies. Seek out those made of heavy metal to achieve even baking and to prevent crusting on the sides of the bar cookies.

Cookie Sheets: The purchase of quality cookie sheets will afford you the greatest reward. The weight should be heavy and the color should be light! Aluminum is the best conductor of heat for high-sugar foods and it won't warp at high baking temperatures. If a pan is warped, loose batters will not spread evenly.

Also available are combinations of stainless steel and aluminum, insulated sheets (which tend to require more baking time), and stainless steel. When purchasing cookie sheets, look for those with only one or two "lips" for grasping. Open sides encourage air circulation around the dough. The size of your oven should be kept in mind when purchasing cookie sheets. For even baking, you should allow 2 inches of oven space around the sheet.

Here is a list of metal baking pans used in this book:

$10\frac{1}{2} \times 15\frac{1}{2} \times 1$-inch jelly roll pan
$12 \times 17 \times 1$-inch Professional half sheet pan
14×17-inch oversize cookie sheet*
12×15-inch standard size cookie sheet*
  *Size will vary according to the manufacturer
$9 \times 13 \times 2$-inch rectangular baking pan
$9 \times 9 \times 2$-inch square baking pan
$8 \times 8 \times 2$-inch square baking pan
4 mini-muffin tins
2 to 4 petite Madeleine pans
2 8-inch metal tart pans with removable bottoms
Note: If using pans with a nonstick surface, a dark metal surface or

made of ovenproof glass, the oven temperature must be reduced by 25 degrees to prevent overbaking.

Cooling Racks

I prefer stainless steel or nonstick cooling racks with small rectangular grids. These provide better support for cooling cookies. Also, smaller cookies are less likely to slip through the cracks. Look for racks that are stable, with "legs" high enough to allow for good air circulation.

Miscellaneous Tools

Offset Spatula: The metal blade of this spatula dips so that the blade is lower than the handle, enabling you to easily release cookies from pans and evenly smooth the surface of bar cookies, icings, glazes, and other toppings. The recommended sizes are 3 ½-inch and 6-inch.

Rubber Spatulas: Sometimes referred to as "scrapers," these come in a variety of sizes. The small 1-inch spatula is handy for scraping out the inside of measuring cups and small containers. The 2-inch mid-range spatula is useful for stirring, blending, and scraping the bottom of bowls. The 2 ¾-inch large or oversize variety is essential for folding ingredients such as chocolate chunks, nuts, and chopped fruit into dough. Its sturdy, larger surface covers a wider area and thoroughly blends ingredients. I recommend purchasing those with a plastic or wooden handle made by Rubbermaid. While all rubber spatulas will scrape a bowl clean, less expensive brands with blades that are either too stiff or too limp will not do the job well. Heat-proof spatulas do not flex well for mixing, but they are ideal to use when melting chocolate.

Whisks: For baking purposes, the longer, tapered sauce whisk is useful for combining dry ingredients with leavening, as well as for blending and stirring, along with numerous other tasks. Balloon whisks draw in air, making them ideal for whipping eggs, heavy cream, and other light mixtures. Look for graduated sizes in the sauce whisks and an 11- to 13-inch balloon whisk for whipping purposes.

Pastry and Goosefeather Brushes: Pastry brushes are indispensable accessories for making cookies. They are used for greasing a pan, as well as for brushing excess flour from dough and for glazing. Flat, natural-bristle brushes with tight ferrules secured with metal or rubber bands, are recommended because they prevent bristles from straying into your food. Brushes in widths of 1, 1½, and 2 inches are the most practical and commonly used. To clean brushes, soak them in very hot soapy water, changing the liquid a few times, especially if still greasy. Do not let the water rise above the metal band. After a thorough rinsing, reshape the bristles. Do not use the same brushes for savory purposes; keep them separate. With good care, your brushes should last for years.

Goosefeather brushes, made from a tightly wrapped cluster of five feathers, are useful for removing excess flour from puff pastry. As with natural bristle brushes, they should be thoroughly cleaned.

Pastry Cutting Wheels (also called Jaggers): There are two styles of pastry wheels, one with a straight blade, sometimes referred to as a pizza cutter, and the other with a jagged or fluted edge. While inter-changeable, I like the attractive zigzag edge the fluted wheel gives to cookies. The straight-blade pastry wheel is the best choice for cutting sticky doughs because the dough does not adhere to the grooves on the fluted wheel. For best results, look for a stainless steel pastry cutter with a sturdy wheel that is firmly secured to the handle to prevent wobbling.

Decorating Equipment: The equipment in this book is limited to a few basic but versatile pieces. Those that I have chosen can create many simple, yet artistic designs. Decorating equipment is available in most upscale cookware shops or stores where cake decorating equipment is sold. The brand that I recommend purchasing is Ateco (see Specialty Sources, page 403). You will want 14-,16-, and 18-inch plastic-coated canvas pastry bags. The suggested decorating tips have the following uses: #804 large round tip for piping cookies; #822 small open star tip for piping ganache and buttercream; #824 large open star tip for piping macaroons; and #805 large round tip for piping cookie dough.

The decorating comb is for making ridges on frosted cookies. Plastic squirt bottles are perfect for piping lines, dots, and other decorations on cookies. A sugar shaker is ideal for evenly distributing granulated and confectioners' sugar over the tops of baked cookies and brownies. Save empty spice bottles or other small containers with fine-holed lids for this purpose, as well.

Cookie Cutters: As with most equipment, quality is worth paying for. I recommend stainless steel or tin-plated cutters that are proportionately heavy for their size, with finely soldered or welded joints. Copper cutters are sturdy as well. To stamp the best cookies, cutters should also have strong handles without any sharp or jagged edges. Many cookie cutter kits are available today, but some of the cutters are flimsy.

Wash and dry the cutters thoroughly after each use. Store them in heavy boxes to protect them from bending out of shape.

Springerle and Speculaas Molds: These intricate, hand-carved wooden molds (see Specialty Sources, page 403), come in a variety of motifs, including animals, flowers, birds, fish, people, and winter scenery. After use, clean the molds with warm soapy water using a mushroom brush or soft-bristled toothbrush. Rinse with clean water and thoroughly dry. The molds may be submerged briefly in water, but *do not soak*. Then carefully wrap for future use.

Cookie Press: With this versatile tool, cookie dough (usually butter-based) is pushed through a barrel-shaped cylinder through a decorative forming plate. Most cookie presses come with up to twenty decorative plates, as well as decorating tips. Some models are available with see-through acrylic plastic, a feature I like. When you make a trip to your next garage sale, if you stumble across a cookie-press with a screw top, don't pass it up. They are the best!

Other Tools Are:

18-inch artist's ruler: For accurate measuring of rolled dough.

Palm size plastic bowl scraper (pastry corne)

Bâtarde (flat-bottomed meat pounder): For smoothing dough.

Square metal mini offset spatula (2¼ x 2¼ inches): For cutting bar cookies.

Ice pick: For breaking up blocks of chocolate.

Chocolate Dipping Fork: These lightweight pronged forks easily balance cookies or confections for dipping in melted chocolate.

Ice Cream Scoop: This is the perfect tool for evenly portioning dough for large cookies. Choose a round scoop with a cog-regulated, spring-release blade. The number 16 scoop is ¼ cup, the ideal size for making oversize cookies like Big Boys (Chapter 3). Look for the number on the release blade. Teaspoon and tablespoon scoops are also available for smaller portions.

Tassie Tamper: An inexpensive, small wooden dowel, this is used to press cream cheese dough evenly into mini-muffin tins. It's available in the gadget departments of houseware stores.

Miscellaneous Equipment

Krumkake Iron: Both electric and stovetop models are available (see Specialty Sources, page 403). The electric model will bake two cookies at a time, imprinting them with an "Old World" decorative design.

The stovetop model, made of cast aluminum, bakes one cookie at a time. Wooden cones are also available for shaping the cookies.

Assorted cookie tins

Disposable aluminum foil containers with lids: In assorted sizes, for storing cookies in freezer.

Plastic wrap

Wax paper

Aluminum foil: Regular, release (nonstick), and 18-inch heavy-duty.

Baking parchment paper

Mini-cupcake liners

Ovens

Conventional, Convection, and Microwave: My students frequently ask what kind of oven I recommend. The optimum arrangement is a gas cooktop with an electric oven. Most professional cooks agree that gas burners produce more intense, easily adjustible heat, yet electric ovens are preferred for their even baking.

Always be selective about the insulation of the oven and the size of the cavity. Since oven space varies from brand to brand, when purchasing a new oven, take your largest cookie sheet to the appliance store to see if it will fit.

Convection ovens are okay to use for baking cookies; however, owing to the circulating air from the oven fan, reduce the temperature by 25 degrees to prevent overbrowning. Be sure to check the baking time as well. Your cookies will often be finished sooner than if baked in a conventional oven. While cookies are not baked in microwave ovens, these are okay to use for melting chocolate and warming glazes. They are also useful for smaller jobs like melting butter, for heating liquids, or for thawing frozen foods. The defrost setting is especially useful for these purposes because you have more control over the heat.

Although today there are many new innovative and costly pieces of baking equipment from which to choose, I'm still old-fashioned at heart. Classic conventional baking continues to be my preference. Still, you should choose the appliance that works best for your situation. Whatever the decision, thoroughly research your options before making a final purchase. This will be time well spent.

Techniques

My primary goal throughout my years of teaching has been to stress the importance of techniques. At first glance, a recipe may seem straightforward, but there are numerous pitfalls hidden within the text of a recipe that lead to mediocre results or even failures. Good baking relies on checks and balances of ingredients. How they are measured, how they are combined, how they are baked, how they are stored, all make a difference in the final result. When you understand a procedure, even one as simple as measuring a cup of flour, you will achieve greater successes.

I teach primarily participation classes and my kitchen is my classroom. In this environment I have had the privilege to observe my students in action. This has given me the opportunity to zero in on procedures written in a recipe that can stymie even the most seasoned bakers. In the techniques that follow, it is my pleasure to share what I have learned from my own years of trial and errors, from my personal teachers, and from many of you.

Ways with Flour and Other Dry Ingredients

Flour is the "muscle man" in baking. It forms the structure to support key ingredients like butter, sugar, and eggs. Throughout my baking career, I have always adhered to my own rule of sifting flour before measuring. However, in working with cookies, I have found that this step has less importance. While it is true that the amount of flour increases when it is strained or sifted, this marginal difference is less crucial to cookie doughs than to other forms of baking.

My cardinal rule—which has not changed—is to *always* spoon the flour into the cup. *Never* dip the cup into the flour. Dipping the cup compacts the flour, and you will have far too much flour in the cookies.

MEASURING DRY INGREDIENTS

Start with an accurate set of dry or graduated measuring cups and a sheet of wax paper, approximately 15 inches in length, placed on your work surface. Spoon the dry ingredient into the appropriate-size dry or graduated measuring cup. (If measuring flour, be sure to fluff it first with a spoon.) Using a straight-bladed object, such as a dough scraper, straight spatula, or dull side of a knife, level the flour by sweeping the utensil straight across the top of the cup. (If measuring quantities less than ¼ cup using measuring spoons, it's okay to dip the spoon into the dry ingredient. The amount is so minimal that there is less chance of the dry ingredient compacting.)

If you are a "shaker," a person who is accustomed to shaking the measuring cup while spooning in flour, stop. Put your measuring cup down on the wax paper and then spoon the dry ingredient into the cup. The simple motion of shaking compacts the flour too much.

STRAINING, SIFTING, AND WHISKING DRY INGREDIENTS

Although it is common practice for manufacturers to label bags of flour "pre-sifted," if a recipe calls for sifting ignore this. The benefits of aerating flour or other dry ingredients cannot be minimized. "Aerating" means passing the dry ingredients through a mesh; the mesh removes lumps and makes the dry ingredients lighter and more powdery. Straining or sifting sets the stage for better blending and absorption of other ingredients. But, most important, straining or sifting blends the dry ingredients with leavening more thoroughly, which is key to achieving a successful result.

It is irrelevant whether you use a sifter or a strainer as long as the dry ingredients pass through a mesh. That mesh can be a medium-gauge strainer or the traditional cylinder-shaped sifter. Because sifters are so poorly made today, I personally prefer a strainer. Generally, I strain over a sheet of wax paper about 15 inches in length.

INCORPORATING LEAVENING WITH DRY INGREDIENTS

My preferred method of blending leavenings—such as baking powder, baking soda, or cream of tartar—into flour is to pass them through a strainer or sifter. This does not apply to recipes where dry ingredients and leavenings are incorporated in a food processor. Begin by using a medium-gauge strainer or sifter placed over a piece of wax paper about 15 inches long. Tear a second sheet of wax paper about the same size and place it next to the first piece. Pass the flour and leavenings through the strainer three times, alternating it back and forth between the pieces of paper. This is a cinch if you lift the paper up and form a funnel to pour the dry ingredients back and forth.

Whisking leavening through flour is another method that can be used in place of straining. I use this technique when smaller amounts of leavenings have to be incorporated. (Larger amounts are better incorporated if they are strained or sifted together three times.)

When grain flours, such as whole wheat or cornmeal, are used in a recipe, strain the leavening through the white flour first, then whisk the grain flour through the white flour and leavenings. Straining grain flour or cornmeal is not recommended because of its coarse texture.

WORKING WITH SUGARS AND OTHER SWEETENERS
Sugar partners with flour and butter as one of the three primary ingredients used in cookie baking. Besides contributing sweetness, sugar adds moistness and tenderness to cookies, and it encourages browning. Many of the recipes in this book use superfine sugar, which melts faster because the granules are smaller. If you are unable to purchase superfine sugar, make your own by grinding granulated sugar in a food processor or a blender. For successful results with your cookies, be sure to use the kind of sugar that is specified in the recipe. If you use sugar substitutes, please refer to books specifically written for these products.

MEASURING WHITE SUGARS
To measure white sugar, a dry or graduated measuring cup is essential. Fill the cup brimming to the top, either with a large spoon or using the dip method. Using a straight-bladed knife, level the top. Because confectioners' sugar is lumpy, strain it before measuring unless the recipe uses a food processor or indicates differently.

MEASURING BROWN SUGAR
Both light and dark brown sugars are used extensively in cookie baking. The sugar must be very *fresh and soft* for successful results. If it is not, use it for another purpose and start with a fresh box (which also must be soft). These sugars harden quickly once they are opened. They should be well sealed, enclosed in plastic wrap, and kept in the refrigerator to retain their softness.

Brown sugars should always be measured in graduated or dry measuring cups. "Lightly packed" brown sugar means that when filling the measuring cup, the sugar should be lightly tamped. When the sugar is inverted, it will retain its shape, but may have some open spaces. When "firmly packed" brown sugar is indicated in a recipe, the sugar must be pressed down firmly into the measuring cup, and if inverted, will have a more compact shape and no open spaces.

After measuring, brown sugar should never be left uncovered for any length of time because a crust will form on the surface. A piece of plastic wrap placed over the cup will keep the surface soft.

Measuring Liquids
Fluid measuring cups should always be used for measuring liquids. The easiest to use is ovenproof glass because the measurements are clearly marked. When measuring liquids, chose a cup nearest to the amount you are measuring. For example, if you are measuring smaller quantities— under ½ cup—don't use a 2- or 4- cup measure. A new addition to the market is a fluid measuring cup introduced by Oxo. The modernistic design allows you to see the liquid level without bending over.

MEASURING THICK SYRUPS
Corn syrup, molasses, honey, and maple syrup are best measured in a dry or graduated measuring cup. Before measuring, it's a good idea to lightly grease the container with vegetable oil or nonstick cooking spray. This prevents the syrup from sticking to the container. To prevent spillage when you pour, always hold the cup directly over the dough or batter.

Ways with Butter, Solid Shortening, and Oils
Butter provides unparalled flavor, delicate color, and extraordinary tenderness and it retains freshness. Butter is sold both salted and unsalted. Salt added to butter acts as a preservative, but it masks its clean, natural flavor. Both salted and unsalted butters have a butterfat content of about 80 percent. In recent years, European-style butters have been introduced to the market. These butters have a higher butterfat content of about 83 percent and are a welcome addition to the baker's pantry. However, because they are richer, the higher butterfat content can make a dough more difficult to handle. All of the recipes in this book use regular, unsalted butter.

Other fats like vegetable shortening and oils can be used as well. When dietary laws must be observed, margarine, preferably unsalted, can be used as a substitute.

Semi-solid fats, like butter and margarine, are classified as plastic fats. These are fats that hold air and are malleable by means of creaming and kneading. Vegetable shortening is a solid fat that also holds air and can be creamed. Oils, on the other hand, are classified as liquid fats. They lack the ability to hold air and cannot be creamed using ordinary kitchen mixing equipment. Since most cookie doughs have a high ratio of fat to flour, the kind of fat used plays a huge roll in cookie baking.

All wheat flour contains protein, which converts to gluten when it comes in contact with moisture or fat. When flour and fat are combined, the fat wraps itself around the starch granules in the wheat flour, shortening the gluten strands. This results in a delicate, melt-in-your-mouth crumb. Oil, because it is fluid, quickly moistens the starch granules, making dough much softer and more difficult to handle.

SUBSTITUTING BUTTER FOR VEGETABLE SHORTENING

While butter can be substituted for vegetable shortening, vegetable shortening is 100 percent fat and butter is about 80 percent fat and 20 percent water and milk solids. Making this substitution often changes the end result. A cookie made with vegetable shortening is more likely to retain its shape and is less likely to spread. The cookie will have a crisp texture, but will lack flavor. On the other hand, cookies made with butter are rich in flavor, but can be less crisp. In recent years, Crisco introduced butter-flavor vegetable shortening, but don't be fooled into thinking you will achieve the same butter flavor. There is nothing that compares to the pure flavor of real butter. *When substituting butter for*

vegetable shortening, if there is liquid in the recipe, reduce the liquid amount by 1 tablespoon per each 4 tablespoons (or one-half stick) of fat.

THE RIGHT TEMPERATURE

The correct temperature of butter, margarine, and vegetable shortening, as well as oil, is crucial when it comes to preparing a cookie dough. Recipe directions that call for butter at "room temperature" can be very misleading. Temperatures of room environments are as variable as the outdoor temperatures at different seasons of the year.

Butter, the most popular of the fats used for cookies, generally should be slightly firm. To determine this, hold a stick of butter in your hand and press it. You should be able to make a slight impression. If butter is too soft, the milk solids separate from the butterfat, making a dough that is too soft, as well. Butter that is too hard will not incorporate easily with other ingredients, producing a dough that is not smooth. When you work with margarine, note that it is softer than butter and should be used in a slightly firmer state. Be wary of using "reduced fat" or "light" substitutions because they do not perform the same.

Vegetable shortening stored at room temperature can be used immediately. If stored in the refrigerator, let it stand for 10 to 15 minutes at room temperature. The same rule applies for vegetable oils.

MEASURING STICK BUTTER AND MARGARINE, VEGETABLE SHORTENING, AND OIL

When measuring stick butter or margarine, note that the recipes in this book specify measurements in tablespoons, up to 1 cup, and/or stick measurements. Stick butter

and margarine are packaged in pre-marked 4-ounce bars. Take note of the wrapping on the stick because the measurements are not always positioned correctly. I recommend opening up the wrapping and dividing the sticks accordingly.

Vegetable shortening is easier to measure in graduated or dry measuring cups rather than liquid measures. After selecting the appropriate-size cup, pack the shortening into the cup, pressing it down to remove any air pockets. Use a straight-edge knife or dough scraper and level the top. As an alternative, vegetable shortening can be measured using the displacement method. For example, if a recipe specifies ½ cup of vegetable shortening, fill a 1-cup liquid measure with ½ cup of water. Then add enough vegetable shortening to raise the water level to 1 cup.

Vegetable shortening is also sold in convenient 1-cup sticks. If you are substituting vegetable shortening for butter, using this type of packaging, the measurement is different because the stick is labeled by volume rather than by weight. One stick of vegetable shortening weighs 7 ounces and is 1 cup by volume, while two sticks of butter weigh 8 ounces and are 1 cup by volume: the butter weighs 1 ounce more. Because vegetable oil is fluid, it should always be measured in liquid measuring cups.

CUBING STICK BUTTER AND MARGARINE

Many cookie recipes use cubed butter or margarine for doughs made either by hand or in a food processor. The easiest way to form cubes is to open a stick of butter or margarine, but do not remove the wrapping, as it keep your hands from becoming greasy. Be sure to do this while the butter or margarine is still cold. The best utensil to use for cubing is a dough scraper, however a long, sharp knife will do. Hold the dough scraper lengthwise or parallel to the stick of butter or margarine and cut down firmly. While it's still on the wrapper, give the butter or margarine a quarter-turn and cut down again lengthwise. Then cut ½-inch slices across the stick, making ½-inch cubes.

STORING BUTTER, MARGARINE, AND VEGETABLE OIL

Butter and margarine should be tightly wrapped and refrigerated away from strong odors. It's okay to take advantage of sales because these dairy items freeze well. If freezing, always label and date the package. Oils can be kept at room temperature, but because they turn rancid easily, I prefer to keep mine tightly covered in the refrigerator.

CLARIFYING BUTTER

Clarified butter is butter that is cooked to separate the center layer of fat from the whey proteins and milk solids. This can be done either on the stovetop or in a microwave. When the butter is melted, a layer of white foam that contains whey proteins, or milk solids, will form on the top. This should be removed with a spoon and discarded. The center layer will be a clear, golden liquid that is 100 percent fat and free of impurities. The remaining bottom layer is a watery substance of milk protein and salts, which are also discarded.

There are many benefits to clarifying butter. The clear butter develops a marvelous, nutty taste that blends beautifully with sugars, spices, and nuts. Because it is composed of only fat, the texture of the cookie is often crispier. In addition, clarified butter has a long shelf life because the impurities have been removed.

When butter is clarified, allow for about a 20 to 25 percent loss in volume. One pound or 2 cups of butter will reduce to slightly more than 1½ cups. Since it can be stored for months in the refrigerator or freezer, it makes sense to clarify a pound at a time. There are two ways to clarify butter.

Stovetop Method: Start with a deep, heavy-bottomed saucepan of an appropriate size. Remove the butter from the wrapping and place in the saucepan. Cook over low heat until white foam (the milk solids) accumulates on the surface. Carefully skim the foam from the surface with a large spoon, repeating until the foam no longer appears. Continue to cook the butter over low heat until the butterfat is clear and the milk proteins have settled to the bottom of the saucepan.

Clarified butter can take from 15 to 40 minutes to make, depending upon how much you are clarifying and the weight of the saucepan. The butter should stand until tepid and then be poured through a fine-mesh strainer placed over a jar. Do not allow the sediment from the bottom of the pot to pass through the strainer. Refrigerate or freeze in a tightly covered glass jar.

Microwave Method: I use this method when a small amount of clarified butter is needed quickly, but the finished product is not as flavorful or as pure as butter that is slowly clarified on the stovetop. Place the appropriate amount of unsalted butter in a microwave-proof container, allowing for the 20 to 25 percent loss of milk solids—for example, 4 tablespoons of whole butter will yield about 3 tablespoons of clarified butter. Choose a container that is deep and large enough to allow for possible eruptions during the melting process. Melt the butter on medium power, then carefully skim the foam (milk solids) that has formed on the top. Let the butter stand at room temperature for 2 to 3 minutes so the milk proteins can sink to the bottom of the container. Then carefully pour off the center layer of fat, discarding the milky liquid at the bottom.

BROWNED BUTTER

Browned butter (*beurre noisette*) is butter that is cooked beyond bright yellow to a rich, golden brown. Butter cooked to this stage has a more intense, nuttier flavor. A word of caution: pay attention to the color of the butter toward the end of the cooking time. It can quickly change from the richly flavored nutty state to one that will taste burned from overcooking.

Handling Eggs

Eggs add color, flavor, and texture as well as stability to dough and batters. The yolk contributes fat and tenderness; the white provides structure. Additionally, both yolks and whites are binders with other ingredients.

Bring eggs to room temperature for 20 to 30 minutes before incorporating them into dough and batters. This will encourage better blending and greater volume if beaten. If you're short on time for immediate use, place the eggs in a bowl of tepid water and let stand for 1 to 2 minutes to remove the chill.

STORING EGGS

Eggs are highly perishable and should be kept in the coldest part of the refrigerator. They should be stored in their original containers, not in refrigerator egg trays, to prevent tastes and odors from penetrating their porous shells. Because salmonella food poisoning can easily be transmitted, proper refrigeration and cleanliness are paramount.

SEPARATING EGGS

Eggs separate better when they are closer to their expiration date and when they are still cold. Always start with clean hands and use the three-bowl method when separating eggs: one to crack the eggs over, the second to empty the whites into, and the third to hold the yolks. For cracking the shell, use the blade of a table knife and firmly tap across the center of the egg. Supporting the egg in your hand, turn it upright. Remove the top portion of the shell and allow the white to flow over the side. The bottom shell becomes the cup to hold the yolk. Holding one shell half in each hand, pass the yolk back and forth, from one shell to the other, tipping the yolk slightly to remove as much of the white as possible. Should the yolk break, do not let any of the yolk droplets fall into the whites. If the whites are to be beaten, even the smallest amount of yolk will reduce the volume. When you break the egg, if any of the shell falls into the egg, try to remove it with a spoon rather than with the eggshell.

All eggs have two chalazae, a large one and a small one. These protein-rich cordlike strands anchor the yolk to the center of the egg. Large chalazae are an indication of freshness. If the egg is heated, whether on the stovetop or in the oven, the chalazae harden and becomes marble-like. The larger chalazae can easily be removed from the uncooked egg yolk with your fingertips. I recommend doing this when making meringue cookies or cookies made with beaten egg whites.

BEATING EGGS

With the exception of meringue-type cookies, cookie doughs and batters are dense and often do not require a lot of beating. In fact, for many recipes overmixing should be avoided. For quicker absorption, if more than two eggs are used, it's a good idea to whisk them in a separate bowl because they will blend in more efficiently.

BEATING EGG WHITES

When egg whites are to be stiffly beaten, always start them at room temperature. The bowl and beaters must be thoroughly washed, with no accumulation of oils on the surface. Cleaning the bowls occasionally with lemon juice or white vinegar to remove this film is a good idea. It's true that a copper bowl does the best job for whipping, however stainless steel bowls perform quite well. Glass and pottery are satisfactory, but these materials do not always create the needed friction for forming air cells. Bowls made of reactive metal, like aluminum, or those made of plastic, should be avoided.

The most common instructions for beating egg whites make reference to three stages: frothy, soft peak, and stiff peak. Because egg whites are often improperly beaten, I introduced a helpful fourth stage that I refer to as "firm peak." This stage falls between soft peak and stiff peak and is especially important when making meringue cookies. The four stages are:

Stage 1—Frothy: Whites are no longer clear, but have developed a foam. At this stage, salt and cream of tartar are commonly added.

Stage 2—Soft Peak: Ridges begin to form on the surface of the egg whites. They are moist and shiny, and when the beater is lifted, the peak of the egg white curves slightly, like the beak of a bird. This is the time to fold them into a batter or to add sugar to form a soft meringue. Although not generally applicable to cookies, egg whites beaten to the soft peak stage provide maximum expansion during baking.

Stage 3—Firm Peak: The ridges on the surface of the egg whites have become very defined, like the back of a sea shell, and are still moist and shiny. At this stage, they stand in firm peaks and are ready for sugar to be added to make a stiff or hard meringue for meringue cookies. Take note that the egg whites pass from stage 2 to stage 3 in a matter of seconds.

Stage 4—Stiff Peak: Sugar has been added and egg whites are beaten to stiff, shiny peaks. If no sugar is used, the whites will be "over-the-hill," dry and lumpy.

To beat egg whites, begin with a stand mixer or hand-held beater on medium-low speed. Add the salt and cream of tartar when the whites reach stage 1, frothy. Salt breaks the albumin of the whites and the cream of tartar stabilizes and whitens them. Increase the mixer speed gradually to medium-high. This gradual increase draws the air in more slowly, giving the whites a stronger structure. High speeds produce egg whites with large, unstable air cells that burst from too much friction, much like a balloon that is over inflated and bursts. Weak structure causes the egg white foam to lose its volume and become watery.

To remedy overly beaten egg whites, add one unbeaten egg white for up to six eggs and whip in briefly to the correct consistency.

Handling Nuts, Coconut, Seeds, and Fruits

Some adults and children do not like textured foods, so at times nuts and seeds can be omitted from a recipe. However, a batter made without them might have an entirely different end result. As an example, because nuts and coconut provide bulk and also perform as "spacers," a brownie or bar cookie made without these ingredients will be more compact. To replace the volume of the ingredient that you are eliminating, you might try substituting ingredients, such as chocolate chips and other flavored varieties of chips. Fortunately, other than flavor, small seeds omitted from a recipe will have minimal effect on a batter or dough.

TOASTING NUTS

Toasting nuts enlivens the oils, which greatly enhances their flavor, as well as adding extra crunchiness. I recommend toasting nuts before they are chopped and thoroughly cooling them before use. When I toast nuts, I like to toast a large batch at once and store them in a jar, refrigerated, ready for use.

Toasted nuts must be cooled before use to allow the rich oils to be reabsorbed. If used when still warm, not only can they cause the butter to melt in a cookie dough or batter but if chopped, they can become pasty.

Oven Toasting: Nuts, which are high in fat, will burn easily, so they should always be toasted on a shallow, heavy-gauge metal pan in a moderate to low oven, 300° to 325°. For even baking, they should be spread in a single layer to avoid crowding. Lining the pan with aluminum foil will save you a trip to the sink. The amount of nuts, their oil content, and their size are all determining factors in how long toasting will take. As an example, sliced almonds toast more quickly than whole almonds. When toasting large amounts of nuts, stir the nuts once or twice during baking for even browning.

To determine when nuts have reached their optimal toasting time, use color and fragrance as a guideline. The obvious sign on blanched or skinless nuts is a slight change in color. For unblanched nuts, fragrance is the best test. When the nuts are just beginning to release aroma, remove them from the oven. Overly roasted nuts are bitter and must be discarded.

When toasting nuts, never mix different varieties on the same pan unless they have similar oil content. Pecans and almonds, for example, would not toast the same. Pignolis (pine nuts) are small, high in oil, and take the least amount of time, 3 to 5 minutes. High-fat nuts like cashews and macadamias take 6 to 8 minutes, while walnuts and pecans take 8 to 10 minutes. Although pistachios are small, they are somewhat soft, so toasting for 6 to 8 minutes is recommended. Hard nuts like hazelnuts and almonds are less oily and require 12 to 15 minutes, or longer, to toast. Brazil nuts and peanuts are rarely toasted before using.

Stovetop Toasting: This quick method is good for small nuts like pignolis (pine nuts) and slivered or sliced almonds. While this is a satisfactory solution when you're in a hurry, there is nothing like the even browning or flavor of oven-toasted nuts. Toast small quantities of nuts in a heavy, ungreased skillet over medium-low heat. Shake the pan often for even browning.

REMOVING THE SKIN FROM NUTS

Hazelnuts: After the nuts are toasted, *while still hot*, empty them onto doubled paper towels. Place a layer of towels on top. Rub the nuts between the layers of towels until the skins loosen. It's okay if a small amount of skin clings to the nut.

Almonds and Pistachios: Blanch the nuts in boiling water, testing them every few minutes to see if the skins have loosened. Pistachio skins will come away from the nut sooner than the skins of almonds. As soon as the nuts are ready, pour them into a strainer and immediately rinse with cold water to stop the cooking process. Empty the nuts onto a pan lined with a double layer of paper towels and blot well with another layer of paper towels. Follow the same directions for removing the hazelnut skins. Then, bake the nuts in a 325° oven on a shallow baking pan until they are dry.

CHOPPING NUTS

Hand chopping produces very uniform pieces with the least amount of oil lost, while nuts chopped in the food processor will be irregular in size and oilier. Because so many cookies use this important ingredient, I will address various ways for working with this multidimensional product. The photographs on page 129 will serve as a guide when you prepare nuts for a recipe.

Hand chopping can be used for all nuts; however, it is especially recommended for high-fat nuts like cashews and macadamias. These higher-fat nuts release more of the nut oils, making chopping more difficult. Brazil nuts, another high-fat nut, are difficult to chop whole because of their size. Before chopping, first cut them in two or three pieces with a paring knife. (A quick time-saver for chopping smaller quantities of nuts, without using equipment, is to place them in a heavy-duty, zippered plastic bag and crush them with a bâtarde, a mallet, or the bottom of a small, heavy saucepan. Be sure to press out the air and seal well before chopping.)

Broken Nuts: Nuts that are split by hand into large, irregular pieces, about ⅜ to ½ inch. Applicable nuts are soft nuts like walnuts and pecans.

Coarsely Chopped Nuts: Place nuts on a cutting board and chop with a chef's knife into the size of dried chickpeas, ¼- to ⅜-inch pieces. Hand chopping produces the most uniform size, with the least amount of oil loss. Alternatively, if you don't have a chef's knife, place the nuts in a wooden bowl and chop them with a crescent-shaped hand chopper.

Medium Chopped Nuts: Chop nuts by hand into pieces slightly less than ¼ inch, much like the size of dried lentils or split peas (or see the food processor method that follows).

Finely Chopped Nuts: Chop nuts by hand into dried-barley-size pieces, about ⅛ inch (or see the food processor method that follows).

Nut Meal: Grind or pulverize nuts to a meallike texture. The ideal home method for making nut meal is with a Mouli hand grater; this procedure produces the most powdery consistency, releasing the least amount of oil, but it is a time-consuming process. Nut meals can be made in a food processor; however, a small amount of flour or sugar must be added to absorb the nut oils.

Chopping Nuts in a Food Processor: Food processors are marvelous time-savers for chopping nuts—just take care not to overprocess. While food processors do not produce uniform pieces, using the pulse button will help control the consistency. More uniform pieces can also be achieved by not overfilling the work bowl.

FOOD PROCESSOR TIPS:

- The steel blade is used for most chopping purposes.
- Try the shredding disk for medium-chopped nuts. This disk produces more even pieces.
- Avoid overfilling the processor bowl. Chop the nuts in small quantities of about ½ to 2 cups at a time, depending on the processor size.
- Use the pulse button to achieve a more evenly chopped nut.
- To help absorb the nut oils released during chopping nuts finely, add a small amount of flour or sugar.

When making a nut meal, pulse first to break up the larger pieces of nuts, then process continuously for the amount of time specified in the recipe. For even chopping, stop the processor occasionally to scrape around the side of the bowl. The nut meal is ready when the powdery mixture begins to clump or cluster around the edge of the bowl. This can take 45 to 60 seconds depending on the amount of nuts in the bowl.

Hard nuts, like hazelnuts and almonds, will take longer to chop than soft nuts, like walnuts and pecans. When chopping nuts for a period of time, always stop the processor to check the size of the nuts and to scrape around the edge of the bowl, if needed.

Here's a great hint for separating the larger pieces of nuts from the nut "dust": After chopping, empty the nuts into a wide-gauge strainer placed over a piece of wax paper. Shake the strainer to allow the smaller particles to fall onto the paper. These particles can be reused for recipes that call for finely chopped nuts. Place them in a tightly sealed container and refrigerate or freeze for later use.

MEASURING NUTS

When I measure nuts, I like to use graduated measuring cups. When you measure nuts, notice how the measurement is written in the recipe. If the recipe calls for "1 cup of nuts, chopped," that means to measure the nuts first and then chop them. If the recipe specifies "1 cup of chopped nuts," *chop them first* and then measure. Since nuts usually reduce in volume after chopping, the measurement will differ because the spaces between the larger pieces disappear. For 1 cup of chopped nuts, begin with 1 generous, full cup of whole nuts.

WORKING WITH ALMOND PASTE

Since the consistency of almond paste is very dense, it is best to use it at room temperature and to break it into smaller pieces to smoothly blend it with other ingredients. Sometimes, the almond paste can be mixed in an electric mixer fitted with the paddle attachment. It can also be chopped in the food processor using the steel blade. Shredding it with a box grater is another alternative. If the almond paste is dried out, it becomes very hard. You can try softening it briefly in a microwave. However, if it doesn't soften and it is a major ingredient in the cookie, I recommend discarding it.

USING COCONUT

Measuring Coconut: The recipes in this book use sweetened, flaked coconut and unsweetened or desiccated coconut, which has a finer, medium-cut flake. To measure the sweetened, flaked coconut, lightly pack it into a dry or graduated measuring cup. Fine-textured unsweetened, desiccated coconut should be poured into the dry measuring cup and leveled.

Toasting Coconut: Empty the sweetened coconut onto a shallow, heavy jelly-roll pan and spread to separate the flakes. Bake in a heated 325° oven for 8 to 10 minutes, tossing the coconut with a fork every so often to ensure even browning. The coconut will crisp as it cools. Watch carefully because it can overbrown quickly at the end of the baking period.

TOASTING SEEDS

Place the seeds in a small skillet and warm over low heat until they are fragrant and begin to brown. Shake the pan periodically to ensure even browning. Cool before using.

PLUMPING DRIED FRUITS

To plump or reconstitute dried fruit, empty it into a heat-proof bowl and cover with boiling water to 1 inch above the level of the fruit. The recipe will specify the appropriate length of standing time; however, the freshness of the fruit will be a determining factor. Older fruit is harder and drier, and

can take longer to soften. Smaller pieces of fruit, like raisins, will plump in a minute or two while larger pieces, such as apricots or prunes, will take longer. When the fruit is ready, empty it into a strainer and rinse briefly with cool water to stop the heating process. Spread the fruit on doubled paper towels. Cover with another layer of doubled paper towels and blot dry. Use as directed in the recipe.

To Macerate Dried Fruits: Plump the fruit first, following the directions above, but do not rinse with cool water. Drain on a double thickness of paper towels, cover with a top double layer of towels, blot dry, and empty into a bowl. The warm fruit will absorb the flavor of the liqueur more effectively. Proceed with the recipe, as directed.

Cutting Dried Fruit: Plumped dried fruit can be diced, sliced, or chopped on a cutting board with a chef's knife. To prevent the fruit from sticking, you can either rinse the knife with warm water or coat it with a little unflavored vegetable oil, from time to time. Fruits that have not been plumped can be cut with either a scissors or a chef's knife depending upon the size of the fruit. It is best to cut raisins with a chef's knife or with a paring knife.

WORKING WITH CITRUS FRUITS

A great frustration of mine is the many types of zesters or graters on the market, each producing a different size and shape of zest. Larger pieces of zest give the least amount of flavor, while finely grated zest gives a more pungent taste because more of the fruit oils are released. If the zest is not grated and measured as intended in the recipe, the balance of flavors

goes awry. The final result of the cookie can be flat or tasteless, while an excess can be overwhelming.

Zesting and Measuring Citrus Fruits: The recipes in this book use zest made with a small, rectangular hand grater, which is my preference (see "Graters," page 380). This is a flat, stainless steel shredder, safe to use, with an easy-to-grip handle. The scalloped cut edges produce a zest that has a moderately concentrated consistency, similar to minced onion, and does not require packing when measured.

Alternatively, if using the grater-zester, a more feathery shred is produced, so press the zest into the measuring spoon with moderate pressure. Additionally, the zest in the recipe should be increased by one-half—that is, 1 teaspoon of zest should be increased to 1½ teaspoons.

When you zest citrus fruits, first wash and thoroughly dry the fruit. Place a piece of wax paper underneath the grater, or grate over an appropriate-size bowl, to catch the zest. Run the fruit down the grater, moving it in one direction against the sharp grates. The pith, which is the white portion underneath the colored skin, is bitter and should never be used.

NOTE THE FOLLOWING EQUIVALENCES:

- A medium, 4-ounce lemon = approximately 3 tablespoons of juice
  1 teaspoon of zest using the hand grater
  1½ teaspoons of zest using grater-zester
- A medium, 10-ounce orange = approximately a scant ½ cup of juice
  2 teaspoons of zest using the hand grater
  1 tablespoon of zest using grater-zester

- A large, 4-ounce lime = approximately 3 tablespoons of juice
1 teaspoon of zest using the hand grater
1½ teaspoons of zest using the grater-zester

After fruit is zested, it deteriorates quickly. To avoid waste, squeeze the juice and freeze it to be used at another time. It will keep in a tightly sealed container for up to six months.

Juicing Citrus Fruits: To juice citrus fruit: roll the fruit back and forth on the counter, exerting gentle pressure to soften the pulp. For the fruit to release the most juice, it is best to have it at room temperature. Softening fruit in the microwave is not recommended because it cooks the fruit.

Working with Chocolate

Chocolate should be treated with respect. It is temperature-sensitive; it reacts to moisture, odors, and to overmixing; if chocolate is overheated, the flavor and texture are compromised. When chocolate is melted, merely a few drops of liquid can change its texture from satiny to gritty. When stored in a cold environment, its beautiful sheen is destroyed; if stored near pungent flavors, chocolate will absorb their essence. Why bother with this temperamental ingredient? Because, there is no other like it!

HOW TO CHOP CHOCOLATE
Chocolate should always be cut into small pieces to ensure even melting. This is crucial to retaining its good flavor and velvety texture. If the chocolate pieces are too large, the surface area becomes overheated before the center has an opportunity to melt.

The size pieces into which chocolate is chopped varies according to its texture. Unsweetened chocolate is the hardest of the dark chocolates, followed by bittersweet and semisweet chocolate. Bulk or block chocolate should be shaved on a cutting board using a chef's knife. Dark chocolates can also be chopped in a food processor because they are firm enough to withstand the heat. If using a processor, for even consistency and to avoid damaging the blade, the chocolate should be cut into pieces no larger than 1 inch before processing. Milk and white chocolate are soft chocolates and should not be chopped in a processor. These delicate chocolates can easily be cut into small pieces with a chef's knife on a cutting board.

Many of the recipes in this book call for 3.5-ounce Lindt candy bars. To dice Lindt or other brands of small candy bars, open the wrapper and place the chocolate on a cutting board. Using a chef's knife, dice the candy into ¼-inch pieces, or other size cubes to be used in place of chocolate chips, or as desired.

Here is a neat trick for cutting up pre-wrapped squares or bars of chocolate. Do not remove the wrapper from the chocolate. Place the paper-wrapped square or bar on a cutting board and pierce it several times with an ice pick. When the paper is removed, the chocolate will be broken into pieces, ready to melt with no mess. The same method works effectively for breaking up small candy bars.

MELTING DARK CHOCOLATES (UNSWEETENED, BITTERSWEET, AND SEMISWEET)
Using a Water Bath: Select a wide, shallow pan, such as a 10-inch skillet, and fill it with ½ inch of hot water, no more. Over low heat, bring the water to a simmer. Place the chopped chocolate in a heat-proof bowl deep and wide enough to prevent water or steam from reaching the chocolate. Place the bowl in the skillet and allow the chocolate to slowly melt. When the chocolate is almost melted, *turn the heat off.* Let the chocolate finish melting slowly, stirring gently from time to time. If the water becomes too cool, reheat it briefly. A small amount of chocolate will quickly melt, while larger amounts will take more time.

Using a Double Boiler: Fill the bottom of the double boiler with 1 to 2 inches of water. Alternatively, any pot can be used with a stainless steel or glass heat-proof bowl placed over it. The bowl should be wider than the pot and should not touch the water. Bring the water to a boil and then reduce it to a simmer. Place the chopped chocolate in the top portion of the double boiler or bowl and set it over the simmering water. When the chocolate is almost melted, turn the heat off and allow the chocolate to finish melting slowly. Stir occasionally and *gently* to be sure the chocolate melts evenly. Care should be taken to prevent steam from reaching the chocolate. Never cover chocolate during or after melting.

Microwave Method: My recommendation for small amounts of chocolate is to melt the chocolate on the defrost setting. Using this low setting, the chocolate melts more evenly, with less risk of overheating. Place the chopped chocolate in an ovenproof glass bowl. Using a defrost setting, melt the chocolate for about 1 minute. Stir with a rubber scraper, then return the bowl to the microwave for another 30 seconds. For larger amounts, heat the chocolate for 1 minute on medium setting. Stir gently with a rubber scraper and return to the microwave, continuing the melting process in 15- to 20-second increments. The time will vary according to the amount of chocolate you are melting and the wattage of your microwave. The chocolate often retains its shape although it is melted, which can be deceiving, so keep a sharp eye on it. It is not necessary for the chocolate to melt completely; it will continue to melt as it stands at room temperature. If it hasn't melted entirely when you're ready to use it, return the chocolate to the microwave for a few seconds. **Oven Melting:** Chopped chocolate can be placed in a shallow oven-proof container in a 225° oven. Stir often, allowing the chocolate to melt slowly. Turn the oven off when the chocolate is almost melted, stir gently and let it stand until completely melted.

MELTING MILK AND WHITE CHOCOLATE

I recommend melting delicate chocolates like milk and white using only the stovetop, water-bath method. These soft chocolates need less heat and less time to melt than dark chocolate. They must be watched carefully because they melt so quickly.

Start with milk or white chocolate cut into small pieces, ¼ to ½ inch. Put the chocolate in a stainless steel bowl and place the bowl in a skillet filled with ½ inch of *warm* water. Let the chocolate stand for a few seconds. Then gently stir with a rubber spatula until the chocolate is melted.

MELTING CHOCOLATE IN LIQUID

It is a myth that chocolate cannot be melted with liquid. It's okay to combine the two ingredients as long as enough liquid is present. Here is the proper ratio to use: For each ounce of bittersweet or semisweet chocolate, use at least 1 ½ teaspoons of liquid. For each ounce of unsweetened chocolate, use at least 2 tablespoons of liquid. Lumping or seizing is a common problem when melted chocolate must be combined with liquid. It's good practice to add the chocolate to the liquid, never the liquid to the chocolate.

For chocolate to blend smoothly into liquid, the chocolate should always be warm. If small pieces of chocolate are present, heat the chocolate slowly, constantly stirring until the mixture is smooth. Here are some chocolate heating tips:

- Always place chocolate in a thoroughly dry bowl. The slightest amount of moisture can cause it to seize.
- Chocolate should be stirred often and gently to ensure even melting.
- Chocolate should never be covered during or after melting because it picks up condensation.
- Chocolate should be melted away from boiling water; steam will cause the chocolate to seize or turn it gritty.
- Melted dark chocolate should never reach a temperature that exceeds 120°. Milk and white chocolate should never reach a temperature that exceeds 110° (these sensitive chocolates burn quickly because they contain milk).

SHAVING AND SLIVERING CHOCOLATE

At times, chocolate is shaved or slivered and added to a cookie dough or batter in an unmelted state. These shards or shavings of chocolate provide interesting contrast between the dark of the chocolate and the light of the cookie dough or batter. Shaved chocolate is finer than slivered chocolate.

When cutting chocolate for slivers or shavings, block or bulk chocolate works best, but 1-ounce squares of chocolate and small candy bars will do in a pinch. All chocolates should be very fresh, otherwise they are too brittle to shave or sliver. Begin with the chocolate placed on a cutting board and, using a chef's knife, cut the block starting at a corner. As the corner becomes wider, rotate the chocolate in another direction to find another corner.

Using a Water Bath

A water bath, also referred to as a *bain-marie,* can be used for both hot and cold mixtures. By surrounding the food with water, the heat is cushioned and protects and prevents the food from overcooking. In cookie baking, the hot water method is used most commonly for melting chocolate. It takes two vessels to make a water bath, one large and the other smaller. For stovetop purposes, a small amount of hot water is placed in a shallow pan, such as a skillet, and heated to a simmer. Set a bowl holding the chocolate into the water. The level of the water should cover no more than one-fourth of the exterior of the inner bowl. Otherwise, the bowl may float or tip.

Water baths are also used for cooling foods quickly. The larger vessel is filled with ice cubes and water and the smaller vessel is set into the center. At times, instead of using the larger vessel, I substitute my kitchen sink, filling it up with an inch or two of water along with some ice cubes. Set the smaller bowl into the ice water and gently stir the mixture to cool it down quickly.

Preparing Pans for Baking

Cookies can be baked on pans that are prepared with butter, margarine, vegetable shortening, vegetable oil, nonstick spray, baking parchment, aluminum foil, Teflon Bakeware Liners, Super Parchment, or other treated liners. Sometimes, cookies are baked on ungreased pans.

How I prepare the pan is determined by the kind of cookie batter or dough with which I am working. Cookie doughs containing a high ratio of butter often can be baked directly on an ungreased baking pan. This is not the case when a cookie batter or dough is very textured because there is a greater risk of sticking. Some rolled cookies made with jam need baking parchment. Sometimes, the 12-inch Release nonstick aluminum foil or the 18-inch heavy-duty aluminum foil can be used in place of parchment. I do not like to use nonstick spray because of the oily residue that remains on the pan after baking.

Following are various finishes that I recommend for preparing baking pans:

- *Butter*—My preference for cookie doughs and batters that require moderate greasing of the pan. Cookies baked on pans greased with butter brown evenly with no "off" taste. At times, butter encourages flavorful, crisp browning on cookie bottoms. Batters and doughs grip to butter, making it easy for them to spread properly. Pans greased with butter are easy to clean and the finish of the pan will be lasting.
- *Butter and flour or cocoa powder*—Ideal for lace cookies and those that are difficult to release from cookie sheets. Perfect for grooved pans, like madeleine tins. Not recommended for bar cookies because of pasty residue that remains on the bottom.
- *Margarine*—Recommended only for those who observe dietary laws.
- *Vegetable shortening*—Not recommended. Not pleasing to the palette.
- *Vegetable oils*—Not recommended. Not pleasing to the palette. Leaves a residue on pans, often making cleaning difficult.
- Nonsick spray—Not pleasing to the palette, but recommended for cookies such as lace cookies or cookies that are difficult to remove from pan. Sometimes, unpleasant film or oily spotting remains on the pan. A nonstick spray containing flour, such as Baker's Joy, is a good choice.
- *Baking parchment*—Ideal for cookies that have a tendency to stick to the pan, although buttering the paper might be necessary at times. Cookies baked on parchment retain their shape more readily and bake evenly. This is not recommended for lining or molding the bottom and sides of square and oblong pans, but it's okay for use on the bottom only. Parchment is difficult to cut on because the paper tears and slides. It's especially functional for baking on jelly roll pans, but awkward to use for spreading thick batters and doughs because the paper lifts. No clean-up required.
- *Aluminum foil*—The 18-inch heavy-duty aluminum foil is ideal for lining or molding the bottom and sides of square and oblong pans. Useful as a lining for cookie sheets but wrapping a small amount of foil under the pan is recommended. The Release nonstick aluminum foil is okay in some instances, but the 12-inch width limits its use. Be sure to use it on the nonstick side. At times, aluminum foil must be buttered or coated with nonstick spray. Baking on either the shiny or dull side is acceptable. No cleanup required.
- *Teflon pan liners*—French Silpat liners or other Teflon-coated liners are ideal for lacey, thin, or fragile cookies that have a tendency to stick. They are pricey, but a worthwhile investment. Easy maintenance.
- *Ungreased pans*—Cookie sheets, jelly roll pans, and mini muffin tins can be left ungreased when a cookie has a high percentage of butter. When making bar cookies, square, oblong, and jelly roll pans must be greased unless otherwise specified in the recipe.

A GUIDE TO BUTTERING PANS

Lightly Buttered: A thin layer of butter is spread on the pan and the butter is barely visible. An example is melted butter spread on a pan with a brush.

Moderately Buttered: Very soft butter is spread on the pan with a pastry brush and the butter is more visible. Do not use melted butter.

Well Buttered: Very soft butter, not melted, is spread on the pan with a pastry brush, making a thicker coating on the surface of the pan; however, the butter should not completely obscure the metal of the pan. (Caution: Care should be taken not to overly butter a pan because as the pan heats in the oven, the butter will ooze over the sides, causing smoking.)

LINING SQUARE AND OBLONG PANS WITH ALUMINUM FOIL

Invert the baking pan on a countertop. Tear off a sheet of 18-inch-wide heavy-duty aluminum foil large enough to cover the bottom and sides of the pan with at least 2 inches extra. Place the foil over the pan, forming it to the shape of the pan. Remove the foil, turn the pan right side up, and insert the aluminum foil liner into the pan. Mold the foil following the lines of the pan, using your knuckles to fit the liner into the corners. Take care not to tear the foil.

Using Baking Pans
COOKIE SHEETS VERSUS JELLY ROLL PANS

In most instances, cookie sheets and jelly roll pans are interchangeable. Throughout this book, in "At a Glance," I recommend the pan that I feel will perform the best. While many cooks and bakers refer to jelly roll pans as cookie sheets, the two pans are not the same. A jelly roll pan always has sides. A cookie sheet is flat except for a turned-up rim for ease of handling. Cookies can take slightly longer to bake on jelly roll pans because the sides of the pan buffer the heat. Sometimes, jelly roll pans are used for making thin bar cookies; releasing flat bar cookies is easier in

these shallow pans. A welcome arrival to the home kitchen is the oversized jelly roll pan, known as the professional or half-sheet pan. These larger pans are made of heavy-gauge aluminum. They have a large capacity and cookies made on them bake extremely well. Sometimes these half-sheet pans can be found in large discount stores, where they can be purchased at a very good price.

I like to use jelly roll pans for cookies that are twice-baked, like biscotti, because the rims on the pans prevent the sliced cookies from sliding off. Baking parchment is especially functional on jelly roll pans because the sides of the pans keep the paper from sliding. (More than one tray of cookies has ended up on my kitchen floor if the pan doesn't have sides.) When I bake with Silpat baking mats, I prefer to use a jelly roll pan.

On the other hand, cookie sheets are preferable for baking thin cookies that require spatulas to remove them for cooling. Because cookie sheets do not have sides, sliding a spatula underneath the cookie is easy. Another advantage to cookie sheets is their ability to hold more cookies. At times, I prefer to use cookie sheets lined with baking parchment. However, the cookie sheets must be dabbed with butter to prevent the parchment from sliding. If cookie sheets are not in your inventory of bakeware, when necessary, invert your jelly roll pans and bake on the back side.

Since an average home kitchen will have a limited number of flat pans, make do with whatever you have and don't let the lack of perfect pans prevent you from baking cookies.

Working with Doughs and Batters
FOLDING AND LIGHTENING

Folding is the process of combining two mixtures of different consistencies with the least amount of air loss. Since maintaining the volume is relevant, one-fourth to one-third of the lighter mixture is first folded into the denser mixture to lighten its consistency. For example, if firmly beaten egg whites have to be folded into a brownie-like batter, a portion of the egg whites is folded in first to "loosen" the batter. This equalizes the consistencies of the two mixtures, making them relatively similar and easier to incorporate.

Temperature of batters is also relevant. Two room-temperature ingredients combine more readily than two cold mixtures. Additionally, if one batter is cold and the other warm, the cold batter should be brought to room temperature so the two can be smoothly blended. To combine the two mixtures smoothly, the cooler mixture should also be lightened by incorporating a portion of the warmer mixture into it.

Whether lightening or folding, the technique is always done by hand, never with an electric mixer or food processor. Be sure to choose a mixing bowl large enough to incorporate the two mixtures without crowding. Always fold with an appropriate-size rubber spatula. When working with large quantities, it is best to use a spatula that is oversized. The job will be done in less time and with less effort.

Here is the technique for folding: Grasp the spatula with the curved side facing down, and cut through the center of the mixture. Move the spatula under the mixture, scraping the bottom of the bowl. Sweep the spatula up the side of the bowl, over the top, and cut through the center again. As you fold, rotate the bowl frequently to evenly blend the mixtures. Occasionally, clean around the entire bowl.

FRAISAGE

Fraisage is a French term meaning "to knead," and is used to incorporate butter and flour, most particularly in doughs with high butter content. Fraisage, when done properly, ensures a tender pastry. Although food processors can also be used to accomplish this kneading technique, machines tend to overwork the dough.

Form the flour–butter mixture into a mound and place on a clean, lightly floured, cool surface such as marble or granite. A countertop will do as well. With the heel of your hand, smear 2 to 3 tablespoons of the dough against the surface, using a 6- to 8-inch outward sweeping motion. Repeat the procedure 2 or 3 times until all of the butter-flour mixture has been blended into a smooth dough.

SPREADING BATTERS AND DOUGHS

Thin batters, which are poured into the pan, should be spread evenly into the corners of the pan with the bottom of an oversized tablespoon. Thick doughs should be dropped in mounds from the tip of a spoon, spacing them equally in the pan. Spread them as evenly as possible with a small offset spatula, distributing them evenly into the corners, as well. For a square pan, I make four mounds, for an oblong pan, I make six mounds, and for a jelly roll pan I make eight mounds. For doughs that are unusually thick, I flour my hands and form the

dough into balls, arranging them evenly in the pan. For these dense doughs, I increase the amount of balls per pan—about nine for a square pan, twelve to fifteen for an oblong pan. This makes the dough easier to spread.

To spread dense dough, flour the heel of your hand and pat the dough to flatten it, working it into the corners of the pan. Lay a strip of plastic wrap or wax paper over the surface of the dough and gently pat it with a bâtarde or the bottom of a glass until it is even. Using a metal dough scraper, the straight side of a plastic bowl scraper, or the blade of a square metal spatula, neaten the edges by inserting the tool between the dough and the edge of the pan. This creates an even edge on the finished cookie and facilitates cutting. To test for evenness of the dough, randomly insert a knife or toothpick into the surface of the dough, then if needed, pat the dough level with your hand.

PORTIONING COOKIE DOUGH EVENLY

Many bakers have difficulty portioning doughs into equal pieces. Here are a few suggestions to help you along. For soft doughs, clean the sides of the bowl with a rubber spatula and, while it is still in the bowl, form it into a mound. Using the rubber spatula, divide the dough into quarters. If the total yield of baked cookies in the recipe is 4 dozen (48 cookies), then each quarter of the dough should yield 12 pieces.

Divide dense dough in the same manner. Working one quarter at a time, place the dough on a lightly floured surface and roll it into a log approximately 12 inches long. Using a dough scraper, score

the log into quarters. Before cutting through, check the total cookie yield of the recipe, then divide by 4 because you will have a total of four logs. Look at the log and determine how many pieces it should be cut into and make a slight depression for each cookie. For example, if a recipe makes 4 dozen (48 cookies), each log should be cut into twelve pieces. Using a dough scraper or a sharp knife, cut through the scored log.

ROLLING SURFACES

Cookie dough can be rolled on many types of surfaces. A large, wooden pastry board, 18 × 24 inches, is the optimum piece of equipment. The board should be anchored to the counter with a piece of rubberized shelf liner cut to an appropriate size and placed underneath. This lining is widely available in most houseware departments. A damp dish towel can be used as an alternative. If you don't have a pastry board, a large cutting board can be used. Pastry and/or cutting boards are the best rolling surfaces to use if you plan on using a pastry cloth because the cloth lies smooth without sliding.

Granite or marble make excellent surfaces for rolling doughs containing a high percentage of butter, such as puff pastry dough. In a pinch, a clean countertop can be used.

HOW TO USE A PASTRY CLOTH AND ROLLING PIN COVER

Rolling cookie dough can be done with ease when you use a pastry cloth and rolling pin cover. The cloth is a rectangular piece of canvas that is treated to prevent the dough from sticking to it. The rolling pin cover or stocking fits over the barrel of a 12-inch ball-bearing rolling pin. Flour is rubbed into the weave of the cloth and the ribs of the stocking to prevent too much flour from being absorbed into the dough. This results in better-tasting and more tender cookies.

It is best to lay the pastry cloth on a large wooden pastry board, about 18 by 24 inches, or a large cutting board. In a pinch you can lay it over a non-skid rubberized shelf liner, available in kitchenware or hardware stores. *Do not lay it directly onto your kitchen counter,* because it will slide and make rolling awkward.

When you are ready to roll, rub three to four tablespoons of all-purpose flour *very well* into the weave to the cloth and about two tablespoons into the rolling pin cover. Be sure to flour an area on the cloth that is larger than the finished size that you plan to roll the cookie dough. Re-flour the pastry cloth and rolling pin cover as needed. (See About Equipment, page 379, for care and laundering instructions.)

SHAPING COOKIE DOUGHS

There are many tricks and techniques to shaping cookie doughs. Most soft cookie doughs should be dropped from the tip of a spoon, not from the side. This will produce a more rounded cookie. Choose a spoon appropriate to the size cookie you are making—that is, a teaspoon for smaller cookies, a tablespoon for larger ones. At times, heaping spoonfuls are okay, too. Push the dough with your fingertip onto the cookie sheet, or use a second spoon to ease it onto the the pan.

Some cookie doughs are chilled before they are shaped by hand. The dough will harden, making it easier to form. If a cookie dough becomes too hard in the refrigerator, simply let it stand at room temperature until it is soft enough to handle. These hand-formed doughs will make more uniform shapes than those that are spoon dropped.

Because kitchen temperatures and seasons have an influence on all cookie doughs, at any time if a dough is too soft to handle, chilling it before shaping is your best bet.

Here are several methods for flattening individual balls of cookie dough:

- Place a bâtarde or a flat-bottomed glass on a square of plastic wrap. Bring the corners of the wrap up and twist it around the handle or top of the glass. A moistened piece of strong paper towel or a dampened linen towel can also be used. Press the bâtarde or glass *gently* on the center of the ball of dough. Then tip the bâtarde slightly away from the center, and using a rotating motion, move the bâtarde around the ball of dough, keeping the most pressure toward the outside of the cookie. If the cookie has not reached the desired thinness, gently press again in the center. Sometimes the dough sticks to the bâtarde or glass. In this case, dip the utensil into flour or granulated or confectioners' sugar, as instructed. If the dough sticks to utensils that have been wrapped with a moistened paper towel or dampened linen towel, change the paper towel to a fresh one and/or move the damp towel to a clean area.
- Avoid flattening cold balls of dough because they will crack around the edges. If you let the balls of dough soften, there will be less risk of the edges cracking.
- Make a cross in the dough ball with a fork dipped in flour.
- Use the heel of your hand dipped in flour.
- Use your fingertips moistened periodically with ice water.

USING COOKIE CUTTERS

Cookie cutters work most efficiently when they are dipped into flour with each cut; however, with firmer doughs, two or three cuts can be accomplished with a single dip of flour. Be sure to keep a shallow bowl filled with flour conveniently at hand. For the cleanest cut, when you make the impression with the cookie cutter, cut straight down—*do not twist.*

When you begin to cut the cookies, start at the top edge of the dough and cut the cookies as close to one another as possible to get the most yield with the first rolling of the dough. When using cutters of various sizes and shapes, evaluate the dough surface and the designs of your cookie cutters to see how to maximize the space.

RE-ROLLING SCRAPS OF DOUGH

Layer the scraps of dough on a sheet of plastic wrap. *Do not form them into a ball.* Bring the corners of the wrap to the center and twist to create a pouch. *Gently* press the pouch with your fingers, but do not form a mass. The dough will come together when it is rolled. Dough can be re-rolled, or if too soft, chilled in the refrigerator for 10 to 15 minutes before re-rolling. Only one re-rolling is recommended because too many rollings will result in a tough cookie.

USING A PASTRY BAG

Pastry bags are commonly used for piping many varieties of cookies, such as spritz, ladyfingers, and macaroons. They are also used to pipe frostings and fillings into cookies. A pastry bag should never be filled to more than one-third of its capacity, so choose accordingly. Place the pastry tip into the bag. Standing the empty bag, tip down, in a tall empty jar or other comparable container will make it easier to fill. Fold the bag over the edge of the jar, forming a cuff one-fourth to one-third down the length of the bag. Fill the bag one-third full of the mixture to be piped, scooping it in with a rubber spatula. Do not overfill. Unfold the cuff of the pastry bag, straighten it, twist it closed, then gently compress the filling to the bottom of the bag.

Holding the bag at the level of the batter or filling with your thumb and forefinger, wrap your fingers around the front of the bag, positioning your thumb across the top of the bag where the opening was twisted. You will use your fingers and thumb to press the mixture out of the bag. Place your opposite hand *underneath* the bag and only use it to steer the movement of the bag. *Avoid squeezing the bag with both hands.* Use only your dominant hand for squeezing, otherwise the filling can overflow from the top if too much force is applied.

A neat trick for keeping your pastry bag clean is to empty the batter or filling onto a sheet of plastic wrap, placing it across the short side about one-third from the end of the sheet. Enclose the mixture by rolling the wrap, like a salami, and twisting the ends. Cut the plastic on one of the sides, about 2 inches from the end of the filling, and insert the cut side into the pastry bag. Twist the top of the bag to close it and press until the filling reaches the end of the bag. Now, proceed with the piping directions given above.

Decorating and Garnishing

EGG WASH

Egg washes are used to produce color or create a shine on the cookie. They are also helpful for securing sugars, chopped nuts, or other trimmings to the dough. Egg washes are also used to seal pieces of dough together.

An egg yolk produces a deep gold color, while the whole egg gives a light golden color. The white provides the least color but the most shine, along with some crispiness. It is best to dilute any part of the egg with cold water, usually 2 teaspoons per egg. Adding a little salt (about ¼ teaspoon per whole egg, or a slightly reduced amount to the separated portion) will make it more fluid, and adding sugar (about 2 teaspoons per egg or egg white) will contribute to the shininess. Lightly beat the egg with a fork in a small container, breaking up the albumen. Beat in the water and/or salt or sugar, if used.

DISTRIBUTING GARNISHES EVENLY OVER DOUGH

Sugar and Spices: Sugar and spices should be placed in a shaker, such as an inexpensive or old salt shaker, spice shaker, or a fine-mesh sugar shaker. If the sugar pours too rapidly, cover some of the holes with tape so less sugar is released.

Rolled cookies need special attention when sugaring because the dough is usually rolled in por-tions. In order to keep the rolling surface clean, after the cookies are cut, remove them to a clean sheet of wax paper, and then egg-wash and sugar them. If the dough is egg-washed and sugared on the rolling surface, the excess will soil the board. For covering large areas, hold the shaker at least 12 inches above the cookies. Holding it too close will cause the sugar to be too concentrated.

Coarse Sugar, Nuts, and Seeds: Coarse sugar, nuts, and seeds also have a tendency to "cluster" when they are sprinkled over dough. To prevent this from happening, put a small amount in the palm of your hand. Make a loose fist, then turn your hand so your thumb faces upward. Holding your fist about 12 inches above the pan, rapidly move it back and forth, releasing a small amount of the seasoning at the same time. Distributing these types of ingredients from a higher level results in a more even distri-bution.

USING GLAZES AND MELTED CHOCOLATE

Some cookies are enhanced by drizzling the tops with glazes in a variety of flavors. Glazes should always be applied to cookies and bar cookies while the cookies are slightly warm. A warm surface allows the glaze to spread more evenly, gives it a better sheen, and helps it adhere. The glaze, which is spread on with the *back* of a spoon, a small offset spatula, the tines of a fork, or a plastic squeeze bottle, must be of a semi-fluid consistency. To check this, fill a spoon with the glaze and pour it back into the bowl. It should pour without the stream breaking.

The temperature of your kitchen and the season of the year are determining factors for achieving the proper consistencies of glazes and/or melted chocolate. Here are some tips that apply to webbing, dipping, and decorating:

- Test the glaze. If it is too fluid, try chilling it.
- Adding a bit more confectioners' sugar may help, provided that sugar is used in the recipe.
- If a glaze is too thick, add a few drops of hot water. (This does not apply to melted chocolate.)
- Place the glaze and/or melted chocolate in a warm water bath while you work to help maintain the consistency.
- If a glaze and/or melted chocolate becomes too thick, warm it briefly on the defrost setting of a microwave oven.

Webbing: This involves making a decorative lined pattern on the tops of individual cookies or bar cookies before they are cut, somewhat like a spider web. The web lines can be made in one direction or criss-crossed. Sometimes, instead of icing, chocolate thinned with a small amount of vegetable oil is used.

To create a webbed finish, use a plastic squeeze bottle or a 4-pronged fork. Fill the squeeze bottle with a warm, pourable glaze that will flow from the tip in a steady stream, but without excessive dripping. If using a fork, dip it regularly into the glaze, letting it drip from the tines.

- Test the icing flow on a piece of wax paper before you begin decorating.
- Practice on a sheet of wax paper to get the right motion.
- Individual cookies should be webbed on a cooling rack with a sheet of wax paper placed underneath, while bar cookies are webbed in the pan before cutting.

Be sure the glaze is dry before you store your cookies. If the glaze is stubborn, place the cookies in the refrigerator for a few minutes to set.

Dipping: Dipping cookies into a glaze or melted chocolate gives them a professional look and secures trimmings such as chopped nuts, coconut, jimmies, nonpareils, dragées, and colored and pearl sugars.

Spread the cookies on a cooling rack with a sheet of wax paper placed underneath to catch the drippings. Also, have some moistened paper towels ready for wiping your hands.

Dip the end or the side of a cookie into the glaze, leaving a thin coating without the surface showing. Trim as desired or leave plain. Set the cookie on the rack to dry. If using more than one flavor or color of glaze and/or melted chocolate, it's best to work these one at a time.

Decorating: Very pretty cookies can be created without too much fuss. Here are some ideas for you to play with:

- Chocolate and vanilla glazes, along with tinted glazes, will give you a broad range of color.
- Use squeeze bottles or disposable pastry bags fitted with a coupler and writing tip.
- If you are using more than one color of glaze, have squeeze bottles filled, ready for decorating. This makes the job easier. These can be filled and stored in the refrigerator and warmed in hot water, as needed.
- Pipe lines, grids, squiggles, and dots.
- Chopped nuts, coconut, jimmies, dragées, nonpareils, and colored and pearl sugars also add fun touches. They should be placed in a deep bowl and applied immediately after dipping.

- Glacé red and green cherries, cut in halves or quarters can be arranged in pretty designs. (Secure with lightly beaten egg white.)
- Pre-made sugar decorations, like tiny icing blossoms, miniature roses, and special-occasion and holiday ornaments, are available from several sources, as are stencils. (See New York Cake and Baking Distributors or Sweet Celebrations Catalog in Specialty Sources, page 403.)

Be sure to let cookies thoroughly dry before storing. Those who are looking for more elaborate, decorative effects should refer to books written specifically for that purpose.

TINTING WITH FOOD COLORING

It is easier to control the depth of color with paste food coloring than liquid food coloring. Place the desired amount of frosting in a small bowl. Dip a toothpick into the paste color and mix it into the frosting. Keep adjusting the color until you achieve the desired shade. Always use food coloring sparingly. You can add more, but it's hard to take away. When using liquid food colorings, add a drop or two to a small amount of frosting first. Then, add that smaller amount to the larger amount, mixing the color in gradually.

Cutting Bar Cookies

Bar cookies should be thoroughly cooled before cutting. In fact, cookies like brownies and lemon squares benefit it they are cut the day after baking. (If you can wait that long.) Cut them with a long, sharp 10-inch slicing knife, or better still, invest in a serrated knife with a blade of 12 to 14 inches. Stores that specialize in cake decorating equipment usually stock them. These longer bladed knives enable you to cut through the cookie in one motion.

When you cut the bar, cut *straight down*. Do not use a sawing motion. Always keep folded paper towels moistened with hot water on hand for wiping the knife after each movement, replacing the towels as needed. A clean blade will make a clean cut. Use a ruler to help you measure evenly before you begin to cut—even the pros do. Rinse your knife blade with hot water periodically, drying it and beginning again.

Freezing Cookie Doughs

If there is one medium in baking that lends itself to freezing, cookie doughs would be at the top of the list. The nature of the dough is such that, in most instances, the finished cookie doesn't suffer. Many doughs can be formed into sausagelike rolls and frozen, ready to be sliced and baked as needed. Freezing cookie doughs is a great convenience and time-saver.

Doughs made with the creamed butter method, such as chocolate chip cookies, are the best candidates for freezing. Most drop and hand-formed cookie doughs fall into this category. Refrigerated doughs, cookie-press doughs, and rolled doughs also work extremely well. Rugalah-style pastries can be frozen, already shaped, ready to be popped into the oven. Buttery, European-style cookie doughs can be frozen, as can biscotti and mandelbrot. Bar cookies made with batters are not recommended for freezing because of their fluid con-

sistency. In addition, meringue and macaroon batters are not good choices for freezing.

Since cookie doughs are so varied, my suggestion is as follows: The next time you make a batch, take a small amount of dough and freeze it for a couple of weeks. Then, bake it. If you get a good result, your question has been answered.

When you freeze the dough, wrap it in plastic and place in a plastic bag, pressing out all the air before sealing. Be sure to label and date your package. Before freezing, it's wise to divide the dough into smaller portions because they will thaw more quickly. All doughs are best thawed in the refrigerator overnight.

In a free-standing freezer, cookie dough will keep for four to six months with temperatures of zero degrees or below. Dough frozen in a side-by-side, or in the bottom or top freezer of a refrigerator, are best used within three months. These types of freezers do not maintain as cold a temperature.

Freezing Baked Cookies

Most baked cookies freeze well. However, those cookies that are finished with chocolate or other glazes that are not garnished with chopped nuts or other trimmings should be garnished after thawing because freezing often impairs the appearance of the glaze. Always freeze cookies according to the type. Crisp cookies should never be mixed with soft or chewy cookies.

I freeze baked cookies by layering them between sheets of wax paper in sturdy, airtight containers. More delicate cookies should be

spread on a jelly roll pan and frozen first before packaging. Each recipe in *Great Cookies* will indicate whether or not freezing is recommended.

The containers for freezing cookies can be aluminum foil, with matching lids, airtight plastic containers, cookie tins, or any substantial container that will give the cookies support. Be sure to use those that seal well and fill them completely to eliminate air space. However, if there is some space between the cookies and the lid, lay a piece of aluminum foil directly on top of the cookies to protect them from exposure to the air. Double-wrapping your cookie containers first with aluminum foil and then in a plastic bag will give the cookies added protection. Always label and date your containers and rotate your stock.

Crisp cookies and those with surfaces that aren't sticky or glazed can be thawed in the refrigerator or at room temperatures in their freezer containers. Soft or chewy cookies should be removed from their containers and spread on jelly roll pans lightly covered with a piece of aluminum foil or wax paper, not plastic wrap. Cookies trimmed with icing, webbed toppings, or sticky surfaces should also be thawed on jelly roll pans. Avoid using plastic wrap because too much condensation forms underneath the surface.

REFRESHING COOKIES

All cookies that have been frozen and then thawed benefit from refreshing. Spread the cookies on jelly roll pans or cookie sheets and reheat in a 325° oven. The length of time will depend on the size of the cookies. For small, thin cookies, 3 to 5 minutes is sufficient; thicker or larger cookies can take up to 8 to 10 minutes. The cookies are ready when you begin to detect a pleasant aroma coming from the oven. Peek occasionally to prevent overbaking. Cool and enjoy!

Many cookies that have not been frozen also benefit from a brief reheating. If you do this shortly before serving, they will taste freshly baked.

Guidelines for Storing Cookies

Although temperatures of kitchens and the care one takes when wrapping baked cookies vary greatly, there are some general guidelines to prevent cookies from becoming prematurely stale. Exposure to air is the common enemy in most cases.

- Crisp cookies are best stored in airtight metal cookie tins. Soft or chewy cookies and bar cookies can be stored in the same way, but should not be mixed with crisp cookies.
- Cookies with preserve toppings or other tacky surfaces should be stored layered between sheets of wax paper. Spray the wax paper with nonstick coating and lay it, coating side down, over the cookies.
- Line the container with wax paper or aluminum foil, using a sheet long enough to fold over the top surface of the cookies. Avoid plastic wrap.
- Place sheets of wax paper between layers of cookies or bars.
- Decorated cookies store best in single layers.

Gift Wrapping

Be as creative as your imagination will allow. The choices are limitless. Remember to package soft cookies separately from crisp cookies. One soft cookie in a batch of crisp cookies will make the crisp cookies soft.

Here are a few ideas to get you started:

- Attractive cookie tins and small baskets are available in craft and discount stores.
- New clay or plastic pots can be obtained from florists or nurseries.
- Decorative gift boxes are sold by card stores.
- Clear cellophane is the best wrap for keeping cookies fresh. Decorative tissue can also be used.
- Beautiful linen napkins or pieces of fabric can be tied around the outside of the container.
- Raffia, wired French ribbon, and other ribbons with holiday or special-occasion motifs make pretty gift packages.
- Don't forget to attach a label or gift card with the name of the cookie.
- Williams-Sonoma has custom, personalized wrap for cookies in their holiday catalog (see Specialty Sources, page 403).

Tips for Mailing and Shipping Cookies

Always mail cookies First Class so they will arrive fresh. Use a sturdy cardboard box or cookie tin that will fit snugly into a slightly larger carton suitable for shipping. Line the outer carton with a cushioned filler such as bubble wrap, shredded paper, or crumpled newspaper. Do not leave empty spaces. Be sure to write "Fragile" in big, bold letters on all sides of the outer carton.

Here is some helpful information to remember:

- Avoid thin, crisp cookies. They crumble easily.
- Avoid cookies with pointed edges; in summertime, avoid frosted cookies or temperature-sensitive recipes.
- Sturdy cookies, such as oatmeal, peanut butter, chocolate chip, biscotti, and bar cookies, are the safest to ship. Make short stacks of cookies (no more than six or eight) and place them in appropriately sized cellophane bags, available at party stores. Tie or seal the tops of the bags as close to the stack of cookies as possible without crushing them.
- Wrap soft cookies separately from crisp cookies.
- Use wax paper or small doilies between layers.
- Pack cookies together closely to eliminate movement.

Troubleshooting

I often refer to cookies as "tricky little critters" because subtle changes in a recipe can bring such different results. Inaccurate measurements, improper ingredients, variables in ovens, and differences in baking equipment, as well as weather conditions, all can have an effect. Here are some hints to help you "tweak" your recipes.

What to try if your

COOKIES SPREAD TOO MUCH

- Start with butter that is not as soft.
- Reduce the amount of butter in the dough.
- Substitute part or all vegetable shortening for butter.
- Reduce the amount of sugar in the dough.
- Use a higher-protein flour (see Flours and Leavenings, page 363).
- Use less liquid in the dough.
- Refrigerate the dough to firm it.
- Do not portion the dough onto hot cookie sheets.
- Increase the oven temperature by 25 degrees.

COOKIES ARE NOT CRISP

- Use part or all vegetable shortening instead of butter.
- Substitute some or all white sugar for brown.
- Add 1 tablespoon light corn syrup and reduce sugar by 1 tablespoon.
- Substitute part or all egg whites for whole eggs.
- The dough was too thick; thin it with a little beaten egg white.
- Reduce the oven temperature by 25 degrees to allow the cookies to spread and crisp.

COOKIES ARE NOT SOFT

- The brown sugar was not fresh.
- Add 1 to 2 tablespoons maple syrup, honey, or light molasses to the dough and reduce sugar by an equal amount.
- Add 1 tablespoon of water to the dough.
- Make the cookies thicker.

- The dough was too thin, causing the cookies to spread and crisp.
- Increase the baking temperature by 25 degrees to prevent the cookies from spreading.
- Reduce the baking time (the centers should appear slightly underbaked).

COOKIES CRUMBLE

- There was too much butter in the dough.
- Substitute part vegetable shortening for butter.
- The dough was undermixed.
- Substitute egg white for liquid.
- There was not enough protein in the flour. (See Flours and Leavenings, page 363.)

COOKIES LACK COLOR

- Substitute egg for liquid.
- Increase the amount of sugar.
- Add 1 tablespoon light or dark corn syrup to the dough and reduce sugar by 1 tablespoon.
- Use dark brown in lieu of light brown sugar.
- Add a pinch of baking soda to the dough.

COOKIES ARE TOO DRY

- The ingredients were not accurately measured.
- There was too much flour in dough.
- The flour contained too much protein. (See Flours and Leavenings, page 363.)
- The oven temperature was too high.
- The cookies were overbaked.

COOKIES ARE OVERBAKED OR UNEVENLY BROWNED

- The oven needs to be calibrated.
- There are hot spots in the oven.
- The cookies were baked on *thin* metal pans.
- The cookies were baked on non-stick or dark metal pans without reducing the oven temperature by 25 degrees.
- The cookie sheets were not reversed top to bottom and front to back during baking.

Specialty Sources

GENERAL

Ateco
August Thomsen Corporation
36 Sea Cliff Avenue
Glen Clove, NY 11542-3699
888-645-7170
Carole Walter's personally designed heavy-weight pastry cloth with rolling pin cover and 12-inch barrel solid Rock Maple ball-bearing rolling pin.

The Baker's Catalogue
P. O. Box 876
Norwich, VT 05055-0876
www.bakerscatalogue.com
www.bakingcircle.com
800-827-6836
High-quality flours, including nut flours, sparkling white sugar, and decorating sugar, nuts, dried and candied fruits, crystallized ginger, Key lime juice, pure maple syrup, Nielsen-Massey vanilla, extracts, and oils. Quality chocolate. Wide range of baking equipment, including cookie cutters, cookie sheets, half and quarter sheet pans, cooking racks, cookie jars, cookie presses, Biscotti pans, teaspoon and tablespoon scoops, pastry boards. Silpat mats, measuring equipment, and chocolate dipping fork.

Bridge Kitchenware
214 East 52nd Street
New York, NY 10022
www.bridgekitchenware.com
800-274-3435
As a chef and restaurant supplier open to the public, Bridge offers a complete line of domestic and imported cookware and bakeware, including decorating equipment, baking accessories, and baking parchment (packaged in sheets) sold in bulk, high-quality strainers, Springerle and Speculaas molds, heavy-duty cookie sheets, rolling pins. Catalog available ($3.00, refundable with first order).

The House on the Hill
P. O. Box 7003
Villa Park, IL 60181
www.houseonthehill.net
630-279-4455
Cookie molds, including historic and Springerle and Speculaas molds and cookie cutters. Catalog available. ($3.00)

La Cuisine
323 Cameron Street
Alexandria, VA 22314
www.lacuisineus.com
800-521-1176
Offers an extensive line of high-quality baking equipment, maple pastry boards, rolling pins, imported wooden spoons and spatulas, cookie presses, decorating equipment and baking accessories, including Springerle and Speculaas molds, extensive line of cookie cutters. Imported and domestic cookie sheets, jelly roll pans, Silpat mats. Catalog available.

New York Cake and Baking Distributors
56 West 22nd Street
New York, NY 10010
www.nycakesupplies.com
212-675-2253
Specialty baking pans, cookie packaging supplies, cookie sheets, large selection of cookie and canapé cutters, cake boxes, and cake rounds, as well as an extensive line of decorating equipment. Rolling pins, Silpat mats, dipping forks, small cupcake liners. Stocks bulk chocolate. Catalog available.

Sur La Table
1765 Sixth Avenue South
Seattle, WA 98134
www.surlatable.com
800-243-0852
An upscale kitchen shop with a complete line of specialty baking pans and accessories, as well as rolling pins, cookie sheets, cookie presses, Springerle molds, cookie cutters, decorating equipment, cookware, kitchen gadgets, small appliances, candy-making supplies, and gift items. Catalog available.

Sweet Celebrations (formerly Maid of Scandinavia)
7009 Washington Avenue South
Edina, MN 55439
www.sweetc.com
888-328-6722
Cake boxes and other packaging materials for baked goods, as well as everything imaginable for decorating, including pearl sugar, sanding sugar, colored sugars, crystal sugar. Cookie presses, rolling pins, Krumkake irons, electric krumkake baker, Silpat mats, small cupcake liners, candy dipping forks. Fine-quality chocolate. Catalog available.

Williams-Sonoma
Mail Order Department
P. O. Box 7456
San Francisco, CA 94120-7456
www.williams-sonoma.com
800-541-2233
"A Catalog for Cooks" features upscale cutting-edge equipment, baking accessories, and giftware. Cookie sheets, cookie cutters, cookie presses, decorating sugars, icing pens, candy cups, novelty gift boxes, and customized paper for packaging cookies. Also a good source for Nielsen-Massey vanilla and premium chocolate for baking. Many items are available through the catalog only.

SPECIALTY INGREDIENTS

Lindt Chocolate
www.lindt-com/USA
Premium chocolate for baking.

Maison Glass, Inc.
P. O. Box 317-H
Scarsdale, NY 10583
www.maisonglass.com
800-822-5564
Professional-quality baking supplies including premium dried and glacé fruits (available year-round), nuts, high-quality nut pastes, and bulk chocolate. Catalog available.

Bibliography

American Heritage. *The American Heritage Cookbook.* New York: Simon & Schuster, 1964.

Anderson, Pam. *The Perfect Recipe.* New York: Houghton Mifflin, 1998.

Betty Crocker's Picture Cookbook. New York: McGraw-Hill, 1950.

Braker, Flo. *Sweet Miniatures.* New York: William Morrow, 1991.

California Culinary Academy. *Cooking A to Z.* California: The Cole Group, 1992.

Child, Julia, Simone Beck, and Louisette Bertholle. *Mastering the Art of French Cooking,* Vol. 1. New York: Alfred A. Knopf, 1961.

Consumers Union Report on Wines and Spirits. Mount Vernon, N.Y.: Consumers Union, 1975.

Corriher, Shirley. *Cookwise.* New York: William Morrow, 1997.

Culinary Arts Institute Encyclopedic Cookbook. Chicago: Culinary Arts Institute, 1948.

Cunningham, Marion. *The Fannie Farmer Baking Book.* New York: Alfred A. Knopf, 1984.

Daley, Regan. *In the Sweet Kitchen.* New York: Artisan, 2001.

Dannenberg, Linda. *Paris Boulangerie Patîsserie.* New York: Clarkson Potter, 1994.

Dupree, Nathalie. *New Southern Cooking.* New York: Alfred A. Knopf, 1986.

Early, Eleanor. *New England Cookbook.* New York: Random House, 1954.

Farm Journal's Country Cookbook. Nell B. Nichols, Editor. New York: Doubleday, 1972.

Farmer, Fannie Merritt. *The Fannie Farmer Cookbook.* Revised by Marion Cunningham. New York: Alfred A. Knopf, 1979.

France, W. J. *The Students Technology of Breadmaking & Flour Confectionary.* London: Rutledge & Kegan Paul, 1960.

Friberg, Bo. *The Professional Pastry Chef.* New York: Van Nostrand Reinhold, 1990.

Grossman's Guide to Beer and Spirits, 6th Edition, Lembeck, 1977.

Healy, Bruce. *The French Cookie Book.* New York: William Morrow, 1994.

Heatter, Maida. *Maida Heatter's Book of Great Cookies.* New York: Alfred A. Knopf, 1977.

Herbst, Sharon Tyler. *The New Food Lovers' Companion* (Second Edition). New York: Barron's, 1995.

Herbst, Ron, and Sharon Tyler Herbst. *Wine Lovers' Companion.* New York: Barron's, 1995.

Malgieri, Nick. *Cookies Unlimited.* New York: Harper Collins, 2000.

Malgieri, Nick. *Great Italian Desserts.* Boston: Little, Brown, 1990.

Mariani, John. *Dictionary of American Food and Drink.* New Haven, Conn.: Ticknor & Fields, 1983.

Marks, Gil. *The World of Jewish Desserts.* New York: Simon & Schuster, 2000.

Medrich, Alice. *Cocolat.* New York: Warner Books, 1990.

Nathan, Joan. *Jewish Cooking in America.* New York: Alfred A. Knopf, 1994.

Ojakangas, Beatrice. *The Great Scandinavian Baking Book.* Boston: Little, Brown, 1988.

Payard, François. *Simply Sensational Desserts.* New York: Broadway Books, 1999.

Pépin, Jacques. *La Technique.* New York: Times Book Co., 1976.

Radecka, Helena. *The Fruit & Nut Book.* New York: McGraw-Hill, 1984.

Rombauer, Irma, and Marion Becker. *The Joy of Cooking.* New York: Bobbs-Merrill, 1975.

Root, Waverly. *Food.* New York: Simon & Schuster, 1980.

Roux, Albert, and Michel Roux. *The Roux Brothers on Patîsserie.* New York: Prentice-Hall, 1986.

Sultan, William J. *Practical Baking.* Westport, Conn.: Avi Publishing, 1986.

Time-Life Foods of the World Series. *The Cooking of Germany.* Richard L. Williams, Series Editor. New York: Time-Life Books, 1969.

Time-Life Foods of the World Series. *Wines and Spirits.* Richard L. Williams, Series Editor. New York: Time-Life Books, 1968.

Walden, Hilaire. *The Great Big Cookie Book.* New York: Lorenz Books, 1998.

Walter, Carole. *Great Cakes.* New York: Clarkson Potter, 1991.

Walter, Carole. *Great Pies & Tarts.* New York: Clarkson Potter, 1998.

Wennberg, G. L. *Desserts, Pastries and Fancy Cakes.* Copenhagen, Denmark: Ivar Forley, 1964.

Woman's Home Companion Cookbook. New York: P. F. Collier & Son Co., 1942.

Acknowledgments

When I began *Great Cookies,* I didn't have a clue that I was about to embark on such a vast subject. It was indeed a challenge, but with the help of an enormously talented team, I was able to bring forth exciting new recipes along with adaptations of popular favorites and timeless cookie classics.

It was through the efforts of my former editor, Roy Finamore, that this magnificent sleek edition came to fruition. His vision coupled with his confidence in me made my dream of a fully illustrated book come true. Roy, thank you for your wisdom, guidance, and friendship. Roy's torch was passed to Chris Pavone, who patiently and articulately helped me smooth out the rough edges in the final stage of the book. Thank you, Chris! You didn't miss a beat.

Judith Weber, my literary agent, has never failed to give sound advice, to be encouraging, and enthusiastic. Many thanks, Judith. Your expertise in the literary field is knowledge to be treasured.

Kathie Finn Redden, my assistant, has been at my side through every page of this book. Her keen wit and humorous Post-its kept me on track and made for hours of laughter. Kathie was an invaluable partner during the photo sessions. She has an artistic eye and an extraordinary sense of taste. She also has marvelous writing skills, and she is organized. Lucky me, Kathie, to have you come into my life. To Kelly Volpe, who was with me in the beginning, my deepest thanks. Your remarkable memory and ability to organize, along with your enthusiasm, went far in helping me get started.

My incredibly talented photographer, Duane Winfield, brought the pages of this book "tastily" alive. Our shootings took place over fifteen months in six photography sessions. Duane and his assistants, Jeff Cate and David Mandel, were a joy to work with at all times. With the patience of Job and his attention to detail, Duane never allowed one crumb to go unnoticed. Duane, no cookbook author could ask for a better photographer.

From the first time I sat with Marysarah Quinn, my art director at Clarkson Potter, I knew I was in very gifted hands. Thank you, Marysarah, for delivering a brilliant work of art. My deepest thanks also go to my publisher, Lauren Shakely, production editor Jean Lynch, production manager Derek McNally, copy editor Carole Berglie, publicity director Leigh Anne Ambrosi, indexer Elizabeth Parsons, Philip Patrick, Katherine Dietrich, and Doug Jones from sales and marketing, as well as Jennifer DeFilippi, Adina Steiman, and Lance Troxel.

Through all my photo sessions, in addition to months of recipe testing, was a dedicated and enthusiastic team of extraordinary people: Debbie Barrett, Judy Epstein, Jeanne Greco, Chiaki Romano, Jim Smith, and Mary Ellen Warner, along with Wendy Dash and Alison Deeb who pinch-hitted when extra hands were needed, you cared about this book as if it were your own. It was a privilege to work with each of you. To young Ali O'Keefe, who aspires to be a pastry chef, thank you for taking time from your homework and a busy social life. You are bursting with talent and I know you will achieve your goal. To my computer wizard, Lorette Cheswick, you truly leave me in awe with your breadth of knowledge. Thank you for getting me through every crisis and for insuring that my book was safe.

To Judy Moore, thank you for the masterful job you did in researching the technical portion of this book. Your thoroughness and concern for perfection did not go unnoticed. My deepest gratitude to my friend Judy Bernhaut for seeking out the charming quotes throughout this book and for her hours spent proofing this manuscript. My thanks also to Nancy Harris, whose computer skills are "par excellence." During the frenzy of the holiday season, Nancy found the time to help me meet my deadline. A special thank you to my friend Sheila Small for the many hours spent on researching rugelach.

My deepest appreciation goes to the super staff of Kings Super Markets Inc.: Director of Marketing Pat Mickell, Manager of the Cooking Studios Susan Loden, and to studio managers Susan Konzen and Sandy Cacioppo. How convenient it was to have an open phone to help me with labeling and other product information! To the outstanding staff associated with the cooking schools, thank you for your genuine interest and willingness to help. You guys are the best!

For technical assistance, I give thanks to master baker and cookbook author Flo Braker, David Carter of Penzeys Spices, Ann Casey from Lindt & Sprungli (USA) Inc., Bob Fink of McAdam Buy-Rite, New York City, cookbook author and entrepreneur Rozanne Gold, master baker and cookbook author George Greenstein, Doug Schneider of August Thomsen Corp., and food personality and cookbook author Arthur Schwartz, host of "Food Talk" WOR Radio, New York City.

To my thousands of students, past and present, I send a special "thank you" for constantly keeping my juices overflowing.

Finally, to those who graciously shared favorite and often treasured recipes, as well as the many who generously gave valuable information to spark my thoughts: my deepest thanks go to: Eleanor Berg, Peggy Berg, the family of Minna Berger, Linda Bogan, James Brackman, Lorette Cheswick, Barbara Chafkin, Nancy Chicarello, Chef Sam DeMarco of District Restaurant, New York City, Jim Duffany, Kim Finkelstein, the family of Rene Fleischer, Marcia Germanow, Pat Graffius, Jeanne Greco, Rita Hirsch, Yocheved Hirsch, Sally Kofke, Ann Koroghian, Doris Kukin, the family of Judie Levenberg, Angela Lisante, Shirley Lynch, Chef Nick Malgieri, Paula Marshall, Joanna Pruess, Kathie Finn Redden, Mary Ellen Robertshaw, Rich Rosenthal, friends of Noel Rozint, Chef Michael Salvatore, Kathleen Sanderson, Stephen Schmidt, Nancy Schwartz, Jim Smith, Athena Sophos, Leslie Sporn, the family of Julia Wolfson, Ruth Wurgaft, Selma Yagoda, and Mary Yorke.

To my husband, Gene, thank you for so patiently putting up with the frustrations of a writer, for enduring the chaos of the photo sessions, and for being my "sounding board" while dining in diners. Your strength and encouragement have meant more to me than words can say.

To our mascot, "Wilson," you may have been just a coconut, but to us you were the "Espirit de Corps."

Index

Conversion Chart

EQUIVALENT IMPERIAL AND METRIC MEASUREMENTS

American cooks use standard containers, the 8-ounce cup and a tablespoon that takes exactly 16 level fillings to fill that cup level. Measuring by cup makes it very difficult to give weight equivalents, as a cup of densely packed butter will weigh considerably more than a cup of flour. The easiest way therefore to deal with cup measurements in recipes is to take the amount by volume rather than by weight. Thus the equation reads:

$1 \; cup = 240 \; ml = 8 \; fl. \; oz.$ $^1/_2 \; cup = 120 \; ml = 4 \; fl. \; oz.$

It is possible to buy a set of American cup measures in major stores around the world.

In the States, butter is often measured in sticks. One stick is the equivalent of 8 tablespoons. One tablespoon of butter is therefore the equivalent to $^1/_2$ ounce/15 grams.

LIQUID MEASURES

Fluid Ounces	U.S.	Imperial	Milliliters
	1 teaspoon	1 teaspoon	5
$^1/_4$	2 teaspoons	1 dessertspoon	10
$^1/_2$	1 tablespoon	1 tablespoon	14
1	2 tablespoons	2 tablespoons	28
2	$^1/_4$ cup	4 tablespoons	56
4	$^1/_2$ cup		110
5		$^1/_4$ pint or 1 gill	140
6	$^3/_4$ cup		170
8	1 cup		225
9			250, $^1/_4$ liter
10	$1^1/_4$ cups	$^1/_2$ pint	280
12	$1^1/_2$ cups		340
15		$^3/_4$ pint	420
16	2 cups		450
18	$2^1/_4$ cups		500, $^1/_2$ liter
20	$2^1/_2$ cups	1 pint	560
24	3 cups		675
25		$1^1/_4$ pints	700
27	$3^1/_2$ cups		750
30	$3^3/_4$ cups	$1^1/_2$ pints	840
32	4 cups or 1 quart		900
35		$1^3/_4$ pints	980
36	$4^1/_2$ cups		1000, 1 liter
40	5 cups	2 pints or 1 quart	1120

SOLID MEASURES

U.S. and Imperial Measures		Metric Measures	
Ounces	Pounds	Grams	Kilos
1		28	
2		56	
$3^1/_2$		100	
4	$^1/_4$	112	
5		140	
6		168	
8	$^1/_2$	225	
9		250	$^1/_4$
12	$^3/_4$	340	
16	1	450	
18		500	$^1/_2$
20	$1^1/_4$	560	
24	$1^1/_2$	675	
27		750	$^3/_4$
28	$1^3/_4$	780	
32	2	900	
36	$2^1/_4$	1000	1
40	$2^1/_2$	1100	
48	3	1350	
54		1500	$1^1/_2$

OVEN TEMPERATURE EQUIVALENTS

Fahrenheit	Celsius	Gas Mark	Description
225	110	$^1/_4$	Cool
250	130	$^1/_2$	
275	140	1	Very Slow
300	150	2	
325	170	3	Slow
350	180	4	Moderate
375	190	5	
400	200	6	Moderately Hot
425	220	7	Fairly Hot
450	230	8	Hot
475	240	9	Very Hot
500	250	10	Extremely Hot

Any broiling recipes can be used with the grill of the oven, but beware of high-temperature grills.

EQUIVALENTS FOR INGREDIENTS

all-purpose flour—plain flour
coarse salt—kitchen salt
cornstarch—cornflour
eggplant—aubergine

half and half—12% fat milk
heavy cream—double cream
light cream—single cream
lima beans—broad beans

scallion—spring onion
unbleached flour—strong, white flour
zest—rind
zucchini—courgettes or marrow